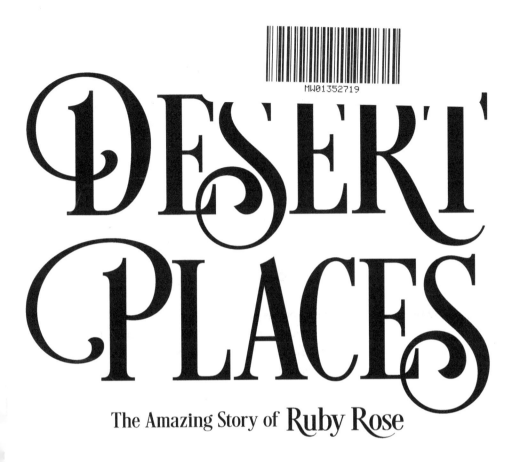

DESERT PLACES

The Amazing Story of Ruby Rose

A Novel

By

Ernest Brawley

This is a work of fiction. All characters, organizations, and events portrayed in this novel are either products of the author's imagination or are used fictitiously.

Copyright © 2022 by Ernest Brawley

All rights reserved. No part of this publication may be reproduced in whole or in part, or stored in a retrieval system, or transmitted in any form or by any means, electronic, mechanical, photocopying, recording, or otherwise, without written permission of the author, except for the inclusion of brief quotations in a review.

For information regarding permission, please write to:
info@barringerpublishing.com
Barringer Publishing, Naples, Florida
www.barringerpublishing.com

Design and layout by Linda S. Duider
Cape Coral, Florida

ISBN: 978-1-954396-30-2
Library of Congress Cataloging-in-Publication Data
Desert Places / Brawley

Printed in U.S.A.

For Chiara and Lenor, with love . . .

They cannot scare me with their empty spaces.
Between stars—on stars where no human race is.
I have it in me so much nearer home.
To scare myself with my own desert places.

—Robert Frost

Part I

Chapter One

Reno Rose was expelled from Brigham Young University in 1930, his senior year, for "dallying" with a married, college nurse old enough to be his mother. His wealthy, devout, Mormon family cut him off as soon as they heard the news, and never spoke to him again. But Reno wouldn't let that stop him. He withdrew the last $200.00 from his account at the Zion National Bank in Provo and hitched a ride into Salt Lake City. There, he hired an infamous counterfeiter named Shorty McPhee to forge a Bachelor of Science degree from BYU's renowned College of Engineering. A week later, he fled south of the border, where in time he found employment as a mining engineer, with the British firm, Rio de Plata, in the state of Hidalgo.

In the year, 1936, when Rio de Plata went bust with a glut in the silver market, Reno took his savings, paid off his common-law wife and brood of little *mestizos*, and caught a train for Arizona.

First thing he did at the Union Pacific Station in Tucson was to have Mexico washed off his back. Then, he had his hair cut, his mustache trimmed pencil-thin, and paid a visit to the station's haberdasher. Thirty dollars lighter, but dressed to kill, he put a crease in his new fedora, lit up a fat cigar, engaged a barefoot Papago Indian boy to carry his bags, and ambled into the Greeley Hotel on South Cherry Avenue where he registered as Captain Reno B. Rose, USA (Res).

He tipped the boy, had his bag sent up to his room, and was just stepping out the door again—heading for a bar and illegal casino he'd heard about on Congress Street—when he caught sight of a beautiful, young woman walking into the lobby on the arm of a slick-looking dude in a white, linen suit and a Panama hat.

The girl was laughing about something the man had said.

"Oh, I declare, Teddy, you just slay me. You really do!"

She shook her head when she laughed, glancing around the room to verify that she had attracted an audience, and her bobbed, platinum blonde hair flared out around her face. It was a perfectly round, powder-white, little face with pink puffy lips, a perky pug nose, forget-me-not blue eyes, and it wore an expression of the purest and most profound self-absorption. And the ring of her vain and trivial laughter sounded clean through the hollow of Reno's hard, foolish heart.

After dinner, he bumped into the couple again in the hallway. Apparently, they were lodged in the room next door. Reno was so intrigued by the woman that he could not resist tiptoeing into his bathroom to spy on them. Down on his knees, with an ear to the toilet seat, he found that he could hear virtually everything. The gist of which was: they were runaway lovers, heading for Palm Springs where Teddy had a job waiting for him in hotel management. The girl, Alma, hoped to meet a Hollywood director who might advance her career as an actress.

Next morning, they were gone, but Reno still could not get Alma out of his mind.

In the week that he lived at the Greeley, he got into the habit of going down to the casino every evening after supper. A former speakeasy, resplendently Victorian, with polished brass fixtures, yellow brocaded wall tapestry, ornate redwood wall panels, beveled mirrors, and crystal chandeliers, it was called "The Excelsior Lounge." Its customers were for the most part loud-talking, tobacco-chewing, local businessmen, ranchers, and railroad men who all seemed to know each other, and they regarded Reno with such extreme suspicion that he found it impossible to strike up even a friendly game of stud poker.

Then one evening, a sandy-haired, well-spoken gentleman in a straw boater hat and a tan, Eastern-cut suit appeared at the bar and engaged several of its regular patrons in conversation. Reno overheard him say that his name was Finney, that he was an attorney from Dallas, and he was here looking for his wife. To be blunt, he said, she had looted his savings account and run off with a handsome charlatan—an ex-convict with a penchant for forgery and petty larceny. The two of them were rumored to have passed this way and he suspected they might have stayed at the Greeley Hotel under false names. Had anyone seen them?

The local gents pushed back their ten-gallon hats, rolled their wads of chewing tobacco from one side of their mouths to the other, spat into the brass cuspidors at their feet, and shook their heads one by one: "Nope, ain't seen hide nor hair of 'em."

Standing by the bar, sipping his rye, Reno was all ears.

Next day, he went down to a printer's shop on the other side of town and had a bunch of calling cards printed up.

Capt. Reno B. Rose
Private Detective
Quick & Discreet Results
GUARANTEED

That evening, he spotted the gentleman from Denver again. "Excuse me, sir," he said, stepping forward smartly. And there was something characteristic in his tone, something partly self-mocking, partly sardonic, that turned heads. "Reno's the name," he went on, proffering his card. "I believe I saw the couple you're looking for, and I'd be happy to be of service, if I may."

The circle which had gathered around the offended husband broke away, and several customers frowned. Others laughed, as if expecting a practical joke. But the sandy-haired gentleman from Dallas seemed delighted that he had struck a spark, delighted even at the note of irony in Reno's tone. He shrugged and smiled disarmingly, as if to say, "Yes, isn't it ridiculous? Another cuckolded husband!" Then he took Reno by the arm, drew him away to the far end of the room, and said, "Please, tell me everything you know. I'm Francis X. Finney. Would you care for a drink?"

Over a whiskey or two, Reno decided that there was more to this well-bred fellow than met the eye. In Finney's pale translucent skin and immense, blue-veined forehead, his watery, wavery, gray eyes and delicately pointed chin, there was something infinitely more complicated than a mere wayward wife.

Could it be? Naw. Reno ruled that out right away. This was no fruit, no fairy. This was a profoundly dishonest man.

Briefly, Reno considered the possibility that Finney was on the make—a huckster out for a mark among the Arizona hayseeds. But he rejected that as well. Finney smelled of something even sleazier. And he reeked of guilty Irish Catholicism. If he was playing some game, it went deeper than that.

"I welcomed the fellow into my home, treated him as a friend in need," Finney was saying. "And she was the one who said she didn't want him around. I swear, there's no explaining it. And you know, without me, she'd be nothing. Took her out of a little hick town in Louisiana and made a lady of her. And now this is how she serves me."

His tone was flat and monotonous, a tad on the nasal side. But there was this maudlin quality to the phrases he chose, and something too in the way he smiled and lingered almost lovingly over the painful aspects of the story: "Not to mention our two little kiddies that she so callously abandoned."

The game the slicker was playing, Reno concluded, was probably with himself.

So, they got to talking. Reno said he had no idea where the couple had gone, but he'd had some success in locating missing persons in the past. Finney wanted to know his fee. A thousand dollars, Reno had said, half up front, half on delivery, plus expenses. Finney said that sounded reasonable, though it didn't at all, and they struck a deal.

Reno left for Palm Springs that night. He found Alma Finnie, nee Stroud, a week later at the Tropicana Palms, registered under the name "Holly Bernard." She was living alone, the hotel bill was past due, the boyfriend was nowhere in evidence, and she was going the rounds downtown looking for a job as a waitress.

She'd been "beat for the yolk," Reno deduced, and started feeling sorry for her, started backsliding, and dithered about sending a telegram to her pathetic, old hubby.

So, he checked into the Tropicana Palms and made her acquaintance at poolside. Her beauty was of the ephemeral kind, he discovered, her body luscious, but a smidge overripe. Yet, for some reason, that only made him want her more—as did the heavy down on her pouting upper lip, the dark roots of her hair, her vulgar, husky laugh, and the apparent trashiness of her antecedents. Breathless with desire, Reno managed only small talk at first. But later he invited confidences.

She was a singer as well as an actress, she said, with experience in several Dallas repertory productions. Her dream was to win the lead in a Hollywood musical. He asked her to sing for him. He found her streetside rendition of *"If You Knew Suzy"* adequate, her effort commendable, and her sincerity appealing, revealing a naive, vulnerable side of her character that he had never suspected before. Yet, he knew, she had missed her bet as the wife of a prosperous lawyer.

Toward evening, when Alma alluded—none too subtly—to her financial distress, he offered to pay her hotel bill. She protested, he insisted, and, by that night, they were bedded down.

Scandalized, the management of the Tropicana Palms evicted them the next morning. They found an even more lavish place, The Warwick Plaza, where they registered as man and wife, and spent the entire month of December 1936 wallowing in one another's arms. They never left the room, rarely got out of bed, and had all their meals sent up by Room Service. They spoke only of bodily functions, learned next to nothing about each other, and could not have cared less. They were like one great, heaving, single-cell animal, one grotesquely long orgasm, and indeed it would have seemed a miracle if they had not conceived a child.

By New Year's Day, 1937, they were deadass broke, and they had decided they were in love.

Reno confessed his role as Finney's private dick.

Alma forgave him. And then they started to conspire.

"My husband is . . . kind of peculiar," she said, in her mock-genteel, Southern accent that never quite convinced but never failed to charm. "Drove me clean out of the house with his foolin' around, thrown' me at his friends, then peekin' through the keyhole to see what's goin' on. That man, I swear, he deserves whatever you care to dish out at him."

That night, Reno sent a telegram: WIFE FOUND STOP COME QUICK STOP.

Finney arrived a couple of days later by train.

"So, where's my Alma at?"

"If you don't mind, Mr. Finney," Reno said, "could I have my month's expenses first? I'm just about bust."

Finney handed him the money, and they took a cab to the Warwick Plaza, where they found Alma wearing a frilly, flesh-colored dressing gown with nothing underneath, what smelled like a half-bottle of perfume, and a great big smile.

"Darlin', I just don't know how you ever goin' find it in your heart to forgive me."

Meekly, Finney accepted her apologies, thanked Reno profusely for his help, and hit him with a thousand in cash plus a hundred-dollar bonus.

Then he entrained for Dallas with his wife.

That night in Yuma, while Finney slept in their Pullman berth, Alma looted his wallet and jumped the train. She caught an express to Los Angeles, met Reno at Union Station, and they celebrated with a champagne breakfast at the Beverly Wilshire Hotel.

"You know," Reno said, abashed and perhaps somewhat alarmed at Alma's dazzling display of duplicity, "I almost feel sorry for the guy."

"Now, Reno, don't you go feelin' sorry for that man," she said, spilling champagne on the lace counterpane in a giggling fit. "I told you what he was like. This how he gets his kicks!"

The following night there was a terrible earthquake. The epicenter was located near Lancaster, in Antelope Valley, fifty miles to the north. But it shook the old Beverly Wilshire to its foundations, broke a lot of glass, and tossed Reno and Alma out on the rug just in time to escape destruction when the chandelier swung itself off its ceiling hook and plunged onto their bed.

In the morning, Reno determined that it must be a sign, if not from God, then at least from Mammon, and convinced Alma to forgo her acting career for the time being and make haste for Lancaster, where they would invest their new capital in the construction business and help rebuild the ravaged towns and villages of Antelope Valley.

Chapter Two

Smoothly rounded, calamine blue, the Tehachapi Mountains swell gently to the north. Spiny, rock-ribbed, green ocher, the San Francisquitos rear up to the south. Between them, the high desert plateau called Antelope Valley splays out in a vast and near perfect isosceles triangle, its base running fifty miles due north along the Southern Pacific Railroad tracks from Palmdale to Mojave, the apex fixed at the convergence of the mountains on a bare windy ridge near Castaic Lake and the Tejon Pass. The plateau is tipped slightly, with its higher, more verdant sections in the west, and its drier sections to the east as it fans out into the great alkaline basin of the Mojave Desert. Cut off from more temperate zones, the climate of the valley inclines toward the continental. In summer, the heat is intense. In winter, the desert is occasionally carpeted with snow. In spring and fall, when pressure differences between the coast and desert are greatest, the plateau's tilted triangular shape acts as a gigantic funnel, accelerating winds from the interior as they seek a way through narrow mountain defiles.

It is called Antelope Valley for the great herds of wild antelope that once ranged its sagebrush floor from end to end. Yet, the Spanish considered it an evil, accursed place—earthquake-prone, full of sinkholes that swallowed men without a trace, and they never went there even to hunt. Until late in the nineteenth century, its only human visitors were nomadic bands of Mojave Indians and twenty-mule-team waggoneers on their way north from Los Angeles to the borax mines in Red Mountain and Boron.

Even into the 1930s, it remained sparsely settled, with some isolated alfalfa farms, cattle ranches, and almond orchards in the west, and a few railroad hamlets in the east. Its chief town, Lancaster, was still surrounded by miles of trackless desert and existed in a purely service capacity, refueling and watering the cars, trucks, trains, and travelers that came through on their way to Death Valley, the High Sierras, and western Nevada.

Reno and Alma arrived there in early 1937. Yet, despite all of Reno's high hopes, he did not do well in the construction business. Earthquake damage was nowhere near as severe as he had anticipated. The Depression wasn't over yet, and he was not the only out-of-work builder attracted to the area. His relationship with his common-law wife, Alma, suffered, and after the babies started to come along, they were rarely on terms of equanimity.

Alma complained of Reno's expensive cigars, and his living beyond their means. She called herself a "poker widow" and never stopped moaning about the kiddies she'd so rashly abandoned in Dallas. She even went so far as to weep over her dear old husband, Francis X. Finney, with whom she would be so much better off now.

For his part, Reno could not abide Alma's whining mouth, her laziness and vanity, her lack of attention to the needs of their children, her chronic hypochondria, her habit of tippling at a hidden bottle of gin all day long, her increasing weight, and her decreasing interest in the physical pleasures which had brought them together in the first place.

By 1941, Reno's business was on the skids. After losing the family home in a disastrous attempt to recoup his losses on the crap tables of Las Vegas, he was lucky enough to be offered a job as construction supervisor for a projected military airfield. It was to accommodate United States Air Force and Royal Air Force pilots for training purposes, and it was to be called "Eagle Field" in honor of the Eagle Squadron of World War I.

After accepting the government's offer and searching Antelope Valley for a possible site, Reno decided on a dry lake six miles west of Lancaster. Why he chose that spot for the air base, when you could land a plane just about anywhere in the desert, no one could explain.

Yet, it was there, at Eagle Field, on December 7, 1941, Pearl Harbor Day, that Alma bore the ugly duckling who would be the last of their brood.

Unlooked for, uncalled for, unlikely product of an imperfect prophylactic and a rare night of conjugal concupiscence, little Ruby Rose arrived kicking and screaming, delivered a month prematurely by an incompetent military quack and a green medical corpsman distracted by the air raid sirens shrieking overhead. Due to the primitive conditions at the air base, still under construction, and the gross malpractice of the attending physician, the birth was exceedingly difficult, and mother and daughter came perilously close to death.

Later, Alma would take their improbable survival as a miracle. And she would cherish her newborn, despite or precisely because of its baleful prospects, as a sign of her own great good fortune.

Reno treated the newborn just as he treated his other children—just as in old age he would treat his pet cats—with habitual indifference, punctuated by sudden outbursts of convivial affection.

Puny, pink-eyed, and colicky, utterly unlike her long-limbed, golden-tressed, older siblings, Ruby was born with a great bald dome, a howling red face, and thick carrot-colored eyebrows that met at the center of her forehead in what her father laughingly described as "Circassian fashion."

Her parents called her "Ruby" because red was what came to mind; it was their favorite color, they had little else in common, and they could agree on absolutely nothing else.

Ruby's big sister, Dee, doted on her from the beginning—changing her, bathing her, dressing her up like a baby doll several times a day. But her brother, Lonnie, resented her incessant bawling which cut into his normal ten hours of sleep a night. And he could never get it through his thick skull that the colic was not her fault, that it was the result of forces—gas and indigestion—that were beyond her control. On one of the rare occasions when Lonnie could be induced to hold his baby sister, when she was almost a year old, he became so distracted by her wailing mouth, her rigid little body and popping eyes, that he dropped her on her head.

No permanent damage was done. But forever after, when contemplating the notion of great heights, Ruby would suffer from a severe form of vertigo. And she would remain convinced throughout the course of her childhood that she was soon to take a great fall, and that nobody, not all the king's horses and all the king's men, would be able to put her back together again.

The Eagle Field construction project was completed in early 1943. But by then, the Department of War required Reno's services elsewhere. So, while Alma, Lonnie, Dee, and Baby Ruby stayed behind in their little construction foreman's house trailer, buffeted by sand, wind, and the slipstreams of rapidly ascending and descending Liberators and Flying Fortresses, the bread winner of the family was sent all over the West, supervising military construction projects. He was absent, therefore, during some of Ruby's most formative experiences.

The wailing of an air raid siren was the first of her conscious memories. It went off somewhere very near, pitched almost beyond endurance. Her brother Lonnie—a shadowy and insubstantial figure until then—suddenly materialized above her crib, frighteningly oversized and real, shouting at the top of his lungs, dancing a mad little jig, and she cried out in fear. But then her big sister Dee appeared, shooed Lonnie away, put a finger to her lips, and whispered, "Hush, baby, hush. We whipped the Germans now and Daddy will be home soon."

The next thing that Ruby would recall was sleeping in her mother's bedroom one night and waking to see a strange man standing outside the trailer in the moonlight, wearing flying boots, a blue-belted military uniform, and an overseas cap tilted down over his brow.

"Pssssssst," he whispered. "Alma!"

Huge, hulking and slit-eyed, with a florid face and a fierce, gingery mustache, the stranger had a funny way of pronouncing her mother's name.

"Whozat? Whozat?" Alma said, rolling swiftly out of bed.

"It's 'arry, love."

"Harry? Harry? Is it really you?"

"Well, it ain't the bleedin' Prince of Wales then, is it?"

"Hot damn!" she cried, stumbling over toys and slippers in the darkness, reaching across the crib to open the window.

"When'd you get in, honey?"

"Winged in from Vic not an hour ago, love," he said. "Flippin' left inboard wanked on us over Frisco. Lost the outboard over Bakersfield, an' I'm a lucky bugger to be standin' 'ere in the bloody flesh. Now let us in, ducks, afore I freeze me fuckin' ballocks off."

She helped him squeeze in through the narrow window and over Ruby's crib. Helped him off with his clothes as well. They hopped into bed together. He crawled on top of her, and soon Mama was making such a racket—moaning and groaning, rocking the trailer violently on its springs—that Ruby assumed the man was trying to hurt her. And she screamed out in terror. Shrieked till she felt her lungs might burst, till Lonnie and Dee were banging at the metal door, the lights in the trailer house next door were going on, and the stranger was cursing under his breath, "Gol blimey, fuck me black an' blue, if this don't take the bloody cake!"

Hitching up his woolen, uniform trousers, he crawled backwards over Ruby's crib, squeezed painfully through the tiny window, and dropped to the ground outside.

"What's the matter, Mama?" Lonnie and Dee kept shouting from beyond the door. "What is it?"

"Go back to bed!" Alma yelled, sobbing, squirming, thrashing about in what Ruby would many years later identify as a paroxysm of aroused but unquenched desire. "It was only a bad dream."

And then, to Ruby's utter amazement, it turned out the stranger was not her daddy after all.

Her daddy was smaller, darker, quicker on his feet, with pouchy, darting, little brown eyes, a sharp nose, thin mustache, and curly black hair that he slicked back with brilliantine. He was always laughing, always talking very smooth and fast, and he wore spiffy-looking clothes: a gray fedora, a blue, pin-striped suit, and shiny black shoes.

Ruby found this out a few months later, when Reno came home from his latest government construction project, threw her up in the air, caught her in his arms and cried, "Whoopie!"

"Guess what, kids?" he said, beaming with happiness, as they crowded around him. "I've been offered a new job."

"Where at, Dad?" Lonnie wanted to know.

"Right here on the base," he said, grinning mischievously. "The garden spot of the Far West."

"Is that right?" Alma said. "What doin'?"

"Now that the war's over, they need a reconstruction supervisor," he said, taking his hat off, flinging it onto the sofa, pivoting gracefully to meet her eyes again. "We're going to convert this place into a vocational institution for the state, with separate male and female facilities."

"Now, would you please tell me," Alma said crankily, "what the go-to-hell is a vocational institution?"

"Well, to be perfectly frank, it's a kind of—" Reno paused for effect—"a prison for the criminally insane."

"For the who?"

"Nut cases to you, Alma," he said, holding up his hands as if to ward off some violent move from his humorless consort. "Now hold your horses, dear. A lot of guys would jump at the chance, now that the government has stopped throwing money around."

"Uh-huh," she said. "And just how long this thing supposed to last?"

"A year, they tell me. Then, I can stay on as a maintenance supervisor if I want. There's a house to go along with it."

And that very afternoon—a rare afternoon in October with not a breath of wind—he took them all on a tour.

Reno, Alma, Lonnie, and Dee, everyone towering over little Ruby, they strolled around the edge of the base, with the great dry lake and the World War II runways on their right, and the neat, khaki, two-story Air Corps barracks on their left.

"Come on, Ruby," Reno said suddenly, laughing, clapping his hands. "Let's see how fast you can run!"

And she didn't think twice but took off like a jackrabbit, heading for the west end of the base, toward great rusting heaps of junked bombers and fighter planes that bobbed up and down in front of her as she ran.

"Run, Ruby, run!" he shouted, and started chasing after her. "Bet I can catch you. Bet I can!"

Hearing her daddy's heavy footsteps pounding along behind her, she increased her speed till it felt she might lift off the runway, might take off and fly like one of those old bombers, and she reached the perimeter of the base long before Reno.

"Whew! You're too fast for me, young lady," he hollered, when he finally drew up beside her, huffing and puffing and slapping his knee. Then he looked at her sharply and pretended to do a double take. "Why, you know, Ruby, for a while there I was beginning to wonder, but here lately you have turned into the prettiest little thing!"

And she shivered with delight.

The Rose's new home, Unit B-20, was located at the end of a long, straight, evenly spaced row of twenty identical Quonset huts whose narrow, metal-canopied, halfmoon-shaped, front porches faced north, and at the end of another equal line of Quonset huts whose curving flanks were exposed to the strong prevailing winds.

Reno claimed that their home's "aerodynamic configuration" would deflect much of the wind's destructive force. But Alma pointed out—correctly, as it turned out—that its serrated metal roof would tend to accentuate the sound of rushing air, resulting in an unholy shrieking noise that would last for the entire duration of the windy season.

"Why, it's nothing but another tin box," she said, shaking her head, resting her fat little fists on the capacious hips of her pink pedal pushers. "In summer, it's goin' be an oven, in winter a refrigerator, just like that damn trailer house. But hell, ever since I met you, Reno, seems like I been livin' backwards, so I guess there ain't no reason to expect any different now."

Ruby, on the other hand, vastly preferred the Quonset hut. It was bigger than the trailer, with a room for her and Dee, and a room for Lonnie as well. And it boasted a little front yard with flagstone steps, a flowerbed, and a patch of grass with a white picket fence. There was even a victory garden in back and a pepper tree with a swing. Yet, for some reason the most vivid impression Ruby had of the Quonset hut was of its kitchen linoleum which was a brilliant blue. She was fixated on that kitchen floor, stared at it, sat on it, played on it for hours, and from then on blue was her favorite color.

Just before they left that day, Dee took her out back and pushed her on the swing. Not too high. Just enough to give her a little thrill.

When they got about halfway home, Alma started limping on her high heels, complaining that her ankles had swollen up and she had to sit down. So, they all sat for a time on a flood control embankment, under a young cottonwood tree, watching Caterpillar tractors digging a gigantic hole in the dry lake bottom, shoveling great piles of rusting war surplus inside, raising great white clouds of alkali dust.

Then an enormous thundering bomber flew overhead, very low. It had six, big, rear-facing, pusher-type engines and six propellors, one of which wasn't spinning.

"The Flying Wing," Reno said, in respectful tones. "Heading for Edwards Air Force Base with one motor out."

The plane disappeared over the horizon. Suddenly, everyone hushed as if listening for something else to happen. But there was only the drone of the Caterpillars across the dry lake, an early owl hooting in a Joshua tree on the bank, truck traffic on nearby Highway 138, the sun hanging low and vermilion above the blue Tehachipis.

Later, Ruby would remember that day as the happiest of her early life.

A not so pleasant time she would remember was one Christmas when Santa left her a shiny, red, American Flyer wagon, and her big brother took her out for a spin.

"Now you be careful with that little girl, Lonnie," Reno said, but Lonnie didn't listen. He never listened to anyone, and he had a mean, teasing streak that was always getting him into trouble.

So, he took her out on the dry lake, whipping around the little sagebrush islands as fast as he could go, skidding the wheels on the dried clay, upsetting her twice, getting her new red, white, and green Christmas dress all dirty, mocking her when she cried.

"Stop, Lonnie, stop, I wanna go home!" she shrieked, but he paid her no mind.

"Wheeeeeeee! Wheeeeeeee!" he went, as if it were all great fun.

And he ran her up a kind of ramp that consisted of an old, engineless, Flying Fortress wing leaning on a hummock of sand and sage.

"Wheeeeeee!" he kept yelling and took her right off the end.

The wagon up ended in mid-air and Ruby felt herself flying, falling, and benumbed by a strong yet uncertain emotion that was neither terror, nor ecstasy but contained a measure of both.

Then everything went black. When she came to, she was lying on the dry lakebed, little worse for wear but with a mouth full of bitter alkaline clay. She jumped up spitting and crying and took off running for the house.

"I'm gonna tell on you, Lonnie! Gonna tell on you!"

"Now hold on a minute, Ruby," he pleaded, suddenly changing his tune, tagging along behind her, pulling the wagon. "Don't tell. Don't tell and I tell you what. I'll give you a nickel, I'll buy you a lollypop."

"Don't want no lollypop," she wailed. "I want my mama!"

"Alright, girl," Lonnie warned. "You tell, and I swear I'll get you back."

"I don't care," she said, hurt to the quick that her big brother could treat her so. "I don't care, I'm gonna tell my mama!"

At home, though, Mama did not seem too interested in Ruby's story. So, she went looking for her daddy. Found him out back in the lean-to shed where he had his little workshop set up. Had his tools, his camp bed, his camp stove, and his portable blueprint table out there; the ones he had carried with him on his travels in Mexico.

"Lonnie hurt me, Lonnie hurt me!" she cried, hurtling into his arms. "Run me clean off the Flying Fortress wing!"

"He *what?*" Reno said, raising off the camp bed where he'd been reading a *Scientific American,* unfastening his big double-tonged belt. "What did you say?"

The funny thing about Ruby's father, from her point of view as a kid, was his educated, well-modulated voice—a voice utterly unlike her mother's or anyone else's at Eagle Field, aside from the Chief Psychiatrist. Even when Reno was trying to be funny, or, on the other hand, even when he was correcting one of the kids, his voice remained at an even pitch, his tone polite and reasonable, his words following each other swiftly and smoothly, with a touch of irony.

"What did you say?" he said again, making her repeat the whole thing. "And where is Lonnie now?"

"He's in the Quonset hut, Daddy, in the hut!" Ruby shrilled, full of righteous indignation, leading him inside by the hand, pointing to where Lonnie lay on his belly, insolently reading a *Norman* comic book on the living room rug. "There he is! There he is!"

Reno didn't even ask the boy whether he was guilty or not. Just walked up and laid his thick leather belt across his butt as hard as he could, one, two, three, four, five, *six* times, raising dust with every wallop.

In this way, Reno was like other parents at Eagle Field, and Ruby found it almost comforting, if she wasn't on the receiving end. But then she started feeling sorry for poor Lonnie, watching him roll and writhe on the floor, gritting his teeth to avoid crying out, switching his legs convulsively to deflect the blows.

"Okay, Daddy, okay!" she cried. "He won't do it no more! He won't do it no more!"

But Reno was into it now, subjecting this great big half-grown lummox to his will, and he wouldn't listen.

"Lonnie, I sincerely hope this will teach you a lesson," he said, panting with his effort, "a lesson to never, never do that to your little sister again."

Lonnie did not say a word the whole time. But he was looking at Ruby, looking hard, every chance he got.

And if looks could kill . . .

A week or so later, she was playing with Gil and Juanita Sanchez, the neighbor kids. They were down in a flood control culvert, up to their knees in brackish white water, hidden behind a stand of stale-smelling cattails and some piled tumbleweeds. They had their pants pulled off, hanging from a little juniper tree on the bank, and they were playing "Doctor & Nurse."

Gil was the doctor. Ruby and Juanita were the nurses. And they were cleaning each other's wounds, splashing water on them, rubbing them to make them feel better. Gil's wound was on the uncircumcised head of his brown and erect little penis. The girls' wounds were located immediately inside the folds of their slick and wet little vaginas. And just as they were about to declare each other "healed" and call it a day, as they'd often done in the past, Lonnie's big leering face and shock of white-blond hair suddenly peered out from behind the piled tumbleweed.

"Well, well, well," he said, as the three of them stood there looking up at him like copulating cats caught suddenly in a flashlight beam. "What've we got here?"

Then he grabbed their jeans from the juniper tree and ran off, shouting cruelly, "You just wait right there, kids, wait and see what's coming!"

None of them had any illusions about where Lonnie was going. He was headed out to fetch Ruby's dad where he was working at the garbage dump. But none of them had the nerve to walk home half-naked through the entire Eagle Field Dependents' Area, not even to save their lives.

So, they just stayed right where they were, clutching the soft, muddy bottom with their tense little toes, too scared to cry, until Reno showed up with Lonnie in tow.

"Okay, kids," Reno said, as calm and polite as ever. "I don't like to be a spoilsport, but could you please come out of there now?"

And they climbed whimpering out of the water, covering their private parts.

"Now, whose idea was this?" Reno demanded, while Lonnie hovered behind him, grinning.

"It was Ruby's idea, Mr. Rose!" Gil said, a truth for which she would never forgive him. "It was all her idea!"

"All right, Gil," Reno said, swatting him hard across his bare brown buttocks. "Why don't you just head on home now? And take your little sister along with you."

"But what about our pants?"

"Should've thought of that when you took 'em off, kid!" Lonnie teased, chasing them off over the embankment.

"You too, Lonnie," Reno said, when he reappeared. "I'd like to talk to the young temptress in private if I may."

"Aw, come on, Dad!"

"I really would appreciate it, Son, if you'd just toddle on out of here," Reno said, and it was quite enough to send Lonnie hastening on his way.

Reno's sudden, unaccountable sincerity and concern effected Ruby in a manner that perhaps opposed his intentions. It frightened her more than any threat might have done, more than any physical beating, because she could not predict its outcome. Trembling, she sat with him on the bank. He turned to her, searching her eyes, quite as if she were some small adult from whom he wished fervently to elicit the truth. He was up so close, he could see the little hairs sprouting from his nostrils and ears, count every whisker on his face, explore the bloodshot swirls within his eyes, smell the cigar on his breath. Yet, he remained as unfathomable to her as the stars.

"You know what you deserve, don't you, Ruby?" Reno said, and for once there was not even a trace of irony in his tone. He seemed almost sad.

"I won't ever do it again, Daddy! Won't ever do it again!"

"You deserve what Lonnie got the other day," he said, grasping her firmly but politely by the arm, guiding her up the bank. "But I think this is too serious for a spanking. So, put your clothes on and sit down here beside me for a while.

"Ruby, I want you to listen very carefully to what I have to tell you," he said, with unaccustomed solemnity. "You're not going to understand all of it now, but you will when you're older. Now, I'm no saint, and neither is your mother. But what I want you to do is—I want you to benefit from our mistakes. What you were doing with Gil and Juanita a while ago is not wrong in itself. Curiosity like that is natural at your age. But you must think of where it might go, what it might lead to. You start playing around like that, especially with a Mexican boy, and it gets around. I'm not prejudiced, but that's the way it is. Then, when you're older, people start to think of you as easy, as cheap. And they start taking advantage of you. Next thing you know, you're married at a young age, and your life is over. I want better things for you, Ruby. The others—Lonnie and Dee—they're good kids, basically, but they don't have what you've got, and they never will. You're my one, my last hope. So don't disappoint me, please. I've already disappointed myself enough for one lifetime."

It was the longest speech he had ever made to her; they were both very moved at the end. She had never seen him cry before. She watched fascinated as the tears welled up, formed droplets, squeezed out the wrinkled corners of his eyes, and glided down his weathered cheeks to the gray stubble on his jaw. Never in her life had she felt so loved. Never had *she* loved so intently. She would have walked through fire for him at that moment, plunged her hand into boiling water. And she firmly intended to take heed of his warning, the full import of which she had only an inkling. She would remember it, understand it someday, behave according to its tenets, and when she was grown, she would be just the kind of girl he desired.

"I'll be good, Daddy, I'll be good!" she cried, inchoately, as he hugged her to his sweaty work shirt. "I promise—I promise."

Yet, the scary thing was, he had revealed such a new and different side of himself that it was like listening to another person talk. He had shown a stranger to her, a stranger she would always love and always believe in, but perhaps never meet again.

Chapter Three

A child of war like Ruby, Max Bauer was born on the day that Hitler's armies invaded France. He came into the world in a wine cellar at the American Hospital in Paris while air raid sirens screamed on the *Avenue de Neuilly* and bombs exploded among the munition barges tied up on the Seine a mile away.

His father, Fritz Bauer, was a German Expressionist painter, driven by the Nazis from his native Hamburg for his part-Jewish blood and his past as a Social Democrat.

His mother, Sybil Prince, was a globe-trotting American socialite, recently disowned by her strait-laced Santa Barbara family for "consorting with artists, Negroes, Jews, and Bohemians."

Sybil and her infant son enjoyed only a short respite in the American Hospital before being forced out by the Nazi *blitzkrieg*. With the German Army at Beauvais in the north and on the Marne to the east, Fritz managed to bribe his little family aboard the last train out of the Gare St. Lazare. Likewise, he was able to get them on the last ferry out of Le Havre and the last Cunard Line passenger liner out of Southampton.

After a period in New York, where Fritz was briefly incarcerated on Ellis Island as an "enemy alien," and an even briefer period in Santa Barbara, where Sybil sorted out her finances, the family moved to Antelope Valley. There, with a small inheritance that she had received long ago from her grandparents, they purchased a small ranch about three miles southwest of Gold Hill. Sybil was suffering from a mild case of tuberculosis, and an arid climate had been prescribed. The prescription turned out to be correct, and by the end of her first year in California her lungs were clear. Only then did they think to fill in the blank space on Baby Bauer's French birth certificate with a *prénom*. They named him, "Max", for Fritz's old friend, Max Ernst. But his mother never called him anything but "Lucky" for the near perfect bliss she had experienced ever since they had reached the sunny slopes of the high desert country.

The little town of Gold Hill, near which Sybil and Max would spend much of their lives, was in the western hinterland of Antelope Valley, yet fortunate enough to be hunkered in close under the northern slopes of the San Francisquito Mountains, and convenient to their seasonal snow runoff. It had started out as a mining camp shortly before the turn of the century, but its veins petered out just after World War I, and its residents took to growing almonds instead.

Afterwards, every February and March, the foothills of the mountains were white with flowering nut trees, the air lush with their pungent bouquet, and the town held its annual Almond Blossom Festival. The older brick and wood frame section of Gold Hill was built directly over the old Calico Mine, on a low rounded butte that heaved up out of the sloping alluvial plain. In the Fifties, the town began to creep out onto the plain, supplanting sagebrush, yucca, creosote, Joshua Trees, and even some of its precious almond orchards with ranch style subdivisions. But growth was uneven, and the town boundaries encompassed an optimistically large area, so the desert kept creeping back in. Overnight, you'd sometimes find vacant lots, baseball diamonds, main thoroughfares, and even the little juniper-fringed graveyard, smothered in sand.

A few miles southeast, on a ridge overlooking the town, a great, ramshackle, mock-Tudor mansion loomed, casting a long shadow over the valley. Constructed in the Twenties for a celebrated ballerina, it had later belonged to a silent movie star named Hillary Bennett, who spent the last forty years of her life holed up inside, virtually incommunicado. Yet, despite its dolorous history and sinister aspect, the place held no mystery or allure for the ordinary folks of the town, and they passed by in their pickup trucks and RV vehicles without even noticing it.

The Bauer's little ranch sat at the foot of some of the tallest peaks in the San Francisquito Range, straddling the mouth of a canyon down which flowed a tiny dry creek that petered out on the floor of the desert a mile or two away. The place was called Sand Canyon, and the ranch house had been constructed in 1907, on a rise above the flashflood line. It was built in the old California-style adobe, whitewashed, long and low, with a veranda that ran all the way across the front, and a patio in back. The view from the veranda, through its trestles of purple wisteria, was exceedingly dramatic, encompassing the snowy crest of Sawmill Mountain on the right, the low cactus and yucca covered rim of the canyon in front, the creek flanked by two long narrow almond orchards below, and the flat, gray, and brown expanse of Antelope Valley off to the left.

The ranch's outbuildings—a barn, a stable, a chicken house, a two-car garage—climbed haphazardly up nearly to the western rim of the canyon. On the sage-brushy ridge to the rear of the house stood an old, wood-framed building which had once been the servants' quarters, then a bunkhouse, and finally the studio of the previous owner, a well-known writer of Western novels. Here, Fritz set up his easels and oils and began to paint. Sybil asked if he wouldn't like to tear out a portion of the roof for a skylight, but he refused. "It is good light," he said, "but it is not my light." He kept all the shades drawn, the doors shut tight, painted by electric light, and his pictures came out looking exactly as they had in Europe: Despite his vivid palette, his startling contrasts, his virile, active shapes and forms, and his abrasive, yet brilliantly conceived sense of harmony, the final effect of his work was bleakness and depression.

Soon after Fritz settled in at the ranch, he had begun to feel touchy and uneasy. It was eerily calm over here in America, compared to the auto-destruction on the other side of the world. Here, the sun came up warm and rosy every morning and slid smoothly into an implausibly azure sky. Birds sang in the almond orchards. Insects buzzed in the alfalfa fields. The coats of domesticated animals glistened in the sunshine. Little Max grew plump and pink on a seemingly endless diet of rich creamy cow's milk. Sybil whistled while she did her morning household chores as if there weren't a care on earth. The lights in the house went on at the flip of a switch. Hot water flooded out of the tap with the flick of a wrist. The car started the instant you pushed the ignition button (it had an automatic transmission, so you didn't even have to trouble yourself to shift the gears). And in town, the stores were packed to overflowing with brightly packaged consumer goods. If one did not read the newspaper, or listen to the radio, or bother to drive the fifty-odd miles into Los Angeles from time to time, one would never guess there was a war going on, that an entire race was being systematically annihilated across the sea. It simply would not sink into Fritz's head that they were all safe and sound. This place, this "California," it was a bit too much for one to swallow. In this age of destruction, what could it have to do with reality? Fritz therefore began to ignore his improbable surroundings and devote his whole attention to painting. He painted as he had never painted before. He painted as if there were no tomorrow, as if any second he would wake up in Auschwitz or Bergen-Belsen. He painted furiously, marvelously, from memory. And when it came time for his first exhibition in America, at the Los Angeles County Art Museum in 1944, he called it "Scenes of War," after Goya.

Despite its timely qualities, however, Fritz's show was not a success. In Los Angeles, he believed, they did not understand his passion, his pain. With the sky always blue, how could they know what he suffered, his *angst?* And, quite apart from that, they did not know the meaning of art, out here. They were social climbers, parvenus. They were looking for big names. They were interested in investment, not perfection. He should have gone to New York, perhaps, where Max Ernst and others of his fellow exiles were knocking them dead. But what could one do? If one was fortunate enough to have landed in a sunny paradise while the rest of the world went up in smoke, dared one ask for more? Nobody ever claimed that art might flourish in a land without cares. So, Fritz went back to work. And from then on, he had no more to do with exhibitions. He resigned himself to a certain period of exile and painted for himself. He painted for posterity. He painted for his beloved old *Deutschland* that would one day rise from the ashes.

After his show at the Los Angeles County Art Museum, Fritz was never again happy in America. And, as the war went on, seemingly endlessly, his sense of alienation and despair increased to the point where it affected his artistic production. Gradually it diminished, in both quantity and quality. Day after day, month after month, year after year, he locked himself in his studio on the hill, listlessly dabbing at canvasses he no longer believed in, staring at his blank wooden walls, pining for his old, pre-Hitlerian homeland, waiting for the war to be over, and for Europe to reconstruct itself sufficiently to make his return possible.

Unfortunately, there was yet another impediment to the eventual achievement of his dream. Sybil was blissful here on the ranch, and she had no wish to drag her little son back to that cold, bleak, hungry place across the sea from which they had so recently escaped at great peril to their lives.

When Fritz saw himself going back to Europe, therefore, it was always alone. He made no secret of it, and if Sybil did not exactly approve, then at least she did not protest too much. It had become self-evident to them soon after they reached California that their marriage had been a mistake. Aside from their obvious dissimilarities of language and culture, they were also divided by their temperaments. In his heart, and despite his Jewish mother, his background as an artist and political activist, Fritz remained a North German burger's son—cold, cautious, methodical, fastidious. Sybil, on the other hand, was by nature ardent, impetuous, disorderly, and rebellious. They were divided even by their age and size. Fritz, though still healthy and vigorous, was a stout little bullet-headed fellow of late middle age. Sybil was a tall, slender, handsome young woman who had been born the year Fritz was serving with the Imperial German Cavalry on the Eastern Front.

They had met in the South of France, where Fritz was teaching a class in "life drawing" at a summer art institute, and Sybil was a nervous, Vassar girl on a *wanderjahr* abroad. It was a classic case. She had lost her father when she was young. He was facing the crisis of his fiftieth year. Add to this the fact that she was an American, an apparent heiress, and he was a refugee, an artist who had never been able to achieve even a semblance of financial independence, and you come up with a match. And it was not an altogether unsuccessful match. For one thing, it produced a fine son who would surely go on to do great things someday. And for another, after the passion had gone out of the marriage, a very strong teacher-pupil relationship remained. Also, to a certain extent, their opposite temperaments balanced out. With the aid of liberal doses of California wine, Sybil was sometimes able to coax a moment of gaiety, or at least levity, out of dour Fritz. And sometimes Fritz was able to induce Sybil to put a little order and forethought into her life. Aside from this, Fritz's sojourn in the Golden State would afford him endless opportunities for carping about the "vulgarity" of America and the inefficiency of its government for the rest of his life.

For her part, Sybil was a life-long romantic, and she would forever cherish the memory of her tragic love affair with a European artist, and her dangerous flight to the New World, just as the flames of war engulfed the Continent.

As Max grew toward boyhood it became increasingly evident whom in the family he would favor. Short and stocky, solid as a rock, he was the image of his father, right down to the Baltic gray eyes. He had inherited Fritz's taciturn nature as well, along with his manual dexterity and organizational skills. But he lacked his parents' imaginative, contemplative side, and from the very beginning had his feet planted firmly in the here and now. Max's instinctive devotion to the real and attainable, his lifelong rejection of the fanciful in all its forms, was a character trait reinforced by early experience and observation. He never saw his parents benefit particularly from their artistic endeavors and concluded therefore that his own path would be straighter. Unfortunately, this set him up for conflict with his parents; for if they had one thing in common, it was their worship of art and culture.

Their first confrontation occurred during Max's fourth year, when he became so obsessed with automobiles for a while that he went around on all fours, with a squeezable rubber horn tied around his neck, honking, screeching his brakes, and swerving wildly about the house, insisting to all who inquired that his name was not Max but "Car." It was then that Fritz, at Sybil's instigation, suddenly put a stop to Max's habit of drawing on little scratchpads whatever popped into his head (usually cars, which he rendered with distressing accuracy), and instituted a twice weekly regimen of hour-long drawing lessons up in his painting studio. But Max turned out to be so inept and recalcitrant at drawing anything but machinery, and so singularly uninterested in recreating the images of nature, that Fritz—after a year of fuming over the child's "willful incompetence"—threw up his hands in disgust and never bothered him with the matter again. Likewise, when Sybil thought it time that Max took dancing lessons and enrolled him in a children's ballet course in Lancaster, the boy proved so resistant to training, and made such a spectacle of himself—lumbering about the dance loft like a Neanderthal, setting all the little girls to tittering behind their hands, putting them off their paces—that the dance mistress was obliged to send him packing after his second lesson. Following a similar experience with a violin teacher, Max's parents gave up on his artistic education.

But the one thing that neither of them would relent on was their monthly trip to the Hollywood Bowl to listen to the Los Angeles Philharmonic. Though Fritz never tired of bemoaning the orchestra's "total lack of distinction and its penchant for movie music," and they sometimes worried about the dent the journey put into their modest family budget, it was the one dose of culture that they allowed themselves, and not even Max's relentless campaign of passive resistance could put them off it... Not at least until he hit upon the device of fidgeting. At first, Max fidgeted only because he was bored and uncomfortable. Yet, after he detected how much his fidgeting provoked his parents, and irritated their fellow listeners, he gradually perfected it into an art. He thought of fiendish ways to make his fold-up chair squeak, to amplify the sound of his feet dragging over the gravel underfoot. Finally, Fritz and Sybil had to throw up their hands and leave him home when they went to the Hollywood Bowl. They hired a fourteen-year-old high school girl named "Preçiosa" to look after him once a month. Preçiosa was the eldest sister of Max's best friend, Carlos "Charlie" Gonçalves, the son of a Portuguese fruit and nut farmer named Pedro Gonçalves.

Though Preçiosa chewed gum constantly, and was none too swift on the uptake, she was uncommonly pretty, with skin exactly the color of, and eyes exactly the shape of, her father's almonds. She used to bring Charlie along with her when she came to babysit and let him and Max watch her when she bathed (the Gonçalves had no indoor plumbing at their place). She did towel dances for them, and a "Dance of the Seven Veils." She let them wash out her panties and brassier and hang them over the gas heater to dry. She let them suck her luscious little nutlike titties and touch her black, crinkly, pubic hair. She let them do just about anything they wanted with her, short of penetrating her, for she was a religious Catholic and feared a mortal sin.

Thus did Max resist all his parents' efforts to bend him to their will. Thus, from an early age did he choose his own sweet way. And to this day, if you'd care to ask him, he probably couldn't name you a Gothic Cathedral, a Renaissance statue, a Baroque painting, a Classical symphony, or Symbolist poem to save his soul. But he could still fix your car, or your motorcycle—body & fender work, or engine repair—and do a good job of it.

Which all goes to say that although Max truly loved his parents and always looked upon their odd foreign ways with tolerance and amusement, he never really trusted their judgement—how could any two people so clearly at odds with their own environment be right? Instinctively, he had made a choice in favor of the values of his friends and neighbors in Antelope Valley, and his parents did not conform to those values. Not only that, but they did also not act, talk, or look like anybody else either. Fritz was the only real artist in Gold Hill, unless you counted the old, silent movie star, Hillary Bennett, who lived as a recluse on the outskirts of town. His German accent was ridiculous, like *"Herr Doktor Profezor"* on the Sid Caesar show. He was absurdly older than Sybil, or any of the other kids' parents, more like a grandpa than a father. And he insisted that Max call him *"Fatti,"* which made all his pals howl with laughter. Sybil wasn't much better, with her snobby upper-class accent, finishing school airs, svelte figure, and stylish clothes, her ignorance of darning, ironing, baking, canning, and all the other housewifely arts, and her total lack of interest in the PTA, the yearly school carnival, or even the Almond Blossom Festival. To make things worse, Max's parents disapproved of just about everything that he and Charlie held dear, including model airplanes, baseball cards, bubble gum, Soap Box Derby racers, yo-yo competitions, sports car magazines, EC Comics, box top collections, Walt Disney movies, and Little League softball. Charlie's folks complained that they—with their beat-out old pickup truck and busy schedule—were always the ones who had to take time out and go to the expense of hauling the boys around to ballgames, after-school activities, Saturday matinees, the city plunge and the county fair, while Fritz and Sybil, who could much better afford the time and money, sat around with their heads in the clouds. And though Max intuited that the Gonçalves' resentment was tempered by an Old-World respect and admiration for their "social betters," he never got over his embarrassment at his parents' strange, imperious ways, and smarted at the fact that he had to apologize for them all the time.

Even so, his childhood could by no means be described as unhappy or deprived. On the contrary, his parents obviously cared for him very deeply, they were always there when he really needed them, and they were quite prepared to devote a great deal of attention to him, if he would only let them. What's more, and despite their ill-concealed indifference to many of his most cherished pursuits, and their disappointment at his lackluster performance in school, they left him with plenty of room to make his own mistakes and discoveries and made only cursory and sporadic attempts to mold him into the carbon copy of themselves that he would clearly never be.

On a certain level, Max was even proud of his parents. They were so much more worldly, literate, and cultivated than anyone else he knew. And they often delighted him with their displays of imagination, especially when they told him bedtime stories. They had started out by reading him make-believe things like *Winnie the Poo*, and *Jemima Puddleduck*, but he quickly grew tired of those, and insisted that they tell him real stories from their own lives. And at this they both excelled. Max would always remember the richly detailed, months long saga of his father's career as a World War I horse soldier, illustrated with bloody, realistic, pencil drawings from the journal he had kept through all his campaigns. Nor would he forget his mother's vivid, tragic account of her break with her family, a depiction that included all the dramatic elements so dear to children's hearts, including a wicked stepmother, a cowardly and deceitful half-brother, a jealous half-sister, and the swindling of our heroine's parental inheritance.

There were other pleasant memories as well. Every evening in warm weather, for instance, the family had a strictly observed "quiet hour" on the veranda. Max loved these times, and he would recall with special fondness all his life the sound of his mother's rocker, the creak of his father's wicker chair, the rattle of ice in their evening drinks, as they sat reading silently or drawing in their sketchpads or simply gazing at the sunset while Max sprawled on the floor below them, grooming his dog, Buster Brown, or working with his building blocks, his Erector Set, or one of his model airplanes. The contentment he experienced at such times was extraordinary, almost passionate, and he felt it go in waves all through him. He felt that everything was in its proper place, that God was in heaven, and all was well on earth.

There was one particularly lovely evening in the late summer that he would never forget—an evening with soft, pink-edged, cotton ball clouds in the sky and just the faintest breath of wind. The air seemed as soft as the clouds, and the temperature was absolute perfection—not the slightest twinge of cold, not the tiniest edge of heat. Max was squatting on the floor, bare-chested, wearing only a pair of cut-off jeans, repairing a model airplane engine, when suddenly all the crickets and nightbirds went silent. Max, Sybil, and Fritz all jerked their heads up at once, but none quickly enough to catch it: A strange white light had flashed across the sky; it had come and gone in the blink of an eye. Max glanced from his mother to his father, seeking an explanation. Fritz raised his eyebrows, shrugged his shoulders, and sniffed the air, as if he might detect the cause with his sense of smell. But Sybil, who read the *Los Angeles Times* every day from cover to cover, smiled knowingly and pointed toward the dark northeastern horizon, toward the distant Colorado River and Las Vegas, Nevada. "Ah!" Fritz exclaimed, in his curious, Middle European intonation, then laughed and—when Max still looked puzzled—deftly sketched in the air with his large, expressive hands a gigantic, mushroom cloud that swelled and boiled and trembled with energy as it rose slowly toward the sky. "Oh!" said the boy, nodding enthusiastically, yet still disinclined not to break their sacred, self-imposed hour of meditation. And they all smiled at each other and went back to what they had been doing before.

The experience left Max feeling even cozier and more contented in his fragile little family circle. The evening seemed to him even more precious for the threat of extinction it contained. Out there across the desert, powerful, destructive forces had been unleashed by the National Nuclear Security Administration, but here, at Sand Canyon Ranch, the crickets had started up again, the nightbirds were calling, and down in the almond orchard the old electric pump was banging away as if it might go on forever.

By 1956, when Max was fifteen years old, Fritz felt that the situation in Germany had improved enough for him to return.

He wrote to the German government in Bonn, and to old friends and paternal relatives in Hamburg, seeking assurances that he would receive his pension as a World War I veteran, that an apartment and part-time art teacher's job would be waiting for him when he arrived. Then, he set about organizing all his paints and pictures, packing them into trunks and clearing out his studio. When he was done, he rented a U-Haul trailer, hitched it to the family station wagon, packed it with his things, and got Sybil and Max to drive him down to San Pedro, where he was to catch his steamer.

Though Max had been apprised of his father's plans for some time, and his parents had repeated to him several times in recent months that soon he would be called upon to be "the man of the house," the reality of Fritz's departure caught him completely unprepared. Even on the dock while his father's stuff was being hoisted aboard, he could not really believe this arrangement was going to be permanent. Apparently, his mother felt much the same way, for even as they visited Fritz in his stateroom that afternoon, toasting him with champagne, wishing him *bon voyage,* she was still talking as if they would all see each other again soon. It was Fritz himself who broke the spell, who insisted—in his cruelly literal-minded way—on confronting the reality of the situation.

"Before I leave," he said, holding them away from him at arm's length, shifting his gaze fondly from one of them to the other, "I would like to make my feelings very clear. I don't like this country, and I will never come here again, if I can help it. But I love you both, in quite different ways, and I will miss you very much, I am sure."

Max and his mother just stood there staring at him for a time, trying to assimilate the meaning of what he said.

Then Sybil spoke, clearly, thinly, shaping each syllable like cracked glass.

"Oh, I don't think you'll miss us for long, Fritz," she said. "You'll pick up right where you left off before the war, and eventually you'll look back on us as just a brief, unhappy interlude in a long and happy European life."

All the way back home to the ranch the two of them were silent, almost embarrassed with each other. But Max felt proud of his mother for what she had said. She had voiced his own feelings exactly, he thought.

They arrived exhausted and turned in early, but at five the next morning, they were awakened by a deep, far-off rumbling. Louder and louder, closer and closer it came. Max peered out his window and saw the leaves in the almond trees start to quiver. Then the foothills seemed to dance up and down. The house began to shake and rattle; dust clouds rose off the open fields, and a crack appeared down the middle of the driveway. A tremendous shock hit the house, shattering windows, raising havoc with the kitchen crockery, and abruptly Max found himself lying flat on his back on a pile of window shards while ceiling plaster rained down on his head.

"Earthquake, Mom!" he hollered. "Earthquake!"

When it was over, he stumbled through the debris of the ranch house to find Sybil cowering under her marital bed.

"Wouldn't you know," she said bitterly, as he pulled her out, "the sonofabitch would get out with the rats?"

Chapter Four

Down the hill from Max and Sybil, at Eagle Field, Ruby Rose began to understand that her world was different from other places. Space was limited in her neighborhood. Quarters were so close that relations with the neighbors were just short of incestuous. Her family resided on the edge of a state prison full of bloodthirsty criminal psychopaths who laughed wackily in the night and banged their metal cups against their cell bars, clamoring to be let out. Not to mention that they were surrounded by a vast, unpopulated desert and a dry lakebed that sometimes filled up without warning and splashed muddily against the Rose's frail, wood frame, back porch.

The first time that Ruby really became aware of the world beyond Eagle Field was on the day she turned nine and was permitted to accompany her brother and sister to Sand Canyon Reservoir. It was one of those golden days of very early summer, after the winds have died down and before the heat comes on. Riding into town through the almond orchards and the Joshua tree forest, she found the landscape somehow crisper, cleaner, less dusty than usual. And the shabby pink and pastel main street of Gold Hill sparkled in the sun.

She sat between her big brother and big sister, proud as punch, moving her sandal-clad feet around in a rapid, complicated dance step to avoid Lonnie's shifting gears, craning her neck to see out the windshield, watching the people strolling around in the streets of the town. The men in straw hats and suntans, the ladies in flower print dresses, bare legs and sandals, no one in uniform, and it seemed to her quite extraordinary.

Then Lonnie drove up Sand Canyon Road. In the dry creek, Ruby could see great piles of white rocks and isolated stands of cottonwoods, desert willows, and maples. An old wood and metal gold trestle snaked down the canyon, suspended on slender, rusting legs, staining the hillsides red. Sand Canyon Dam, though constructed of heavy, reinforced concrete, seemed to her thrillingly fragile in its rounded Art Deco contours and stylistic flourishes, as if it might burst its confines at any moment and send a wall of water down the canyon, sweeping away everything in its path. For the last three or four miles, the road wound up the steep chaparral walls of Portal Ridge, switching back and forth in tight curves, hanging over alarming cliffs with no guard rails.

Then Lonnie lit up a joint, toked at it long and hard, while trying to drive with one hand.

Done, he flicked the butt out the window, put a demonic look on his handsome, jut-jawed face, and jammed his foot down hard on the accelerator.

"Hey, let's see how fast we can go!" he hollered. "Whadaya say? Whadaya say?"

"Come on, Lonnie, quit goofin' around," Dee replied, grinning foolishly, "You're gonna get us in a wreck."

At first, it wasn't so bad because they were going uphill, and Lonnie's old Ford had seen better days. Then they reached the summit, tipped downward, and Ruby's stomach went hollow. The landscape—the brown, murky little body of water far below, the gray stony mountains surrounding it—wheeled dizzily from one side of the car to the other. The engine wound out in second gear. The tires squealed. The brakes protested, smelling of burnt friction lining.

Broadsiding around the sharpest of the switchback curves, they skidded to the brink of a two-hundred-foot cliff, then careened to the mountain side of the road again, scraping the side of the car on solid rock.

Ruby moaned, gritted her teeth, sucked air.

Dee's habitual passivity turned to panic.

Yet, neither cried out, nor begged Lonnie to relent; they knew it would only make him worse.

"I'm outta control!" he yowled, spinning his brodie knob back and forth. "Look out, world, I'm outta control!"

The edge coming ever nearer. The emptiness below like a vast hungry face. Now, like Humpty-Dumpty, Ruby would die, just as she had always known she would die, shatter into a million pieces, and not God in his heaven nor anyone else would ever be able to put her back together again.

The image was at once terrible and beautiful.

And when by some miracle the car made it to the bottom, and Lonnie parked in the Antelope Valley Water District parking lot, and everything went back to normal, Ruby experienced something akin to disappointment.

They changed into their swimsuits in the car.

Dee and Ruby sat in back.

Lonnie sat in front, peeking, making fun of them: "Peach Fuzz! Peach Fuzz!"

Then they walked down to the reservoir and spread their picnic things on the beach.

Later, Ruby convinced Dee to help her make a sandcastle. Ruby did the rough work on it, hauling mud from the shore and packing it into strong high walls, chattering to her big sister all the while. Dee did the fine work, constructing gateways, passages, porticos, and towers, sticking little white pebbles around the edges to create the illusion of ramparts.

Dee was a large, plump, pallid girl, not unpretty in her short, straw-blond pageboy and her red, two-piece bathing suit, but with a nature so placid and vague that Ruby didn't know quite what to make of her.

Dee would do just about anything she asked. Spent hours dressing her, combing her hair, talking baby talk to her, and routinely took the place of her alcoholic mother around the house. Yet, Ruby always had the feeling that Dee did not see her clearly. She seemed to look straight through her most of the time, failing to respond to repeated questions. Not that this was much different from anyone else in the family. They were all preoccupied and self-indulgent to a greater or lesser extent, and tended to treat Ruby like a household pet, or a piece of furniture for which they felt a thoughtless affection.

For Dee, Ruby existed rightly enough, but only as a kind of dimly perceived ideal, a character in the dreamworld where she spent most of her time. Sometimes, when Ruby put on one of the frantic little mime-shows or Shirley Temple song-and-dance routines that she had devised as a means of attracting her family's ever-flagging attention, Dee would laugh and clap along with the rest. Yet other times she would flash Ruby with an almost paranoid look, as if it were somehow seditious or subversive that her little moppet, her puppet, her baby doll, should perform so well outside the orbit of her mistress.

Ruby worked on the sandcastle for an hour or so, then stopped to watch her big brother swim out to the float and put on a diving show.

Lonnie was a fantastic diver, an inspired water comic as well, and he made the beachgoers gasp aloud over his antics. Golden hair flying, brown muscular body gleaming in the sun, he went off the high dive platform frontwards, backwards, sideways, slipping and twisting and somersaulting, barking like a seal, flipping his wings like a penguin, cavorting like a dolphin.

Finished, he swaggered out of the water, bowing to the wonder-struck onlookers, grinning triumphantly.

Tall, sleek, and tan, he seemed to his small sister beautiful and awful, winsome as a young Nazi Olympic star she had once seen in an old *LIFE* magazine.

Then he came over, stood on their sandcastle, crushing its walls and porticos, and shook himself off, getting Ruby and Dee all wet.

"Come on, quit it, Lonnie," Dee said mildly. "That's cold."

"Oooooooh!" Ruby went. She liked it. It made her feel good all over. "Someday," she said, "I'm gonna be big like you and Dee."

"Don't count on it, shrimp," Lonnie said, and slipped into the water again. "See you next lifetime, kids!"

And he swam way, way, way out, until they could not see him anymore.

Ruby and Dee waited and waited and waited, but their brother never came back.

The County Sheriff dragged Sand Canyon Reservoir for two days, but never found him. There was even some doubt that he was dead at all, for a boy matching his description was seen hiking over Portal Ridge the following day, and Dee found some of his clothes missing from his room.

Suspicions increased when it turned out that he was flunking all his classes in school, he was wanted for questioning in a burglary and vandalism case, he had gotten a fifteen-year-old Palmdale girl in trouble and her family was threatening to press statutory rape charges if he didn't marry her.

The sheriff was convinced that Lonnie had committed suicide, but the Roses had their doubts. It was just like Lonnie to set it up like that, and then have a macabre last laugh on them all.

Three months later they received a telegram from Parks Air Force Base in Dublin, California: SORRY FOR THE SCARE STOP JOINED AIR FORCE STOP DOING WELL STOP WILL WRITE MORE SOON STOP.

After Lonnie was gone, Ruby felt more alone than ever. But at the time, her feelings were mixed. On the one hand, she was sad to see him go and blamed herself to a certain extent for the curses and maledictions she had flung at him in the past. On the other hand, she could not help but breathe a sigh of relief that their unequal combat would now end in peace. At the same time, there was this other feeling that had come over her, very strong, a feeling that something was done now, something was gone, something that could never be again.

And it wasn't just her big brother.

When Lonnie went away, he took a great big chunk of Ruby's childhood along with him. And in the months that followed his disappearance, all her childish illusions fell away one by one. No longer could she ignore that her father came home from work only rarely and slept alone, that her mother cared for little but her daily bottle of gin, that Dee harbored sullen resentment against both her parents and could not wait to get out on her own. No longer could Ruby close her eyes to the fact that her family was not like other families at Eagle Field, that somehow it had gone dreadfully wrong.

Imperfect as the Rose family might have been, Alma was still at its core. Everyone reacted to her; she was the flaccid dough that held them together. Yet Alma wasn't there. Where she should have been there was just this great omnivorous hole, like the mouth of a vacuum cleaner, that sucked things in but never gave anything back.

The truth was, Ruby never had a mother. Dee was the only mother she ever knew. And Dee fell for a fast-talking Airman E-4 from Edwards AFB, not four months after Lonnie's disappearance, and ran off with him to Loring AFB in Caribou, Maine.

Dee asked Ruby to come with her—begged her, even. Then wrote tearful pleading letters after she was gone. And Ruby was torn. But in the end, she preferred, as she would express it later in writing, "a sordid reality of my own to the rosy, nebulous dreams of someone else."

Dee divorced the airman six months after the wedding, married a transient, heavy equipment operator twenty years her senior, had three kids in quick succession, in three different Eastern states, and ended up on welfare in Florida, divorced again. She never remarried, and when Lonnie visited her, while he was stationed at Homestead AFB, he wrote that she had taken up with a Seminole Indian and "gone to pot."

Alone with Alma from the age of ten, Ruby became the mother of her mother. From that time on, there was rarely a minute when Alma was not drunk and raving, or sick and hung over, or when she felt up to housework, shopping, cooking, or putting herself to bed.

"What's wrong, Mama?" Ruby asked, on the evening that her sister fled, as Alma lay sprawled on the blue kitchen floor like a gargantuan baby girl—pink, plump, half-naked—with her bottle between her legs. "What's the matter?"

"Here, Honey, come and help Mama to bed," she whined. "Your old man, he's no help. And Lonnie and Dee, they just taken it all out of me, I reckon."

Alma still had moments of semi-lucidity now and again—fleeting moments, usually in the early morning—when she would call Ruby into her room and sit her down in front of her on the bed and brush her hair.

"Damn, but I do love that long red hair of yours," she would say, stroking it gently from the crown of her head to her waist. "Reminds me of my sister, Sue Ellen's. Now, I want you to always take care of that, honey. You hear? It's your greatest asset."

Ruby loved these sessions in her mother's bedroom, loved being stroked and fondled and talked to, because it was such a rare treat. At such times, frantic to get some hold on Alma, some fix on whom she once might have been, she would quiz her relentlessly about her past.

"What did you want to be when you were a little girl, Mama?"

"Why, I always wanted to be an actress, hon. Down home, I was always dressin' up in my mama's old clothes, runnin' around the house playin' make-believe, singin' and dancin', just like you."

"How come you wanted to be an actress?"

"Hell, I don't know. Just didn't know any better, I guess. We was poor white trash. Only got to the movies about once a year. It was silent then, with Clara Bow and Hillary Bennett. *Now, that looks like a pretty nice way to make a livin'*, I'd say to myself, like it was the easiest thing in the world, *I think I wanna do that*."

"But you never got to be an actress."

"Why sure I did, honey. But only amateur productions, after I got married and went up to Dallas."

"What was his name?"

"Who's that, hon?"

"The man you got married to first."

"Finney. Francis X."

"Where's he at now?'

"He's remarried now, I believe, but I ain't heard where they stayin'."

"How'd you meet him?"

"He come through town with a wad of cash and a big Pierce Arrow. Put up at the hotel. Stepped out to the picture show. I saw him to his seat."

"You were an usherette?"

"Yep."

"Then what?"

"Well, that man was so high-toned, we never seen the like in our little town. Just clean swept me off my feet."

"Did you have children with him?"

"Course I did."

"How many?"

"Two, two boys. Luther and Fred."

"What'd they look like?"

"Towheaded. Slow to walk. Luther, the oldest, he was a fat little thing. Always puttin' up a squall. Had colic, I think, just like you. Fred, he was quicker at everything, and he had the sweetest nature. Put him to breast and he never let out a peep. But he had weak lungs. Nearly lost him when he was two. Pneumonia. Sat by his side in the hospital room for three days and three nights, prayin' my heart out, and finally he come through."

"Where do they live now, Mama?"

"Don't rightly know, honey. They all grown up now."

"Don't you miss them?"

"I tell you, sometimes it's more than I can bear."

Alma's expressions of feeling were not fully convincing to Ruby, because her recollections of her previous life seemed so vague, so sparse in detail. If you loved somebody, she figured, you would remember every little thing about them. And she wondered how much her mother would think of her, after she was grown and gone. *I bet she'll remember my red hair*, she thought, *and that's about it.* Yet, when Ruby asked for the little heart-shaped locket that her mother had always worn, until its gold chain snapped on her fat neck, Alma gave it to her without ceremony. She could not remember, she said, if it had been given to her by Reno or by Francis X.

Later, it came to Ruby that her mother had probably always been the same. Probably had as little interchange with the Finneys as she had with the Roses. She was like a willful child, always, wrapped up in a cocoon of infantile self-absorption.

Unlike a normal child, however, Alma did not grow more lucid and thoughtful with the passing years. On the contrary, she regressed at approximately the same rate that her daughter matured. There was a time in Ruby's earliest youth when their mental ages coincided, perhaps. But, by the time Ruby learned how to read at the Eagle Field dependents' school, Alma had given up reading even the funny papers. By the time Ruby learned how to add and subtract and figure out the weekly household budget, Alma had forgotten how to count past twenty. By the time Ruby was old enough to do the shopping at the commissary, Alma had declared herself an "invalid" and taken to her bed. And, by the time Ruby found a way to restrict her mother's supplies of alcohol, it was already too late. Alma had to be diapered and changed like an infant, and soon she regressed to the womb and beyond.

It happened, as Ruby conceived it later, as an adult, "on a brisk, blustery day in early March after a rare desert rain, with plump little moisty-edged clouds skittering across an enormous cobalt sky, and almonds blossoming on the foothills of the San Francisquitos, snowfields gleaming spectacularly on the smooth southern flanks of the Tehachapis."

She got off the Gold Hill Junior High School bus with Gil and Juanita Sanchez, Sally Porter, Eddie Marczaly, and some other kids, and started off down the blacktop road past a line of leafless cottonwood trees, "their spindly, tightly-twisted branches like fine gray lace, like the skeletons of spiders."

They passed a work gang of inmates guarded by a grizzled black custodian.

They passed a flock of ravens "that hung in the wind not a foot above the sage and swooped every few moments to feast in the blink of an eye on the living harvest of the desert floor."

They passed a sign that said:

EAGLE FIELD VOCATIONAL INSTITUTION
TRESPASSERS PROSECUTED TO THE LIMIT OF THE LAW

Ruby was in no hurry. And Eddie, Sally, Gil, Juanita, and the other kids, absorbed in a discussion about a TV program called *Your Hit Parade,* with Snooky Lanson and Rosemary Clooney, left her quickly behind.

She dawdled along, kicking pebbles, counting traffic reflectors. The red clay shoulder of the road was slippery underfoot, and soggy, dwarf pine needles clung to her rubber soles. The sun felt warm on her right cheek, but the north wind blew cold against the left one. The air smelled of damp sage and almond blossom—a dry land after rain.

She was wearing white Spalding shoes, rolled bobbysocks, tartan pedal pushers, a gray woolen sweater with her mother's little gold locket showing, a blue duffel coat, and a long bouncy ponytail under a voyageur cap.

At first sight, perhaps, she looked a typical adolescent. But there was something about her that was special, remarkable, she believed. Though she moved slowly, wistfully along the road there was a springy, uncommon energy to her step, a dancer's unconscious grace, and a kind of natural theatricality about her entire appearance that set her apart. And when she glanced at her reflection in the mud puddles, she looked so cute, so quintessentially American—with her red hair and freckled face, her big blue eyes, turned up nose and generous mouth—that she thought she would make a perfect Coca Cola ad someday, or that some Hollywood talent scout might discover her having a cherry soda in Rear's Drugstore in Gold Hill and sign her up for a contract at MGM or Paramount.

On the bus that day, she had felt nervous and preoccupied, wondering how she was going to manage her mother this time. But now that she was nearly home, it came to her suddenly, right in the middle of her reverie about a movie career, that she had nothing more to fear.

Just like that it came.

At home, she would find her mother dead.

Drawing up to the entrance of the dependents' housing area, she saw a boy she knew. He was sitting on the grass, packing his newspapers into a white canvas *Los Angeles Mirror* bag. He was not a tall boy for his age, nor particularly handsome, but very solid and dependable looking, with fine brown hair, broad Germanic features, and an intent look on his face. He did not live at Eagle Field, yet he had been enterprising enough to obtain the *Times-Mirror* concession for the dependents' housing area, and he came here to fold and deliver his papers.

His name was Max Bauer. He was a Freshman at Antelope Valley Joint Union High School in Lancaster. He lived near Gold Hill. He came from a family of war refugees. And for a long time now, Ruby had been fascinated by all his activities.

Every day, summer and winter, he would coast on his bike down the long gentle incline from his home in Sand Canyon. Later, his elegant, ash blond mother—a mother who became Ruby's own in dreams—would pick him up in her station wagon for the trip back.

In summer, Ruby used to watch from her front yard as Max pedaled his bike up to the front gate, parked it by the visitors' reception office, walked out to the county road and loitered on the shoulder, waving his thumb at passing cars till one of them gave him a lift. Then she wouldn't see him again for hours. She imagined him hanging out in Lancaster, leafing through girlie magazines in the bus station rack, buying himself a root beer float at the Frosty Freeze, passing the time of day with the *Times-Mirror* distributor, Mr. Beresford, on Ovington Street, and she would envy Max his masculine independence with her whole soul. Then late in the afternoon, she would look up from her hedge-clipping or hanging out the clothes or watering the flowers or sitting around gossiping with Juanita or Sally or whatever she was doing, and she would see him getting dropped off at the crossroads, slamming the car door, waving goodbye, hoisting the huge, heavy-looking bundle of newspapers onto his large square shoulder, and walking onto the grounds.

Later in the year, when school started, she noticed that he coasted his bike down in the morning, caught the big, yellow, Greyhound-type, Antelope Valley Joint Union High School bus with the Eagle Field kids at the corner and brought his papers back from town with him on the bus's return trip in the afternoon. He walked down the road with them on his shoulder, slung the bundle on the grass, cut the twine with one strong swipe of his Swiss Army Knife, and folded the papers up in perfect squares so they would throw better. Then he packed them carefully in the bag he wore around his muscular neck and set off down the long rows of shiny aluminum Quonset huts, whistling or singing a song under his breath, maybe The Crows' "Oh Gee," or Fats Domino's "Goin' to the River," or something else she liked.

Sometimes, he asked her if she wanted to tag along with him and learn his route in case he ever got sick.

"Naw," she always said.

"Why not?"

"It's not for girls."

But today she had decided that she was going to stop and have a chat.

"Say, I wonder," she said, as soon as she had plopped down beside him on the grass, "could you come home with me for a minute? I'm worried about my mom."

"Okay, but only for a minute," he said. He had a shy, sensitive smile that Ruby liked, and despite his foreign birth spoke in the flat, reassuring Western drawl of inland California. "My customers get mad if they don't have their papers by five."

They approached the Quonset hut warily, Max with his load of tabloids, Ruby with her bag of books.

"I'm afraid something's wrong," she said. "It's just this feeling I've got."

She opened the kitchen door, peered into the darkness.

"Mom?" she said. "Mom?"

"You want me to go in with you?"

"Would you?" she said, and she tiptoed into the kitchen.

Max was right behind her, and she was acutely aware of the drama unfolding: they stage-whispered to each other like visitors to a funeral home, and Ruby nearly lost her cookies when Max suddenly switched on the overhead light.

"Mom? Mom?"

"Where is she, do you think?"

"I don't know, maybe in there," she said, and led him into the bedroom.

They found her sitting in bed, propped up with pillows, just as she had been when Ruby left for school that morning. Her eyes were shut, the bowl of Cream of Wheat that Ruby had prepared for her breakfast was still sitting on the tray in her lap, and the big, old, family cat, Nestor, was still purring beside her on the bed.

But the cat had drained the bowl of its milk, Alma's pallor was of a kind with the untouched remains, an empty bottle of Gordon's Bombay Dry Gin lay just beyond her blue swollen fingers, there was no sign of breath, and the room smelled distinctly of physical corruption.

"Mom?" she said again. "Mom?"

And then, with Max peering over her shoulder, she leaned far across the stained and rumpled sheets to look deeply into her mama's face. It was a tiny, once-pretty face—a face in which traces of Ruby's own young face could still be seen—bloated beyond all proportion by years of drink, with great clammy white-green jowls that dwarfed and mocked her delicate features, and a pink cupid's bow mouth that was turned down now in an obscene little smirk of self-satisfaction. More than anything she resembled a character in a book that had frightened Ruby as a child: THE FROG QUEEN, all fat and green and sassy after just having gulped down a great fly.

"I think she's dead," Max said. "We better get help."

They ran next door to the Sanchez hut. Mrs. Sanchez called Reno. Reno came home from work, took one look at Alma, and called the Duty Resident. The Resident examined her and called the Chief Physician.

While all this was going on, Ruby was in Juanita's bedroom, where she had been consigned in her "bereavement." Reclining there amid carnival prizes, plastic dolls, and gay-colored Mexican blankets, breathing cheap perfume, while Juanita and Sally sighed, patted her hands, smoothed her hair, and whispered condolences, Ruby was not so much bereaved as dumbfounded that her premonition had come so astonishingly close to the mark.

"Shush, you two, shush," she whispered back at them, finally, after she'd managed to absorb what had happened.

And proceeded to imagine for them in vivid detail the long' black hearse that would come to take Alma away, and all the things that would happen later: After the funeral, she and her dad would drive back to Eagle Field, reminiscing about happier times in the past. Then at home, they would have a glass of Kool Aid together and switch on the TV.

"It's better this way," Reno would say.

And forever after, Ruby would count the beginning of her own life from the day that her mother lost hers. She and her dad would get along fine on their own, she said, and when he was home, she would look after him better than any wife. Sometimes, he would stay out all night playing poker with the boys or visiting a lady friend, in which case Ruby would quietly do her homework, fix herself something to eat, spend a couple of hours practicing dance steps with Juanita and Sally or singing with the radio, then put herself to bed with a book, preferably a good 'showbiz' biography, like *Gypsy,* or *I'll Cry Tomorrow.*

Reno would appreciate her independence and self-reliance and reward her if not with overwhelming affection, then at least with his trust and respect.

Other times, he would be gone for days on end, but Ruby would just take it in stride. She would pass her time alone studying photos in movie and fashion magazines and holding forth in front of the mirror for hours on end, preening and mugging and putting on dumb shows, experimenting with her mother's old clothes, her make-up kit and jewelry, creating a new, livelier, more interesting, and appealing adult personality for herself.

She would get Mr. Michael Marczaly, the Director of Recreational Therapy at Eagle Field, to give her private tutoring in drama, dance, and singing. She would pay him with her babysitting money and swear him to secrecy. Only Juanita and Sally would know the truth. If Ruby brought out "The New Me" too fast the other kids would call her a phony.

She would wait for exactly the right moment.

On her first day of high school, the time would be ripe.

And in fact, it all came to pass just as Ruby imagined it. Except when the Chief Physician arrived, he found that her mother still displayed weak signs of life.

An ambulance came, and it took her away to the Antelope Valley Community Hospital in Lancaster, where Alma lingered, like a black cloud of guilt over her daughter's life, for six long, long weeks.

Chapter Five

A few days after Max helped Ruby out with her mother, he held a "business meeting" with his mother in Fritz's old studio. He was sixteen now, he said, so she could now rely on him for help and advice. They could not go on forever, just coasting along, eating out of cans heated over a hotplate, bathing in the half-destroyed bathroom of the ranch house. It was time they put their heads together and came up with a permanent solution to their housing problem.

The ranch house was beyond all hope of repair, he said, but the studio could be added onto. He proposed that they loot the ranch house, the stables and barn for material, including lumber, window frames, flooring, roofing, kitchen, and bathroom fixtures, and use it to expand the studio into a small two-bedroom house.

"But how're we going to do that, Lucky?" Sybil protested. "We're not carpenters, and we can't afford to hire one."

"Mr. Gonçalves could do it, and Charlie and I could help."

"But how do you know he could do it?"

"Charlie said."

"What does Charlie know about these things?"

"His dad built their place from scratch, so why couldn't he do ours?"

"Well, for one thing, Mr. Gonçalves has his own farm to run."

"In winter, he barely works at all, Charlie says."

"And how would we ever pay him?"

"We don't have to pay him cash," Max said, and suggested that they sign over a quarter-acre of their almond trees to Mr. Gonçalves in return for his labor and expertise.

"Why darling," Sybil said, her long narrow face lighting up for the first time since Fritz left town, warming Max to the very cockles of his heart, "I think that's a perfectly marvelous idea!"

The Gonçalves family lived in a little, tin-roofed, unpainted, clapboard house at the end of a dirt road in the narrow upper reaches of the canyon, overshadowed by steep mountain walls and Sand Canyon Dam. Charlie—a great beefy fellow with a mass of curly black hair and the rugged aquiline features of a Roman foot soldier—slept on a straw-stuffed mattress in the barn, surrounded by almond lugs and gunny sacks. And Max had always thought the Gonçalves home the most exotic of places, full of wondrous and unexpected delights. There was a windmill pump with the sweetest water he had ever tasted, and an outhouse with a real, carved halfmoon. There was a herd of black and white goats that ate tin cans, a Jersey cow that gave the most deliciously unpasteurized milk, a homicidal, barnyard rooster, and a loud little yellow donkey named "Canary" with a razorback and the kick of a Cape Buffalo. Pigs, hens, ducks, turkeys, and half-wild dogs roamed the dirt front yard, fighting and raising a flurry over scraps flung casually from the kitchen window. The family pickup looked like the product of an archaeological dig. The big, fat mama of the house, Alicia, had but a single tooth in her head and spoke barely a word of English but laughed uproariously at everything you said. Preçiosa ran around in a torn pink and white housecoat that invited prurient pubescent glances. And the father, who wore handmade Mexican riding boots and fancy Western gear while his womenfolk ran around barefoot, was as vain as a gamecock and handsome as a Marlboro Man.

There was no phone at the Gonçalves home. Indeed, they had only received electricity the year before. So, Max and his mom took a stroll up to their place one evening after dinner. Mr. Gonçalves—or "Pete" as he was known in Gold Hill—met them at the gate and invited them in. All smiles and bows, he sat them down at the kitchen table under the single overhanging lightbulb. And while Alicia, Preçiosa, and Charlie hovered nervously in the background, whispering in Azores Portuguese, he offered Sybil a glass of his homemade wine. Then, so distracted was Pete to have this distinguished lady in his home, he strutted about the kitchen for several minutes spouting nonsense, "Hope you don't mind the place, Ma'am, it ain't much, but it's home sweet home," before he thought to pour the wine that he held in his hand. Once it was poured, however, and Sybil had pressed him to sit down and listen to her proposal, he was all business.

"Well, you can bet I'm the man for the job, Ma'am, and I will have some time on my hands, come December," he said, furrowing his low dark brow in a parody of deep reflection, "but I don't see how I can do it for anything like a quarter-acre of almond trees."

In the end, Pete settled for a half-acre of almonds, and they struck a deal.

He set to work with Max and Charlie during Christmas vacation, and the job went so well—at least according to his own lights—that he reckoned they'd be done by the first of April.

Yet, as time went on, Pete became increasingly troubled and distracted by Sybil, and he had difficulty focusing on the job at hand. He followed her with his dark, heavy-lidded eyes wherever she went. He forgot what he was about whenever she passed by. He crushed his thumb with the hammer one time when she was merely handing him up some nails. He expressed his admiration for her beauty quite openly—right in front of the boys who worked beside him—and began pursuing her with sweet nothings and wildflowers he picked on his way to work.

In the beginning, Sybil just laughed and treated it all as a joke. Then, she affected pique. Then, outright anger. When none of these seemed to work, she pretended to acquiesce, at least on a platonic level, "Oh, Pete, you say the kindest things, and I just know that we'll always be good friends and neighbors." But that turned out to be her biggest mistake, for Pete resented her patronizing tone, and reacted by walking off the job, calling her a tease, and then coming back to redouble his ardent proposals.

Implausible as it may seem, Sybil was tempted once or twice, for she was lonely; she had not been courted in years, and never with such Latin persistence and concentration. But at last, her good sense prevailed, and she turned him down in no uncertain terms.

"Pete, I don't want to ever hear you talk like this again. If you do, I'll tell your wife."

When it thus became clear to Pete that all his efforts had gone for naught, he moped about for only a day or two and then put on a show of complete indifference, singing Azores folksongs in his beautiful tenor, and swinging his hammer as if he had not a care in the world.

He finished the job—to his own satisfaction—by the first of April as he had predicted. Sybil paid him off with the half-acre of almonds. Max and Charlie breathed a collective sigh of relief and resumed a friendship which had been suspended by unspoken mutual consent during the courtship. And that would probably have been the end of it if Pete had been half as capable and responsible a builder as his son had represented him to be.

With their attention focused for so long on Pete's romantic improprieties, Max and his mom had failed to notice that the construction work on their house left much to be desired. Huge gaps remained in the wallboards and wide spaces between the windows and frames, through which the wind howled night and day. The roof leaked rain in such volumes that even during a brief April shower all of Sybil's pots, pans and buckets were not enough to contain it. The house stuck out at funny angles all around, and spiders, lizards, snakes, and field mice came up through the cracks to nest in the odd little crooks and crannies of the eccentric floorplan. The bathroom tilted downhill at such an angle that inadvertently dropped hairpins, cosmetic jars, and combs skittered across the tile by force of gravity. When you turned on the shower, the water came out brown as peat.

Yet, confronted with his negligence, Pete turned surly and disclaimed all responsibility for repairs, maintaining that he had already worked off his half-acre of almonds, that he had been given inferior materials as well as inexperienced help, and problems of this kind could only be expected since he had been forced to work under such intolerable conditions. He refused to even accept an extra hourly wage to set things right, on the grounds that his pride was hurt. And in any case, his hands were full at his own place and would be until next winter. Then, when Sybil pushed him, alluding to possible legal proceedings, he threatened unnamed reprisals, "We're all alone out here, Mrs. Bauer, and you never know what might happen."

After that, the families had nothing to do with each other, refusing even to recognize each other when they passed in their cars on Sand Canyon Road. The bad feelings reached down even to Max and Charlie, who snubbed each other wherever they chanced to meet.

When mutual school friends asked why they were no longer buddies, Max replied, "Because Charlie's old man is a crook and a lecher."

"Well, I don't know what no lecher is," Charlie said when he heard about the conversation. "And my old man ain't perfect, but at least my old lady ain't no prickteaser."

Max attempted to defend his mother's honor, one evening after football practice, but he was no match for the larger boy and ended up with a broken nose. He lied to his mother about where he'd taken the damage. "In football practice," he said. And she was too discreet to voice her suspicions. But she sensed the truth.

"You're such a good, good boy, Max, more than any mother deserves," she said, on the way to the doctor's office, running a long slender hand through his thin lank hair. "And I don't want you to go blaming yourself for anything that happened with the house. "Okay?"

But she needn't have worried, for Max was far too practical-minded and resilient to spend much time lamenting the past or even the loss of his oldest friend. So, while his nose healed, he began casting about for some way to make things right.

The year before, he had obtained a driver's license. Then, with the proceeds of his paper route, he had bought himself a pickup truck and expanded his business to Rosamond, Willow Springs, and beyond. Now, he decided he could hold down a second part-time job, and he contracted with a dairy outlet in Palmdale to deliver milk door to door in the Gold Hill area. Rising every morning before dawn, he drove his truck into Palmdale in the dark and finished his twenty-mile milk run just in time for his first period shop class. Meanwhile, his mother had found a job as a weekend restaurant hostess at the Calico Inn in Lancaster. With the additional income, they decided that they could now afford a competent workman to do a proper job on their home.

Max remembered that Ruby Rose had once told him her dad was a builder with a degree in Civil Engineering from BYU. He knew that she was grateful to him for standing by in her trying time with her mother, so he decided to seek her advice.

Ruby was fifteen now, and in the months since she started high school, she had transformed herself by some mysterious means from a skinny, freckle-faced little carrothead into a real beauty, with the self-confidence to match.

To Max, her new bubbly personality, red lipstick, curled eyelashes, and trendsetting clothes were all part of a transparent act, a pathetic attempt to compensate with a bit of fluff and flounce for a squalid background. And he felt genuinely sorry for her when he saw her strutting her stuff in the schoolyard, thrusting out her little, budding breasts, talking too loud and fast, trying to get herself noticed, admired, and loved. Yet, he had to admit, the general effect was electric.

Which all goes to say that not only had Ruby become attractive to Max but she had also become virtually inaccessible to him.

So, he approached her tremulously, with much delay and confusion, one afternoon when she was getting off the bus at Eagle Field.

"S-Say, Ruby," he stuttered, intoxicated by her *eau-de-cologne*, blushing to his collarbone, "We got some work up at our place, and I was wondering if your dad still does construction work on the side."

"I don't believe so, Max," she replied, in her new extra careful diction, dazzling him with her smile. "But I wouldn't mind asking him for you."

As it turned out, she was right about her dad. He had no further interest in construction work, he said. But Ruby talked him into driving up and talking to Sybil anyway, just as a favor to herself. Reno looked the place over—looked Sybil over as well, a bit too thoroughly for Max's taste—assessed the home's structural problems and declared them to be nearly past remedy. But he agreed to try and set things straight on account of Max, who had been so kind to his daughter in her distress. His only conditions were that he be paid carpenter's union wages and that he be allowed to work weekends and after hours.

Sybil agreed, Reno set to work, and with Max assisting him, he was able to put the house to rights within a couple of months.

Yet, that was not the most remarkable of his achievements.

He had a brief affair with Max's mother, during which Sybil—whose long-dormant appetites had perhaps been whetted by Pete's attempted seduction—utterly lost her head for a few days, mooning after Reno on the job, calling him "my Mellors" out loud, quoting from D.H. Lawrence's *Lady Chatterley's Lover*, and virtually ignoring her son's existence. She even let Reno spend a few nights in her marriage bed, an occurrence that was not lost on the neighboring Gonçalves family—for Pete was surely the culprit who slashed Reno's tires and poured sand down his gas tank. And Reno caused Max such pain that he hid his head under the pillow to muffle his cries when he heard the springs start squeaking in the room next door.

Like many such conflagrations, however, the affair extinguished itself—burning up of its own white heat—as swiftly and mysteriously as it had ignited in the first place, leaving its participants much as they had been before. They were even friendly afterwards, only a bit stiffer with each other, more businesslike.

Reno finished his job. Sybil paid him off with the proceeds of Max's milk run and her new job at Lancaster's Calico Inn, and that was that.

The only thing Max ever heard his mother say of the matter was in a telephone conversation he overheard a few weeks later by chance.

"I had no idea how good it could be with someone who doesn't think, who just goes ahead and does it like an animal," she said to one of her former Vassar classmates who now lived in Beverly Hills. "But what do you talk about afterwards? Drywall? Roofing? Asphalt tile?"

So, in the end there was no harm done, from Max's point of view. His mother had her little fling, the house was snug and comfortable, he'd learned a thing or two about carpentry and life—not the least of which was to always expect the unexpected—and he'd managed to draw closer to Ruby, who sympathized with his misgivings over the affair.

"Your mom's a classy lady," she said one day as she helped him fold his papers after school. "I mean, I'd give anything for a mother like her. But I just couldn't figure out what she could see in a guy like my dad."

"Well, I don't know," Max replied, emboldened now that the affair was safely over. "You're not a bad looking bunch. I mean, I could see *myself* getting carried away, if I didn't watch out."

"Oh Max, I don't want you to think of me that way," she said, squeezing his hand. "I want us to be really good friends."

So, to Max's unutterable disappointment, they became confidants. And all the rest of the way through high school, he was obliged to listen to Ruby's heartaches over boyfriends, her complaints about girlfriends, her triumphs as class officer, newspaper editor, drama star and Homecoming Queen, while he, loving her, lent an everlasting ear.

Chapter Six

Reno never noticed when Ruby got her period, but about three years later he must have caught a glimpse of the Kotex box in her dresser drawer because suddenly one day he came up to her and said, "Shall we go out for a ride, honey? I think it's time we had a little talk."

He drove her into Lancaster to see a movie called "Mom & Dad," and all the way he hemmed and hawed, for once at a loss for words.

"Well," he said finally, as they were nearing the outskirts of town, "I guess you heard about all that sex stuff in school already. Right?"

"Sure, Dad," she said. "Just this one thing I haven't figured out yet."

"Yeah?"

"Where does the baby come out, from the front or the back?"

Reno spluttered and foamed for half a minute before he decided that she was pulling his leg.

"Hey, that's nothing to joke about!"

"Oh, you men, you all make such a fuss about it," she said.

Truth was, though, Ruby still didn't have a very clear idea of how it all worked, and she was in no hurry to find out. Her mother had made no attempt to enlighten her while she was alive. It was not the sort of thing she would ask in one of her infrequent letters to Dee. And anyhow, the way Mrs. Sanchez told it, men were the ones who got all the fun out of it, women all the trouble. She had figured out for herself how to deal with her period—with a little help from Juanita and Sally—and she could do the same with the rest of it. And if she had need of masculine advice, she was sure that her drama coach, Michael Marczaly, would be a far more reliable source than Reno.

But the funny thing about Michael, she thought, if you stood him up against Reno and asked anyone at Eagle Field who was the most trustworthy, they would surely pick Reno.

Slight, drawn, pasty-white, with great glittering green eyes, a wide, sensual red mouth, and a halo of frizzy, yellow hair, Michael looked a bit like "The Joker" in the *Batman* comic strip, and he was famous at the institution for his perverse wit. He reminded Ruby somewhat of her brother, Lonnie, though they looked nothing alike and, on the surface, appeared to have little in common. It was a certain hyper-critical way of looking at things, a profound dissatisfaction with life that they veiled in chronic sarcasm. But with Michael, it was all on a much higher and more rarified plane. As a kid, he had sung and danced in the chorus lines of some of the greatest Broadway musicals of the late thirties and early forties. After the war, he had put himself through the UCLA drama department playing in a Westwood piano bar. There, unfortunately, he had acquired a taste for hard liquor. But he was not a social drinker, nor a secret drinker like Alma. He went on binges like a sailor. Every few months his wife Veronika—a physical therapist at Eagle Field—would get a call from some bar in Hollywood and have to drive down with a friend and haul him back dead drunk. And soon after they reached home, all of Eagle Field would know. Everyone indulged Michael, though. Apparently, they considered his binges colorful.

Veronika was a large, dark woman with close-cropped gray hair, bloodhound eyes, a vast porous nose, thick sensitive lips, and a loud abrasive voice. Yet her sum was far more attractive than her parts, and she had the steady temperament and briskly efficient manner that a man like Michael would find indispensable. They had met in Brooklyn when they were kids then ran into each other again at a San Diego military hospital during the war, when Veronika was a WAVE chief petty officer in the physical therapy department and Michael was a Marine Lance Corporal recovering from a case of combat fatigue. They had a son named Eddie, a year younger than Ruby, whom they treated much like a pair of Marine non-coms might treat a promising young recruit, alternately ridiculing his achievements and proclaiming their faith in his brilliant future. And Eddie responded just as an oft offended and sometimes encouraged recruit might, with frequent professions of fealty and occasional surreptitious betrayals. It was Eddie, therefore, who told all the neighbors every time Michael went out on another of his binges. In altercations with outsiders, however, the family instinctively closed ranks and presented a united front, refusing to admit—even in the face of incontrovertible evidence to the contrary—that any of them might ever be in the wrong. As loud and contentious Hungarian New Yorkers with ill-concealed left-liberal political opinions, the Marczalys were regarded by the residents of Eagle Field as odd-balls and pinkos. But they were tolerated, uneasily, for their intelligence, their sense of irony, and their exceptional qualities of innovation.

Michael's course in recreational therapy at Eagle Field's "Pre-Release Unit," for instance, was like no other such program in the country at that time. On the catalogue of the institution's activities, it was listed as a course in "Dramatic Expression." In fact, he ran it more like a professional acting course, with elements of what would later be termed "psychodrama." To begin with, he had his patients stand up and tell their deepest secrets—things they'd never revealed before. Then he tried to get them to achieve a certain distance from their material, to see its humorous side and transform it into comedy, using other members of the cast as characters. And finally, he had them seek a common theme. What emerged almost inevitably was an irreverent sketch of family life, or an impudent spoof of life in a state institution.

After establishing a theme, Michael had his students develop their own musical scores and choreography. Meanwhile, he trained them physically every day in the techniques of dance, singing, tumbling and acrobatics.

He worked them mercilessly.

Anyone who gave less than one hundred percent was given the boot.

His students hated him at first. They regressed and threw tantrums in class and denounced him to the administration. But they ended up worshipping him, willing to go through fire for him, and a good deal further along on the road to recovery.

Michael's annual comic reviews in the Eagle Field gymnasium were the talk of the valley, sold out weeks in advance.

Ruby had come to him as a wide-eyed fourteen-year-old, with none of the usual preconceived notions of what a drama course should be, and she was not at all put off by his unconventional teaching technique. Nor did she resist exposing her innermost secrets. On the contrary, she treated him to her entire life story, from her birth in a Red Cross tent to her attendance at her mother's "death bed," all in one great manic gasp.

After hearing her out, Michael decided that his first task was, as he put it, "to channel all that energy and enthusiasm and give shape to your memory and imagination."

A willing and able student, open to all suggestions, Ruby made quick progress.

Along the way, she fell a little in love with Michael. She studied his every gesture. She imitated his walk, his talk, his sly smile, the highly stylized, almost mime-like way he moved his body and used his eyes. She even imitated his soft, persuasive Brooklyn accent, and his caustic way with words.

To defuse what might have become an awkward situation, Michael took her home one night to have dinner with his wife and kid. And soon, Ruby was like part of the family, the daughter the Marczalys never had. She spent hours at their place, watching television, playing chess, Scrabble, and Bridge. She went on vacation with them, with Reno's grateful blessings, to Yosemite and Sequoia National Forest in the summer of her sophomore year in high school, to Big Bear Lake at Christmas vacation of her junior year, to San Clemente Beach State Park at Easter time.

Veronika took her under her wing, taught her everything she would need to know about homemaking, gave her the only copy of *The Joy of Cooking* she would ever own, and frankly apprised her of all she had never learned of human reproduction.

Yet, as far as her stage training was concerned, Ruby felt that now—in 1959, in the summer before her senior year—she had gone as far as she could with Michael's private coaching, and she was anxious to take a further step.

"What I need," she said one Sunday afternoon as they sat together on his worn davenport, while Veronika and Eddie mounted butterflies on the kitchenette table behind them, "is the experience of total theater."

"You know," Michael replied, shaking his head, "sometimes when I listen to you, Ruby, it's like hearing an echo, or listening to a broken record with my own voice on it."

"Then why do you bother teaching me these things?"

"Not to have you spout them back at me half-digested," he said. "How about your high school drama course? What're you doing next term?"

"*The Importance of Being Earnest* and it bores me stiff. You know what I'd really like to do, Michael?"

"No, and I'm afraid to ask."

"I'd like to try out for this year's comic review."

"What, at the Pre-Release Unit? Are you kidding me? They'd have you for dinner out there."

"I thought you said they weren't considered inmates or patients anymore. They are 'students,' ready to get let out into the general population. I thought they were cured of their criminal insanity."

"Cured? I don't know about that. I know that after repeated sessions of electro-therapy and massive doses of modern medication they're somewhat stabilized for the moment. But 'cured' I wouldn't call them."

"Well," she said, shifting her eyes rapidly from Michael to her own wildly gesticulating hands, "who says I don't have problems of my own to work out?"

"Problems you may have, love. But think of what these people have experienced. Madness. Delusion. Abuse. Being locked up in a state prison."

"Are you kidding? I've spent my whole life in this place!"

"You'd be resented," he persisted. And he looked her over critically, but with unmistakable pride and pleasure too. "You would be a disruption, an alien element, and I don't know where that would lead us."

"Tell you what, Michael," Ruby said, fretting, twisting in her seat. "Let's make a deal. If I can wangle a visitor's pass, you'll let me come out and have a look around. Okay? And if I cause the least bit of trouble, I'll be gone in a flash."

Michael threw up his hands and laughed. When he laughed, he was bigger than life. His eyes screwed up into tiny, green, Magyar slits; his mouth flew open, his tongue glistened red, his chest heaved, and he went "Har har har!" But after you got to know him, you found that he was not so much mirthful as an expert parodist of mirth. And your heart went out to him in the same way it went out to circus clowns and stand-up comedians.

"All right, you win, you win! But you know, love? You know what the mystery is to me? Why in God's name are you willing to go through all this to pursue a career in show business? I mean," he whispered, with an eloquent, eye-rolling glance at his dumpy wife, his nerdy four-eyed kid, his dilapidated Quonset hut, "look at what it got me."

The Pre-Release Unit turned out to be just another Quonset hut like all the rest, with the sun glaring off its metal roof and the sand piled up along its curved aerodynamic walls. But, at least, it was outside the barbed wire fence. Ruby drove her dad's pickup out there one morning in June, presented her forged visitor's pass to the custodian, inquired as to the whereabouts of Mr. Marczaly, and was conducted next door to the old bomber hangar where Michael held his rehearsals. It was an enormous echoing space, with laser-like shafts of white sunlight beaming down through rivet-holes in the rusty tin roof. Birds made their nests in its steel beam rafters, whistling and flitting from one to the other, and the whole place smelled faintly of their droppings.

A song-and-dance number was in progress when Ruby walked in. Michael was standing just below the makeshift wooden stage, directing a singer and a group of eighteen dancers dressed in black and white stripes and clanging chains. Michael's drama class was the only place at Eagle Field where male and female inmates were permitted to interact, and his cast consisted of nine men and nine women.

A spidery little Chicana pianist played a catchy, syncopated, Brechtian theme in the background. The singer, standing at center stage, was a hugely fat but rather fey black man with an outrageous falsetto voice that he used as a musical instrument, scatting deftly up and down the scales in counterpoint to the melody. The dancers were evenly divided between Black, White, and Latino, and ranged in age from not much older than Ruby to not much younger than Michael. All of them, male and female, had had their hair cropped unevenly, close to the scalp, and they were an extraordinarily unsavory lot, with enough cross eyes, buck teeth, cauliflower ears, spastic twitches, limps, double joints, knock knees, and pigeon toes between them to furnish a small nut house of their own. As dancers they were well-rehearsed rather than proficient, a fact that worked to their advantage in this case, for their desperate look and heavy foot-stomping packed a powerful emotional appeal, especially when contrasted to the humorous, rinky-dink, background music.

These are real prisoners, Ruby said to herself. *Not actors dressed up like prisoners.* And she knew that Michael had been right. There was no place for her here. No matter what she had suffered, she knew no suffering like this.

Finally, Michael called a break, caught her eye, and took her aside.

"I see what you mean," she said, as they stood together on the tarmac outside. He passed his cigarette to her. She had never smoked, but she took a drag without coughing or showing any surprise. "Never seen a scarier bunch of people in my whole life."

"Oh," said Michael, laughing, taking his cigarette back, "you don't think this is the way they really are, do you? Jesus, I'm glad to hear they're so convincing."

"You mean to say . . . ? My God!" she said. "You know what, Michael? If I could work with a cast like this, I could work with anyone!"

"Yeah, well I've been thinking," he said, and then he looked at her in a way he never had before, took another puff at the cigarette, reached over, and stuck it between her lips. "Maybe there's a thing or two you could learn out here after all."

So, he pulled some strings with the administration, fudged a bit on her age, vocational experience, and artistic accomplishments, and got her a summer job as his student aid.

On the way out to work the first day in his car, Michael leaned over to Ruby, patted her on the thigh, and said, "You know, I've got this theory of group dynamics. You take a lot of people and put them together in a small area for a long enough time and they sort themselves out into certain roles. I call them King, Queen, Fool, Knave, Poet, Wise Man, Sorceress and Pawns. The King, the Queen and the other big players are always in competition. They try to win the pawns over to their side. They form alliances and power blocs and play one off against the other. Or they get a pawn to be front man and manipulate things from behind the scenes. What I'm trying to say, love, things out there are not always what they seem. Get what I mean?"

"Sure," she said, but it took her a week of work at the hangar, helping with the costumes and make-up, moving props and scenery, to understand what he was talking about.

The King, she figured, was this big, blustering, Norwegian guy named Ip who thought a great deal of himself and bullied everyone. And he had a funny little humpbacked, long-haired Mission Indian sidekick named Billy Blood whom he kept around as his fool. Enid, the hugely fat Black man whose falsetto was so impressive, was the Queen, in terms of his sexual preferences as well as his apparent romantic attachment to Ip. The knave was a sleazy little rat-faced Boston Irishman named Darcy who spent lots of time complaining and trying without much success to create dissension among the others. Nat Goldman, a Talmudic-looking fellow with a long gray beard who was forever offering unwanted opinions and advice, was the "wise man." The poet was Dillon, a cadaverous, goateed, beatnik type who was always spouting long-winded quotations that turned out to be non-sequiturs. Cecilia Marquez, the pianist, was the sorceress. She read palms, saw the future in cards, and interpreted dreams. The other prisoners were clearly just folks, with little impact on anyone.

On the other hand, Ruby could discover no evidence of "power blocs," "conspiracies" or the cynical use of "pawns." In fact, the inmates seemed unfailingly polite and considerate—with Darcy's egregious exception—and despite their various character quirks they were as "normal" as any other large group of people working together in a confined area.

"How do you know when they're playing straight with you?" Ruby asked Michael, one evening as he dropped her off at her house.

"You don't," he said. "As a rule of thumb though just assume they're not. They wear many hats, love. You get past a few, and you think you're down to hair and bone, but there's always another one under that."

"How do I make contact with them? I mean, how do I get them to let down their guard?"

"Tell you what I do," he said. Then he crossed his eyes, made a face, and whispered into her ear, "I pretend to be one of them, use their own mad logic on them."

As an exercise, Ruby decided to follow Michael's example. She thought about it for a long time, and eventually she figured out how to do it—She acted just like her normal self, except that she imagined herself always walking on an inch or two of ice. Communication between her and the prisoners improved immediately, and in time she was able to confirm that their relations were as byzantine as Michael had suggested.

There was one unforeseen result, however.

The more Ruby tried to conform to crazy ways, the more the craziness rubbed off. It got to the point where it was second nature. Even after-hours, she kept walking around on ice. Her father and friends started to look at her strangely and ask if she was feeling all right.

Observing Michael from her new perspective, she discovered why he'd always seemed so different—It had rubbed off on him as well.

From then on, she always felt a tiny bit uncomfortable in his presence.

"I think you can start trying things out on stage now," he said to her after she had been on the job a month. "But it's going to be touchy with the inmates. We'll have to approach it delicately. I tell you what. Why don't you try to work out a little skit? Show it to me and we'll polish it up together. Remember, though, don't try to get too fancy. Go for the simplest, most blatant interpretation of the experience. Then turn it on its head, do something unexpected with it. That's how you make comedy."

Ruby thought about the project for over a week but could not produce anything she liked. Disillusioned, she called Michael over one Saturday evening when her dad was out on the town. Sitting at the kitchen table together till nearly midnight, chain smoking cigarettes and getting bombed on Reno's rye whiskey, they put their heads together and tried to invoke something from her past, no matter how far-fetched or ridiculous, that might serve as the basis of a skit.

Ruby came up with a few things she thought might do, but Michael kept trying to trivialize them. He wanted to condense her mortal struggle with her brother Lonnie to a comic ride in a little red wagon, wanted to transform her experience with Gil and Juanita in the flood control culvert into a dialogue between a couple of seventeenth century Puritan children: "I'll show you my arm," says the little girl, playing coyly with the long, black sleeve of her hooded cloak, "if you show me yours." He was particularly excited by the idea of dressing his adult actors up as juveniles and have them affect childish voices.

"It's a proven crowd-pleaser," he said, "as old the snows."

"Sounds like corn to me," Ruby said.

And suddenly, she thought of her mother. Through the buzz of alcohol in her ears it seemed that she could almost hear her calling, "Ruby, get in here this minute. You hear?"

Leaving Michael in the kitchen with the last of the booze, she weaved into the bedroom, slid open Alma's closet door, and the first thing that struck her eye was a satin, party dress from the 1930s. A fleshy beige in color, still smelling faintly of Alma's perfume, it was long, almost ankle length, very slinky and vampy looking, with a low-cut bodice, a belted waist, and a lacy white fringe about the neck.

Ruby picked it up like a message from the past and laid it out on the bed. She stripped to her panties and bra and prepared for a visit from the dead.

Pulling it on over her head, feeling it slither down her breasts and hips, she could feel herself slipping away, falling into a spiral, into the abyss, with Alma's face at the bottom.

She panicked, clutched frantically at the rim of herself.

Yet, right in the middle of it all, she was dying to capture it, the essence of the illusion, and fashion it to her own ends.

She let go.

Her mother invaded and took control.

Smiling Alma's little cupid bow smile, Ruby swayed out to the kitchen to rejoin Michael.

"Well, land sakes alive, y'all never guess who I run into this afternoon at the picture show!" she exclaimed, and he gasped in recognition.

"Ruby, you're a born mimic," he said, after she had gone through an extemporaneous ten-minute monologue. "You got her down perfect. But to be frank, love, it's heavy stuff. I mean, the purpose of our show is to dispel horror, not invoke it. Right? What am I trying to say? How can we create a skit from this material that'll work for us?"

What he wanted to do, it turned out, was reduce all of Ruby's rich, blackly humorous evocation of Alma's tragic life to a routine in which a little girl helps her tipsy mother and father home from a wedding party and the roles of parents and child are reversed.

And Ruby would not go for it.

For a moment it even seemed to her that he might be jealous of her talent.

"Listen, I've been thinking," she said. "You were probably right in the first place, Michael. I mean, what am I doing, butting in on your show out there?"

That seemed to set him back in his chair for a moment. Then a boozy, maudlin look came over his face. Sighing and shaking his head, he leaned toward her till he was nearly touching her breasts.

"Ruby, Ruby, Ruby," he murmured.

His neck and shoulders were thin and bony under his T-shirt. And she could smell him. He smelled of liquor. But under that, there was something sweet and sour, like Chinese food. He raised his long narrow head to gaze moodily into her eyes and she became acutely aware of the color and texture of his facial skin. It was dry and yellowish and from a distance it looked smooth. But up close, under the kitchen's fluorescent light, you could see a thousand tiny wrinkles around his thin mouth and slanting, yellow eyes. And beneath his weakish chin, the flesh hung down like the wattles of a chicken.

Catching his breath almost painfully, as if he feared a heart attack, he reached for her then, slid his sweaty, scaley hand around the smooth, satiny waist of her mother's dress.

"Look, Michael, what I'm trying to say is this," she said, squirming out of his grasp, rising unsteadily from the table. "I'm normal, right? I'm healthy. What has the Pre-Release Unit got to do with me or my future?"

"Well, if that's the way you feel, love," he said, pushing to his feet. "Why even bother hanging around?"

"Actually, I was just going to bring that up."

"Hell," he said, starting for the door, "you'd probably do better at the Frosty Freeze or the A & W Root Beer stand. At least financially."

"Probably would."

"Then go right ahead."

"You won't be mad, Michael? Really not?"

"Mad?" he said. "What've I got to be mad about?"

She let him out the door and watched him teeter around the corner, heard his sandals scrunching in the sand toward his home three lines down, heard his squeaky screen door swing open and slam shut.

And she lingered a moment on the dark porch, listening to other night sounds: pepper tree branches rustling in the backyard, Mrs. Sanchez's bedsheets flapping on the line next door, the low rattling of water coolers in the windows of Quonset huts, truck traffic on the highway a quarter mile away, and a propjet in the sky.

It was incredibly hot outside for this time of night, incredibly dry. The wind singed her face, seared her lungs. She stepped into the yard to look up at the sky. There was only the merest sliver of moon, and a million stars.

It was August, the month of the shooting stars.

She waited until she saw one and made a wish.

After that, things were never the same for Ruby and Michael, and the emotional distance between them grew to the point where their relations were merely correct. But she still confided in his wife as to a mother and continued as his private student, and with his help she was among the final contestants in the state high school Dramatic Interpretation Championship, the following March.

Alone on stage at the El Monte Legion Auditorium in Alma's dress, with her hair permed and peroxided, lashes fake, face powdered white, cheeks rouged round like a baby doll, mouth like a bruised fruit, voice husky, Southern, she enthralled Michael, Veronika, Reno, Max, Juanita, and thousands of others with her performance of *Streetcar Named Desire.*

And suddenly, she was transfixed, impaled on a pinnacle of light, transformed by the witchcraft of her own words into Blanche DuBois herself: *"I can smell the sea air. The rest of my time I'm going to spend on the sea. And when I die, I'm going to die on the sea. You know what I shall die of? I shall die of eating an unwashed grape one day out on the ocean. I will die with my hand in the hand of some nice-looking ship's doctor, a very young one with a small blond mustache and a big silver watch. 'Poor lady.' They'll say. 'The quinine did her no good. That unwashed grape has transported her soul to heaven.'"*

Afterwards, looking into that vast sea of faces (defined, given purpose, and meaning in the mirror of those adoring eyes), the air electrified around her by the thunder of applause, Ruby began to shudder, to grow weak in the knees. Yet, she was able to turn even her own excess of emotion to dramatic account and stayed perfectly in character as she reeled off stage, leaving them all wondering, whispering after her, wanting more.

Chapter Seven

One chilly but magical morning in early spring, not long after Ruby's performance of *Streetcar Named Desire* at the El Monte Legion Auditorium, Max was out hunting rabbits on Portal Ridge. Strolling along with his shotgun cradled in his arm, not paying much attention to much, he was just sort of gazing out over the valley. From that altitude, two thousand feet above his mother's place in Sand Canyon, he could see clean across Antelope Valley and out into the Mojave Basin for a hundred miles. To the north, he could see beyond the Tehachapi Range to Centennial Ridge in the snowy Sierras, to the east beyond Barstow and Daggett to the great silver dunes of Stoddard Valley and Jackhammer Gap. And wherever he looked there was something different going on.

That's what Max loved about the desert. It looked so tedious, but it was amazingly subtle and varied and it had a million moods.

From where he stood, he could observe tiny B-47's practicing take-offs and landings at George AFB in Victorville, jet fighters rocketing the barren hills of the Naval Ordnance Test

Range in Inyokern, and the creaky, old Flying Wing making passes over Edwards AFB on Muroc Dry Lake.

He could track the shadows of westerly rain squalls as they stalked the desert like dark insidious thoughts, raising powdery white dust storms on the alkali flats.

Another half hour, another trick of the light, and the plain transformed into a vast coral sea, with Saddleback Butte, Black Butte, Long Butte, Red Butte, Indian Butte and Rocky Butte thrusting from its unruffled surface like an archipelago of precipitous volcanic islands, each aptly named.

Enjoying the view, and the tangy scent of wild oat on the wind, Max had almost forgotten what he was doing up there on that yellow, treeless ridge when a big, spotted catamount with glaring red eyes, a bobtail, and tufted white ears, came tearing around a boulder, hot on the trail of a cottontail.

All three spotted each other at once, but the rabbit had the quickest reflexes. While Max and the bobcat froze in their tracks, too startled to do anything but stare, the cottontail shot between Max's legs and ran down a hole.

Two or three seconds later, Max and the cat finally translated thought into action.

Max raised his shotgun and prepared to fire.

The cat screamed, leapt into the air, twisting and flailing like Tom in a *Tom & Jerry* cartoon, and came down running full tilt in the opposite direction.

Max lunged forward and let go with both barrels just as the cat flung itself over the razorback southern ridgeline.

He knew he'd hit something because he could see the fur fly, and when the cat lit, it started listing a mite to the right, and had this tendency to bowl over the clumps of creosote and sage rather than leap over them or slip around as it normally might.

So, Max took off after the cat, trailed it down the ridge and into Bitterroot Canyon. It was a dry canyon, with an even floor and steep walls of chaparral, but there was some underground water because a line of stunted willows and patches of antelope grass ran down along the clay bottom. So, it was no effort at all to follow the spoor. It was like a long, weaving pattern of red ink spots across a plane of rough, white, construction paper, or like one of Fritz's paintings of his later period, slides of which he was always sending over from Hamburg, along with pictures of his new German wife and step-kids.

Max jogged along with his 16 Gauge Remington at port arms. Not a sound in the world but his heavy, ragged breathing, and the echo of his crunching bootsteps on the walls all around.

The canyon narrowed. The chaparral and the underground water petered out. The air went still and flat. Even the smell of vegetation seemed to fade.

The sun blazed down on the crown of Max's cowboy hat, on his flannel shirt. He began to sweat under his arms.

The white sand floor of the canyon glared in the sunlight, hurting his eyes. The walls closed in, grew steeper, turned to yellow sandstone.

He found the cat at a bend in the dry creek bed, holed up in the shade of a soft sandstone boulder with the size, shape, and color of a reclining African camel. Panting, wheezing, growling, its blood pooling out on the sand, it glared out at Max from the shallow darkness, its little tufted eyes like red points of light.

"Well, my friend," Max said, sighing, "I guess this is it."

But then it occurred to him that in the excitement he had forgotten to reload. So, he had to break the gun, palm the expended shells, drop them in his shirt pocket, fish around for a couple of fresh ones, load and lock and prepare to fire, while all the time eyeball to eyeball with the suffering, bleeding cat.

"I guess this is it," he said again, sadly, because up close you could see that it was really an awfully pretty cat, young and healthy, with a muscular white chest, a shiny spotted dun coat and paws too big for its size. Hefty for its species, it would have gotten even heftier in a season or two, if Max hadn't gut-shot it from behind with his 16 Gauge and then had to put it out of its misery.

The double shotgun blast resounded again and again, getting softer and softer as it rolled down the canyon.

After the dust had settled, and the walls quit echoing, the cat was dead, its head hanging on by only a thread.

Max approached respectfully, even reverently, but before he could make contact another sound startled him.

He whirled, shotgun at the ready, and stood frozen in mid-pace for half a minute, straining to hear. Then it came again, and he stomped his foot and laughed in relief when he recognized it as the bleating of a young lamb or goat kid coming from far away, from behind walls of stone.

Torn by competing impulses, Max held a moment longer, then elected to abandon the cat for the time being and investigate this new phenomenon. He remembered that Pete Gonçalves ran a few head of goats and left them out on the open range up Portal Ridge. Perhaps this was one of them.

"Maybe this is how I can make things up with the Portugees," he said aloud.

It went against Max's nature to hold a permanent grudge, or to court trouble with his neighbors. With disorder in your own backyard, he figured, how could you make sense of the world at large?

So, he followed the sound of the bleating goat farther than he had ever gone before, till the canyon tapered to an arroyo, a ravine, a deep mountain crevice with high, smooth, yellow walls that sometimes met in an acute triangle over his head. Followed it right to its dead end at a dry waterfall, then backtracked when he caught a snatch of the bleating again. Found a crack in the wall that he had missed before. Squeezed in and heard the goat again, very close.

The crack opened after a few feet, became a cramped little straitened cave with gray and brown smoke stains on the roof.

Around a turn and he found the goat in a circle of soft, dusty light that filtered down through a crack in the ceiling. A tiny black and white ewe, only about a month or two old, it was trembling violently, blowing hard, but seemed more scared than hurt, for it bleated lustily and scampered around a bend when he reached out to grab it by the ear.

Max went after the goat, saw light ahead, and followed it into a hidden canyon.

The instant he reached the place he sensed that it was very old. And there was something "illicit" about it that affected him profoundly.

At first—and despite his qualities of healthy skepticism and common sense—he was almost frightened of the hidden canyon.

It had once been a sacred place, he thought, and it was meant to stay that way. Exploring its constricted precincts, he kept half-expecting the ghosts of prehistoric Indians to pop out from behind every abutment of rock. Yet, once he had discovered all its secrets, he decided that his presence had disturbed no souls, loosed no skeletons, and was perhaps even meant to be.

It was a blind canyon, he found, with a flat loamy bottom and hundred-foot, perpendicular, sandstone walls. Three shallow, smoke-darkened caves scarred the yellow surface of the eastern wall at about the height of a small man. Inside, Max expected to encounter hieroglyphs and stick figures depicting extinct animals, but in fact there were only the remains of ancient campfires.

The canyon's most remarkable aspect—in this bone-dry land—was the fact that it held ground water. A small, clear pool with a white sand bottom emerged near the sunny southern face, providing sustenance to a tiny plot of grass and a stand of little canyon maples with white and brown mottled limbs and the most delicate furry leaves.

Forgetting the goat for a moment, Max stripped off his clothes and bathed in the pool, the water of which he found tepid and sweet to the taste.

Renewed, refreshed, he crawled out, lay in the grass, in a patch of sun, and fell asleep, dreaming of prehistoric cave dwellers and beautiful redheaded, freckle-faced Indian maidens dressed in the skins of catamounts, and woke in a puddle of semen.

He would bring Ruby here someday, he thought. She would not be able to resist him then.

And he named the place in her honor.

Later Max found the little goat, hoisted it up on his shoulders and carried it out through the cave. Carried it all the way to Bitterroot Canyon. But when he reached the dromedary rock, the cat was gone.

No trail. No bloody indentation in the sand. No marks of it having been dragged away.

It was just gone.

For the first time in his life, Max questioned the evidence of his own eyes. And he wondered if the cat was not just a figment of his imagination. For an instant he even considered the possibility that it was a supernatural sign, with some significance relating to the secret canyon.

Then he began to doubt the existence of the canyon itself, so strongly that he traipsed all the way back again with the kid on his shoulders to assure himself of Ruby Canyon's concrete reality.

Then, puzzling over the riddle on the way back to his pickup truck, he decided that some larger animal or another hunter had happened along in his absence. But what animal? What hunter? And why erase every trace of the cat's existence?

Max never solved the mystery of the cat. And he would wonder about it, from time to time, for the rest of his long life.

He loaded the goat into the bed of the pickup, tied it down with twine, and drove to the Gonçalves' place.

Pete wasn't home, but Charlie was, and he came out of the house with a great big, shit-eating, Portagee grin on his face, like maybe he wanted to make friends again.

"Well, I'll be good goddamned," he said, when he saw the ewe. "We been lookin' for that little critter from here to Kingdom Come. Where the fuck did you find her?"

"I tell you, man, the way it looked to me," Max said, grinning back, "she was about halfway to Paradise."

Chapter Eight

Ruby knew she would win that night at the El Monte Legion Auditorium, and she did—a thousand dollars in cash or a year's drama scholarship to UCLA.

She took the cash.

Having no intention of waiting a year before launching her acting career, she bought herself a used '47 Chevy for a hundred dollars and prepared to light out for Hollywood as soon as she graduated from high school, in June 1960.

She told no one of her plans, not even Reno. She hated the thought of saying goodbye, and she was not good at taking advice. She would send everyone a postcard once she got settled.

But then one day in April, she was standing out front of her Quonset hut, watering the lawn in one of her dad's old work shirts and a pair of jeans, when Juanita Sanchez came shimmying across from her place in a pair of white, form-fitting capri pants, a tight black sweater, and high-heeled gold sandals.

"Hey, doll, we gotta talk," she said, grinning lewdly, popping gum. "Know what I mean?"

"What's up?"

"Well, you know, my brother, he keeps trying to line me up with Max Bauer, and I just wanna know where you're at."

"Where I'm at?"

"Yeah. I mean, he's cute. But like if you got eyes..."

"What makes you think that?"

"Come on, it's written all over your face."

"Oh," Ruby said, shading her eyes from the sun, "well, uh..."

And then she had to think fast.

Though she and Max had always stayed close, they had run in different high school sets. Later, while he was going to Junior College, he took over the barn behind his mother's place and went into business as an auto mechanic with Charlie Gonçalves. Now business was so good he'd had to quit J.C. and hire Gil Sanchez to help.

Ruby didn't see much of Max anymore, and she missed the long heart-to-hearts they used to have. Sometimes she would see him roar by the front gate on his motorcycle, his hair flying, and she would think how cool he looked in his tear-drop shades and black leather jacket.

But that was about as far as she had taken the matter.

And so, it came as a surprise even to herself when she responded to Juanita's question by blushing to the base of her neck and stammering, "Well, yes, I think, yes, I'm sorry but yes."

After that, she felt she had no choice.

So, the next time Max came by on his bike, she waved at him, and he circled to her fence.

"Hey," he said, smiling, rapping his pipes. "You are looking good, girl."

She was barefoot, in a low-cut, tight-waisted pale blue sundress with spaghetti straps, and fully aware that he was not mistaken.

"Thanks, Max," she said, beaming her best Miss America at him. "But say, you're not looking so bad yourself."

"You doing anything next Sunday? "

"Nothing much."

"Want to go to the races?" he asked. And then he laughed for no reason.

Men often did that with her. But she liked Max's laugh, a light uncomplicated laugh that made you want to laugh back. And he had the most beautiful white teeth. Thin dry lips. A crooked prominent nose. Strong jaw. Heavy beard. He looked older than his age. Incipient crow's feet around his narrow, gray eyes. A high sunburnt forehead with the beginnings of three wavy creases that crinkled up when he smiled. He looked like a cowboy or a railroad brakeman. Looked like he belonged outdoors.

Ruby liked that.

"What races?" she asked.

"Motorcycle races, up in Newhall. I'm gonna be riding."

"Didn't know you raced."

"Sure. Week before last I won my heat."

"No kidding?" she said. "Okay, sure, why not?"

Next Sunday and they wailed over the San Francisquitos at seventy and eighty miles an hour, the motor roaring, the machine vibrating on its knobby tires like it might shake apart.

On the curves, sometimes they were leaning so far over that their boots were but inches from the sizzling roadway, and the backsides of mountains that Ruby had spent her life looking at went by in a blue, funky blur.

Clinging to Max with her knees and arms, pressing her head and nose between his shoulder blades, she could smell—through her own smell of fear—the piquant, peculiar odor of his leather jacket, a smell of male sweat, animal fat, and engine oil.

She loved that smell.

He pulled off the freeway at the Newhall Municipal Airport where they had a half-mile steeplechase track set up, a combination of dirt and tarmac, wooden jumps, and water obstacles.

Max left Ruby off at the bleachers and went around to sign in, get his number, and wait his turn at the starting line.

It was strictly an amateur affair, he had said. Anyone with the $25 entry fee was welcome.

Unhappy in the bleachers, itching to get closer to the action, Ruby ran down to the track and stood behind a hay bail at the southeast corner with a bunch of loud, beer-drinking bikers and their molls.

Watching for Max, she saw him pull up to the starting line in the second heat with about thirty other riders, all of them wearing leather pants and jackets and steel-toed boots. They sat there for a time, revving their engines, making an infernal racket. Then a little man in a red, baseball cap dropped a black and white checkered flag, the crowd cheered, and they were off in a deafening roar and a cloud of acrid black smoke that swirled up and engulfed the stands.

Screaming down the straightaway, anonymous in their helmets and smoked visors, aiming directly at Ruby, the riders looked evil, war like as if they might keep right on going and smack her flat, grind her into the asphalt like a toad. Then at the last possible instant they geared down and slid into the turns straight-legged, steel toes sparking out behind. And hit it again on the other side, their rear wheels fishtailing, front ones rising off the ground, spinning wildly. Some of the riders ran into each other on the curve, or careened off the walls, fighting to keep their balance. Others fell skidding in the dust and lay still, their engines winding out, while already the leaders of the pack were at the other end, hurtling obstacles, splashing through muddy knee-deep water, racing back through the heat waves on the straightaway again.

It seemed to Ruby such a dangerous, futile endeavor, going round and round that silly track. What with the dust and noise and exhaust smoke and the fact that the riders all wore black and were constantly lapping each other on the track, she could hardly tell one from the other, and she was never sure where Max was in the pack.

Yet, she could not deny that the spectacle was stirring, in the same mindless way that she supposed duels and jousts were stirring, and other vainglorious pursuits that women followed with skittering hearts.

Max won the heat, but Ruby didn't even know it till she saw him standing on the victor's platform, smiling shyly, his helmet on his hip, accepting the kiss of the pretty, blond, mistress of ceremonies.

Whooping for joy, Ruby ran across the track and up onto the platform to implant a second kiss on his weary, blackened face.

She had meant the kiss to be brief and chaste. She had pictured it that way in her mind. But something—his smell of oil and machines, a program encoded in her genes—shattered the picture, changed it all around. And she let him crush her to him right there before the dignitaries, kiss her as she had never been kissed before, while the crowd roared its approval.

And then all the way back over the mountains that day she asked herself why.

What it was, she decided at last, was his intensity, his will, his ability to absorb himself in a single endeavor to the exclusion of all else.

Under everything, she thought, he was like herself.

At Soledad Pass, he angled west off the freeway on Anaverde Mountain Road, heading for Gold Hill. The freehold plots beside the highway were poor in these parts, scattered across the steep north slopes and windy ridgelines like airliner crash sites or the sets of post nuclear holocaust films: dented metal house trailers with roughhewn wooden extensions and rabbit hutches out back, lived-in vans and ex-school buses with butane tanks lashed to their sides, abandoned cars, obsolete farm implements, war surplus equipment of uncertain function, all of it lying tilted at odd angles and rusting in the chicken-pecked yards behind dwarf juniper windbreak, scraggly cactus plantings, and piled tumbleweed.

Ruby remembered that the old movie actress, Hillary Bennett, lived on a hill near here, so when she saw a mailbox with BENNETT stenciled on the side, she impulsively asked Max to stop and ride up the driveway.

"How come?" he wanted to know. "What I hear, she doesn't like visitors."

"True, but if I can convince her we have something in common, maybe she'll talk."

"What'll you talk about?"

"Hollywood," Ruby said. "What else?"

Miss Bennett lived in a big, old, ramshackle Tudor-style house with white timbered walls and a fake thatch roof. It should have looked out-of-place on this rough windy ridge above the desert. But California had a way of absorbing such apparent anomalies, of assimilating them into its general tacky modernity without a seam.

The driveway was deeply rutted and eroded, partly overgrown with sagebrush. "NO TRESPASSING! BEWARE OF DOG!" said a sign nailed to a bedraggled cottonwood tree. There was no car out front, the garden was unkept, and the place had a forlorn, abandoned look. But a dog barked from inside the house as they pulled up, and Ruby could see the old woman—a wavy-haired redhead like herself—peeking out from behind the pea-green drapery of the front picture window.

"What happened to her son?" Ruby asked, as she swung off the bike. "Didn't she use to have a son?"

"Yeah, but he hasn't been around in years."

"What about that old Negro servant she used to have?"

"He died."

"But how does she get money? How does she eat?"

"What I hear, the bank sends her cash by messenger about once a month, and she gets a weekly delivery from Safeway in Lancaster. I used to deliver her milk, but she cut that out when her cook took off."

"You ever see her?"

"Naw, not really. Just when she peeked out, like she's doing now."

Ruby glanced at the front window and spotted her.

"Miss Bennett!"

"Go away!"

"Please, Miss Bennett. I'm an actress. I'm going to Hollywood soon. And I'd like your advice."

For a long time, there was no response, then Ruby heard the front door's lock click open.

"All right, come in, but I only have a minute," the old woman said. "And wait till I lock up the dog."

Disbelieving her own good fortune, Ruby jumped off the bike, left Max behind, pushed open the heavy, old creaking door, and stepped inside.

Adjusting her eyes to the darkness, she found herself alone in a large, cluttered, Tudor antechamber, with hardwood floors, whitewashed oak-paneled walls, and a high-beamed ceiling. All the blinds were drawn, and the heat, the airlessness, the smell of dog, and accumulated dirt, nearly overwhelmed her.

"Miss Bennett?"

"In here!" the old lady shouted, grumpily, and Ruby followed her voice through the dark, jumbled rooms to a kind of parlor.

The old actress was seated on an uncomfortable-looking Victorian chesterfield before a vast, empty, stone fireplace. The tattered Persian carpet in front of her was cluttered with magazines and newspapers, none of which seemed more recent than World War II. Miss Bennett herself was leafing distractedly through an old issue of *LIFE*. Though how she could read it in the yellowish gloom Ruby had no idea.

"I—I'm so sorry to intrude, Miss Bennett, but . . ."

"Never mind, never mind," she said, throwing her magazine down, rising swiftly to shake Ruby's hand, yet avoiding her eyes. "As I said, I only have a moment, so why don't you just sit down here beside me, young lady, and tell me what it is you want to know."

Miss Bennett's low, nervous voice, her sudden movements, her strong handshake, and her thin figure were of a woman several decades younger, and Ruby's first impression was one of astonishment.

But after she had sat beside her a few moments, her impression changed to one of horror, for Miss Bennett's sharp little face and thin prominent nose had collapsed around her false teeth in such a way as to give her a witchlike appearance, and her skin was covered with an eczema or skin cancer of such raw severity that it made her face glow red.

"As I said, Miss Bennett, I'm an aspiring actress and I'm going to Hollywood soon to try my luck, so I'd like to know what it was like for you in the early days."

"Well, it was wonderful," the old lady said, in that easy, fluent, yet curiously passionless manner of people who've recounted their life story a thousand times in interviews. "I arrived from New York, where I'd been brought up, without a sou. And my first day in town, I was in the May Company Department Store, applying for a job, when a customer stepped on my foot. 'Oh, I'm so terribly sorry,' he said. 'Is there anything I can do?' As it happened, the man who stepped on my foot was Rupert Wagner, the famous director. I'd have recognized him anywhere. So, 'Yes,' I said, 'there is something you can do, Mr. Wagner. You can give me a screen test.' Well, he looked me over very carefully. Then he winked, and he said, 'Young lady, I think I can do even better than that.' He was shooting a jungle picture at the time in Griffith Park and his female lead—a drug addict if you want to know the truth—had just come down with hepatitis. He put me in her place that very afternoon. The picture was called *The Jungle Cruiser* and it was a big success. The press made a big to-do about my looks. I was deluged with offers, signed a contract with old Sam Goldwyn, and the rest is history."

Miss Bennett rose as soon as she had finished, letting Ruby know that her audience was at an end. Yet, still she avoided looking her in the eye.

"Oh, that was a great story, Miss Bennett, and I'll remember it always," Ruby said, smiling politely, though in fact she had found it disappointingly unexceptional. "I'd just like to ask one more thing before I go. Have you got any advice, anything you can tell me that I should know, that would make my life easier in Hollywood?"

"What's your stage name, dear?"

"Uh, Ruby Rose."

"Hmm. Not bad. A bit flashy. But so are you. So, keep it. Now listen. Here's my advice. And don't forget it." The old woman stared past Ruby and cackled to herself, as if at some bittersweet memory of long ago. "Keep your mouth shut, your eyes open, a price tag on everything including your privates, and don't take any wooden nickels."

Ruby would recall Hillary Bennett's parting words verbatim and repeat them to listeners many times in the future, evoking hilarity that never ceased to please her, even when she was as old as the woman she mocked.

After their day at the races, Max and Ruby went out together often. And every Saturday afternoon he would come by her Quonset hut to take her for a ride on his bike. She loved those Saturday rides. He took her places she had never been before—Red Rock Canyon, Devil's Postpile, Mount Baldy, Roy Roger's Castle, Castaic Lake, Desert Hot Springs, Joshua Tree State Park—and she awaited them all week with great anticipation. But one Saturday, he took her a way they had never been before, a wild and lonely way down Portal Ridge toward Bitterroot Canyon, and she grew suspicious of his intentions.

"Hey, where we headed?"

"Got something to show you."

"What's that?"

"Long story," he said. "Want to hear it?"

He pulled over to the side by the dry creek bed. They climbed off the bike and sat on the hard clay bank, fooling with willow switches, poking them into ant holes, watching a black and yellow lizard sunning on a rock.

"Not long ago, I was out hunting rabbits on Portal Ridge, and I shot this bobcat," he began.

Max's way with words was new to Ruby, like a gift he had been saving for just this moment. It occurred to her that he was smarter and more sophisticated, more like his parents, than he had ever let on. And she loved him for it; it was the one thing she had found lacking in him. At the same time, she knew he had chosen to reveal himself now precisely because she would love him for it. And though she liked his story well enough, especially the part about the secret canyon, she felt a perverse desire to ridicule him when he was done, to belittle his discovery.

"So, you named the place for me, huh?" she said. "What'd you call it? Motherless Gulch?"

"I'm not going to tell you that," he replied very seriously. "Not till you've seen it for yourself."

"Look Max," she said, taking a deep breath. "I don't think I'm ready for this yet.

"Ready for what?"

"This," she said, pressing her hand first to her own heart, then to his.

"Why not?"

"You'll laugh if I tell you."

"No, I won't."

"It's this vow that I've made."

"What kind of vow?"

"You promise you won't laugh?"

"I promise."

"I've sworn to stay a virgin," she said, "until I get my first big break in the movies."

And he burst out laughing. But he did not take her to his secret canyon that day. And though it soon got around town that they were "going steady," she never tired of reminding him that their scene was strictly a temporary thing.

He took no offense. Maybe he didn't believe her. He seemed to have total self-confidence in her regard, and to fundamentally misjudge the power of her ambition.

"You'll come back," he said once, "when you're tired of running around."

"I'm not going to *be* running around," she responded. "I'm going to be pursuing my career. And you sound awfully sure that I'm going to fail."

"No," he said. "I'm just sure of where you belong."

"Well, if we ever do tie the knot, I want to tell you right now that I am not going to give up my name."

"What?" he said, incredulous. "I don't get it."

"Which do you think has more *panache*, 'Mrs. Bauer' or 'Ruby Rose, Superstar'?"

"Get outta here!"

"I'm serious, Max. If you want me, you gotta take me as I am."

"I'm starting to think that might be kind of hard to do."

"Get used to it!" she said, laughing, slapping him on the shoulder.

After that, Ruby and Max went through the motions of a typical early 1960s romance. They started out by double dating with other couples—Gil Sanchez and Sally Porter, Juanita

Sanchez and Charlie Gonçalves—but quickly progressed to the next stage, which was total involvement in each other to the exclusion of all others.

She rarely saw Michael or his family anymore and had little time for her father.

Instead, night after night, she went out to park with Max in the desert.

Remembering her sister's experience with men, and what her father had told her when she was very young, Ruby fought Max every inch of the way. But he was clever, and patient, and he seemed to understand instinctively how to move her.

He went about it manually, and with infinite care.

In the beginning, therefore, love was not so much a spiritual manifestation to Ruby as a physical one, and she measured it solely by its effects on her body. Yet with each slow, careful step, each new physical response, her resistance weakened, and her love grew.

It grew like a germ, a seed, a benign virus in her virgin womb. She could *feel* it growing, and it absorbed all her consciousness. Her imagination took on a life of its own, separate from her plans and intentions.

At school, at home alone, she daydreamed of making love. She had the most vivid sensations of it. She could see herself doing it from every camera angle. She could feel him inside her. She nearly had orgasms thinking of it, then loathed herself and picked fights with Max when he came over to visit.

Yet, he never hit back at her, never argued, or resisted. Just kept on his slow, imperturbable way.

First, he touched her breasts on the outside of her clothes, lightly with his fingertips. Then, many hours of make-out time elapsed before he was ready for the next step, which was squeezing her breasts gently and rubbing her nipples with the flat of his hand. Next, he slipped that calm, cool hand of his inside her bra, opened the clasps from behind, pulled up her sweater—an inch or two more each date—then finally stuck his head down and sucked her breasts till she had to beg him to stop.

Fascinated by what they were doing together, hypnotized by Max's subtle hands, his educated fingers, she felt the little virus growing like mad. Desperate, she reminded herself that there was still hope because at the rate Max was proceeding, she would graduate from high school and be long gone before he reached his goal.

Then he stepped up the pace.

As Max explored Ruby's body, so she explored the contours of his mind. She was neither a psychologist nor any sort of poet or philosopher. Her efforts to interpret Max's personality were based purely upon empirical observation. He was brave because he was willing to defy death at the racetrack, thoughtful because he rarely failed to bring her flowers, intelligent because he knew more of science, mechanics, business, politics, agriculture, and the principals of organization than she, loyal because he had promised his mother Sybil that he would never leave her, respected and admired because his friends Gil and Charlie seemed to hang on his every word, generous because he always paid her way, honest because when she found a ten dollar bill in the movie theater, he made her turn it over to the management, loving because his eyes lit up whenever he saw her and he never seemed to get enough of her, understanding because he did not resent her increasingly perfunctory resistance to a seduction that was probably already a foregone conclusion, tender because he had absolutely the softest, most magical touch of any man she had ever dreamed of.

"You must have a way with animals," she said one time.

"Yeah," he replied, then laughed. "All kinds."

But what she liked most about Max was that he never tried to do what so many other boys had foolishly tried to do before—compete with her on her own terms, talk over her, cut her short, boss her around. He seemed perfectly content with the natural order of things—he in the role of audience, Ruby as star—except in the sexual arena.

Ran his tickling fingers down her belly, down her thigh and up her dress, outside her panties, inside her panties, outside on her curly patch of red pubic hair, inside at last, making her all creamy wet.

Sunday afternoons, they would drive out onto the dry lakes in his pickup truck, park behind sagebrush islands, and she would smell his mother's Sunday Roast on his breath, meaty, bloody, and warm. She loved the smell, and it was on Sundays that they usually progressed a step further. It was on a Sunday in early June, in fact, when they progressed to that place beyond which there is nowhere left to go, except the ultimate.

"Let me take you to my secret canyon," he whispered, and Ruby felt too weak to answer either yes or no.

They rode to Bitterroot Canyon in his pickup. Then he rolled his bike down off the truck bed and they took off cross country, raising a plume of white sand along the dry creek bed, blowing the silence of the walls with the proliferous echo of their exhaust.

He parked where the canyon dead-ended and led her up an arroyo, into a cave that got narrower and narrower.

She grew frightened and started to pull back.

But he talked to her smoothly, quietly, like a man with a balky mare.

"Easy now, easy now."

Talked her right out of her own world and into his.

He had said Ruby Canyon was magic. But to Ruby herself it seemed not so magic as cinematic. Its sand floor was implausibly smooth and white. Its walls seemed inordinately high and precipitous. Its pool too clear and round. Its atmosphere fuzzy and romanticized, like a Cecil B. DeMille set. The flawless blue ribbon of sky above the walls seemed merely part of the lighting. Even Max, leading her inside, appeared not as his familiar self but as an actor playing the role of someone larger, stronger, older, wiser.

Frightened again, Ruby broke away from him and started to run. He raced after her, caught her, spun her around like a doll, crushed her, kissed her, ground his teeth against her lips.

It all seemed like part of the script.

A delicious feeling of languor overcame her, and she melted in his arms.

He picked her up, carried her to the pool, laid her on the grass beside the water, reached behind her, released the catch on her halter top.

Her breasts spilled out in his hands.

But she wanted more of him than just that.

She wanted everything, she thought.

Naked, he was muscular and hairy, her opposite pole. He bent and licked her toes, ran his tongue to her breasts and down again, spread her legs, licked her clit till she whimpered and cried his name, then rose, his mouth wet with her juices, to kiss her face.

She reached for him and drew him in. It hurt for only an instant and then filled her with a feeling of destiny. She saw the future and it was him. But she could not figure out yet how he was to fit in.

"I love you," he said, and came inside her.

Chapter Nine

Finally, Ruby was ready to leave for Hollywood.

She had cried and kissed Reno goodbye and seen him off to work.

She had loaded her car and embraced Max for the umpteenth time and promised her undying love.

She started the engine and put it in gear. The car rolled forward, and she was about to wave bye to Max when they were both blinded momentarily by a tremendous flash of light.

She slammed on her brakes just as a powerful shockwave struck, rocking the car violently on its springs, cracking the rear window, knocking Max clean off his feet.

An atom bomb, or what sounded like one, went off directly overhead, and a great roiling ball of fire appeared in the sky, seeming to feed off its own energy mass, attracting lightning out of the void. Monstrous clouds of smoke, naphthylamine black, billowed out from its fringes, and shiny, metallic, confetti-like stuff came fluttering down. Mixed up in it all Ruby could see what looked like parachutes.

"Get down! Get down!" Max shouted, racing up to the car, leaping inside, throwing her to the floor.

And there they huddled, trembling for their lives, for what seemed an eon, while the silvery confetti grew into great tumbling shards of aluminum aircraft debris that landed all around them, shaking the earth when it hit, crashing into hangars and Quonset huts, causing fires and secondary explosions.

The parachutists came down last, after Ruby and Max had crawled out of the car and all the danger was past.

One of them landed near the front gate where Max used to fold his newspapers.

Another hit the dry lake where Lonnie used to take her in the little red wagon.

Another came down in the pepper tree just behind Ruby's Quonset hut: a Black boy, only a year or two older than Ruby, and frail as a reed, he was swinging with his military boots not a foot above the ground. And he seemed remarkably untouched by the disaster, except for the smoke stains on his blue-gray jumpsuit. His eyes were closed, there was a peaceful expression on his handsome, sensitive face, and he appeared to be merely unconscious.

Max whipped out his Swiss Army knife, cut him down, and laid him on the grass. Ruby took his head in her lap and leaned over him, feeling for his pulse. She was so close to him she could see the shaving bumps on his face, the dried line of spittle that ran out the side of his mouth, a tiny scar on his right eyelid, his long and beautiful black lashes. He seemed so real to her, so alive, so young, but he had no pulse. *It's not fair, not fair,* she kept thinking, *because I've got life to spare.* She closed her eyes, pressed her forehead to his, concentrated with all her might, trying to beam some of her spare life into him.

Then Max put an ear to his chest and shook his head.

"He's gone," he said, and went in to phone the police.

But the police already knew.

The Flying Wing had exploded in flight over Eagle Field and plunged to earth, taking its entire crew along with it.

Shaken by the experience, haunted by an image of the Black boy hanging in the pepper tree, Ruby put off leaving for Hollywood for a week. She told Max she wanted it kept secret from their friends, as she had kept her original leave-taking secret. But Max let it slip to Charlie one morning on the job. Charlie told his live-in girlfriend, Juanita. And Juanita conspired with Sally to throw a tasteless going-away party at the Desert Lanes Bowling Alley in Lancaster that confirmed all Ruby's worst fears about such events.

Reno got her alone in the corner by the bar and presented his date for the evening—a frumpy middle-aged car hop named Sweety McCann whom Ruby had never met before—as his future bride.

"With you gone, honey," he said, "I need someone else to take care of me now."

Juanita, in her cups, gave voice to lengthy and tearful recriminations concerning Ruby's previous intention of leaving town without saying goodbye to her best and oldest friend.

Michael sulked all evening, sipping at a bottle of vodka concealed in his coat pocket, then bellowed out, just as everyone was leaving, "You're going all the way, Ruby baby! All the way!

And you might not think so, but I had it too once. Yeah, I had it to!"

Max apologized for giving her secret away, and presented her, on his mother's behalf, with an antique Hermes hatbox filled with theatrical makeup. But she blew up anyway, and accused him of having a hidden agenda, of taking pleasure in making her feel guilty.

"You know," she said, on the way home, "maybe we ought to think about dating other people for a while."

"Whatever's right," he said, shrugging it off. But she had hit him where it hurt.

Then, as luck would have it, she had carburetor trouble the next day on the way to L.A. Had to swallow her pride, phone Max at the garage, get him to drive up Angeles Crest in his pickup truck, and tow her all the way back to Gold Hill. Max "experienced delays," as he said, finding a replacement part, and Ruby was made to suffer the perils of the second goodbye.

Everyone came around to apologize, to get maudlin again and deny what they had said at the party and blame their behavior on drink and an excess of emotion.

"I just hope you'll be able to forgive me someday!" Juanita cried."

"Don't hesitate to call me day or night," Michael said. "You get into any trouble; I'll be down in a flash."

Reno claimed he'd never had any intention of marrying Sweety McCann; it was only a joke.

Max admitted that maybe there was a grain of truth in the notion that he secretly wanted her to stay.

In short, they made her life so miserable that she was able to leave them at last.

Ruby arrived in Hollywood, in June of 1960, with six hundred dollars in travelers' checks, a suitcase, Sybil's Hermes hatbox, and her beat-out Chevy.

She got herself a room in a motel-style apartment complex on Franklin Avenue in East Hollywood, ate from cans, and set herself the goal of making it big before the money ran out. As she would put it later, in a written account: "Having spent a lifetime dreaming of a movie career, I had yet only the vaguest notion of how to make one happen, and I was astonishingly naive about my chances."

Her initial step, according to Michael's instructions, was to have some glossy photos of herself made up. The next was to find an agent. But the first six photographers she tried either instantly put the make on her or asked her to pose in the nude. Then, after she'd finally had her portraits shot by a friendly homosexual, none of the agents she looked up would respond to her telephone calls.

She discussed the matter with her next-door neighbor, Birgitta, a former Miss Minnesota, and was not encouraged by what she learned.

"There's only one way, babe, unless you got pull."

"How's that?"

"On your back."

Disheartened, depressed, Ruby phoned Michael to ask his advice, and he insisted on coming down to counsel her in person.

He called her from a Hollywood bar a week later, at one o'clock in the morning

"Say, good-lookin'," he slurred, "how's 'bout comin' down and havin' a lil' drink?"

"Sure," she said, despite her misgivings. "Be right over."

When she got to the place—a big, brassy, jazz spot on La Brea Boulevard called "The Blue Mirror"—Michael was sitting in at the piano, singing an Al Hibble derived pop rendition of "Time Goes by So Slowly" while the regular performer took a break.

"Oh, my love, my darling," he sang off-key, grimacing with schmaltzy passion, *"I've hungered for your kiss, a long, lonely time. Time goes by so slowly, and time can do so much. Are you still mine? I need your love. I need your love. God speed your love to me."*

And what struck Ruby about him was not so much his disheveled appearance—he looked as if he had slept in his checkered suit—or his state of sloppy sentimental inebriation, but the fact that he seemed so *diminished*. At one time, Michael had seemed monumental to her, as fixed and solid as the stars in their firmament. Yet here he was—just another Hollywood has-been or never-was—a ludicrous picture, even, with his sallow skin, red lips, wild eyes, and frizzy yellow hair, boring this sophisticated, multi-racial audience with an embarrassing performance of music that held no appeal for them in the first place.

Easing him out from behind the piano, Ruby convinced him to ride home with her for a cup of coffee.

"Listen, you know, you're gonna have to sober up if you want to drive back over those mountains."

In her car, Michael passed from his manic stage to his maudlin one, babbling incoherently about his lost chances. For a while, he faded out entirely, his head banging against the car's window frame. But as soon as they were in the door of her place, he got a second wind.

"You used to want me," he whispered in her ear, nearly wilting her with his breath. "Now I want you."

"You don't know what you're talking about," Ruby said, slithering out of his clutches.

"Oh, yes I do," he said, humping up to her from behind, grabbing her around the breast and belly. "And I want it now."

Ruby was repelled by his touch. He smelled stale and old. And he was so deadly serious, so out of character, as he stood panting and writhing behind her.

Suddenly, he was biting her on the back of the neck, thrusting at her with his pelvis, jerking her backwards from the hips. There was nothing tender in the gesture. It was coarse and brutal, like a stranger in an alley.

"For Christ's sake, Michael, stop this!" she said, but he wouldn't hear, and clamped his teeth down harder, hurting her, drawing blood. "No, please, no!"

A mirror hung on the wall in front of them, just above her chest of drawers. Ruby could have looked for Michael's reflection there, or her own, as he slammed her face down on the chest with one hand, jerked her skirt up with the other, tore her panties aside, and violated her from the rear.

But she shut her eyes tight.

She did not want to see it.

It was like some blind unthinking force, an act of God, battering her with unreasonable, unanswerable authority.

In her mind's eye, however, she could see it all: She was dressed as her mother again, in a long fleshy beige dress. Swaying with drink, pouting her little cupid's bow mouth, she was just asking for it, everyone would say.

It was over in a minute. Michael passed out on the sofa, and there was nothing she could do to wake him.

"He's on another one of his benders," she said, when she phoned Veronika a few minutes later. "I'm letting him sleep it off at my place and I'll send him home tomorrow."

Then she locked herself in the bathroom and showered till the water ran cold. Unable to bear the sight of her own body, she dressed in jeans and a sweatshirt and huddled on the cold bathroom tile for the rest of the night.

In the morning, Michael slept late and awakened with a colossal hangover.

"Oh my God!" he moaned, stumbling into the kitchenette where she was brewing coffee. "What happened to me?"

"Isn't it obvious?" she said, feeding him tomato juice and aspirins.

"Ruby, I can't tell you how much I appreciate your help," he said, so sincerely, so genuinely remorseful, that she concluded he had no memory of the night before. "Jesus! No telling what I might've done to myself."

"Don't mention it, Michael," she replied, straight-faced. It was easy for her. He was no longer a person. She neither hated him nor pitied him. She observed him. "But honestly, you were no trouble at all."

"Even so, if there's ever any way..."

"Well, thank you. There *is* one thing I wanted to ask you."

"Right," he said, smiling suddenly, rubbing his hands together, making a great show of enthusiasm. "We gotta put our heads together on this movie thing."

"Actually, I've kind of put that on the back burner since I talked to you last."

"Oh?" he said, and there was something in his manner—something tepid and hesitant—that led her to suspect that he recalled more about last night than he let on. "I think Max has gotten me pregnant, and I want to get an abortion."

"I see," he said, and Ruby could have sworn that she detected a note of relief in his tone. "Well, that's tough, love. I'll ask around and see what we can turn up."

True to his word, Michael talked it over with Veronika as soon as he got home. Veronika sought advice from her coworkers and inmate helpers at Eagle Field, obtained an emergency leave from her job, and arrived in East Hollywood the next day.

"Sweetheart, I'm here to help you get your act back together," she said, as soon as she was in the door, and arranged for a visit to a GYN that very afternoon. Then, having ascertained that Ruby was indeed six weeks pregnant, she set out to find an abortionist. Within twenty-four hours, through the friend of a friend of a friend, she had acquired the name of a "Dr. Martin" in Tijuana.

The abortionist, as it turned out, was a plump, elderly, American woman with a round, rosy face glowing with good health, a pair of kindly, crinkly, blue eyes, and a brand-new pink cinderblock clinic on a barren, garbage-strewn hill above the tumbledown Mexican city.

"Welcome, welcome!" she said, exuding candor and good intentions, as she greeted them in her office. "Won't you sit down? Is there anything I can get you?"

Dr. Martin wore a spotless medical smock, an air of brisk professionalism, and a smile so wide and honest—but of such a peculiar intensity—that it nearly qualified as beatific. Her appearance was so wholesome, in fact, and so utterly unexpected, that it put Ruby instantly on guard, and heightened her already intolerable level of anxiety. Yet inside the surgery room, Dr. Martin was so tirelessly thoughtful and humane, anticipating every fear and desire—even letting Veronika stand by the table and hold her hand right up until the operation began—that Ruby decided to just relax and put her feet up in the stirrups and go with the flow.

Working under the sheets, explaining the procedure step by step, the old woman performed the abortion with such remarkable aplomb and painlessness and dispatch that when she announced its completion Ruby exclaimed, "What? What? You mean it's gone? I can't believe it! That's all there is to it?"

"That's right, honey," said Dr. Martin, beaming at her benevolently. "Your baby's in God's hands now."

All the way back up the freeway, Veronika was extra sweet to Ruby, patting her on the leg, warning her of the dangers of post-partum depression, counseling her to put the entire episode behind her as quickly as possible. But the instant they hit Franklin Avenue in East Hollywood the smile dropped off her face.

"Now that I've seen you through this thing," she said, in a flat, emotionless tone more startling and frightening to Ruby than any sneer might have been, "I want to tell you how I really feel."

"I don't understand," Ruby said, her heart failing, for she already suspected the worst. "What do you mean?"

"Oh, please. Michael has already told me everything."

"Everything?"

"Of course," she said, pulling into the parking lot of Ruby's apartment complex, leaving the motor running. "He always does. It's part of why he goes off like that in the first place. And I can grant him that."

"Did he tell you he raped me?" Ruby burst out. "Did he say that?"

"But with you," Veronika went on, not hearing, "with you I just can't. It's too much to ask."

Ruby thought of a million things to say, but none of them seemed right. Suddenly it seemed cruel and unworthy to force the truth on Veronika. She had been like a mother to her. How could she tell her that Michael had grown undesirable to other women? How could she confront her with the brutality of a man she needed to protect and admire?

Watching her back around and pull out of the parking lot, Ruby felt not merely shame, and pity for Veronika, and rage against Michael. What she felt most was loneliness.

She called Max that night, and his voice sounded so calm and reasonable, so sure, and rock-solid, that she wanted to reach out and touch him across the telephone line. She thought of her father, of her brother Lonnie, of Michael.

Max was the only man she would ever trust again.

"You mad at me?" she asked, after she had told him about the abortion.

"Let's say I'm disappointed."

"There's just no way I could have it now."

"I understand," he said. "But I don't have to like it."

"I don't like it either. But there it is."

"How much did it cost?"

"A lot."

"I'll wire you some money."

"I could use it.

"When am I going to see you next?"

"Not yet," she said. "I'm still a little queasy, and I need time to sort things out down here."

Ruby took Max's money, 'midnighted' out of her motel room, and moved into her car, eating at drive-in restaurants, sleeping in the back seat, doing her make-up in the rearview mirror, going to the toilet in service stations, bathing in the surf at Santa Monica and rinsing off in the beachside showers provided by the state.

She hadn't gotten her period yet, and she was still getting sick in the mornings, having to stop the car and throw up by the side of the freeway, but it never occurred to her to doubt the surgical skill of Dr. Martin, or the success of the abortion.

Meanwhile, she had settled on a strategy to break into the movies. She did not have time for a subtle approach, she figured. Her money would not hold out that long. She had to do something simple and direct.

She started hanging out at the Paramount, Warner Brothers, 20th Century Fox, and MGM lots in the mornings, when all the directors were coming to work, approaching them with her glossies and a personal sales pitch. But she was not the only aspiring actress with that idea, she discovered. Nor did the directors seem charmed when they were accosted at the front gate. Once she even got herself forcibly ejected from MGM by security police.

At that point, she determined to go for broke, all or nothing. She asked herself which movie director she admired and respected most. It was Otto Preminger, she decided. She had seen him interviewed once by Edward R. Murrow, and she had been delighted by his droll wit, his bald dome, his suavely arrogant European manner, and his penchant for shocking people and shaking them up. Her favorite of his films was "Saint Joan." She had followed its development since 1956, when Preminger began his celebrated quest for a young unknown to play the role of Joan of Arc. After reading that he had interviewed fifteen thousand young women all over the world and settled at last on Jean Seberg, a seventeen-year-old druggist's daughter from Marshalltown, Iowa, Ruby had dreamed of affecting a similarly remarkable and glamorous change in her own life.

Despite all its advance publicity, however, *Saint Joan* was not an artistic or financial success. Hollywood critics, pundits and gossip mongers pounced on the haughty Mr. Preminger, reveling in his failure.

Yet, through it all, Ruby remained his faithful fan. At the Deseret Theater in Lancaster, most of the audience had departed out of boredom before the film was half over, but Ruby sat riveted during the entire performance. And at the end—when Jean Seberg, small and frail, her hair cut short like a boy—mounted the pyre, and a radiant light descended upon her, and the clock in the church tower struck the hour of her burning, Ruby wept alone in the theater until it was empty, till the manager had to come along and ask her to leave.

Shortly thereafter, drawn perversely to the inspiration and evil of the Church, she had gone through a brief "Catholic" period, attending Mass with Juanita at Saint Bernard's in Lancaster.

Years later, in the middle of a chill, foggy night, parked on a quiet street in the Beverly Hills flats with all the doors locked, lying on the tattered back seat under her winter coat with a wad of clothes for a pillow, listening to the tall royal palms rattling in the wind off the Pacific, reflecting on the career of Otto Preminger, she decided that the great director was just waiting to discover Ruby Rose.

The next morning, over coffee at McDonald's, she read in Sheila Graham's gossip column in the *Hollywood Reporter* that the distinguished director was in town for a few days, staying with his brother Ingo while he dickered with MGM over a property entitled *Exodus*. And it seemed to her a miraculously fortuitous coincidence.

She looked up Ingo Preminger in the phone book, found that he was an actors' and directors' agent with offices on sunset Boulevard in Hollywood and a residence on Manzanita

Drive in Bel Air, and drove directly up to his private home, a large, whitewashed, tile-roofed Spanish Revival place partially obscured by banana trees.

Her intention had been to deal with the matter forthrightly, to go right up and knock at the front door and ask for Otto Preminger. Yet, faced with the reality of the situation, she found herself petrified, unable to think of anything save the director's infamous hauteur, his power to reduce importunate inferiors to a state of tears with a single withering glance. So, she just sat there in her car for twenty-four hours, smoking cigarettes, watching everyone who came and went. And though she never caught a glimpse of Otto Preminger, she did in fact make the acquaintance of his brother Ingo's tall, stunning, blond, Austrian wife.

"Hi, I am Mrs. Preminger, and your car... I wonder if you could move it," she called out, clumping awkwardly down the sloping red brick driveway in silver spike heels and a silver cocktail dress, after Ruby had ignored several impassioned pleas from her maid and gardener. "I don't want to call the security patrol, darling," she went on, in a remarkably off hand and familiar tone, peering in Ruby's side window, regarding without apparent interest the junk food wrappers and coke bottles littering the floor, the clothing and underwear piled up on the back seat. "But, you know, I am having a soirée tonight, and this space I need for my guests."

"I'm sorry," Ruby replied, "but I'm waiting for Otto Preminger."

"But Otto is in Palm Springs for the weekend," Mrs. Preminger said, smiling affably, while at the same time vigorously shaking her head. "Why do you wish to speak with him?"

"It's about a role in his next movie, *Exodus*."

"I see. Well, give me your name and phone number, and I will have him contact you."

"I don't have time for that," Ruby protested. "Why don't you give me his address in Palm Springs?"

"Ah," said Mrs. Preminger, patiently, shaking her head again, "but you know this is something I cannot do."

"Then I'll just have to stay right here."

"Come, come, darling . . . please?"

"I don't have any choice," Ruby said, starting to cry. "I've promised myself that I'm either going to be an actress or die."

"I understand," Mrs. Preminger said, still not unkindly, as she turned to go. "But I have needs also, and privacy is one."

Ruby thought Mrs. Preminger was going to call the police on her. Yet not an hour later, she struggled back down to the car in her silver high heels and cocktail dress, leaned in the window again and said, "I am probably mad to do this, darling, but do you need a job?"

"Well, yes, I suppose that's the general idea."

"Then listen. My serving woman has just called in. 'Sick,' she says. So, to help with the party tonight I need someone nice. Have you any experience in that line?"

"Sure," said Ruby, on impulse, though she hadn't at all. "When do I start?"

"Right now," said Mrs. Preminger. "But your car you will park in back."

"Is Mr. Preminger going to be there tonight?"

"No, darling, he will not be. Nor will Ingo. And when my guests are trying to relax, I prefer you do not pester them with business talk."

Ruby tried to keep to Mrs. Preminger's rule that night. Avoiding the guests, and the more formal serving tasks, she tried to make herself useful in the kitchen. It was a lovely Spanish-style kitchen, combining the most modern appliances with rough stone floors, rustic whitewashed walls, and heavy oak ceiling beams from which baskets, utensils, gourds and bunches of tomatoes and garlic were suspended. To Ruby, it was a pleasure to do dishes in Mrs. Preminger's kitchen, for even the window over the sink provided a glamorous view of the teardrop-shaped swimming pool and the lights of Beverly Hills.

Toward the end of the evening, however, visitors began to appear in the kitchen, guests looking for ice, or drinks, or soda water, or just idle conversation. One of these was a tall, craggy, wispy-haired old Englishman in a red ascot, blue blazer, white duck trousers, and canvas yachting shoes. His name was Miles Burnham, he said, mixing himself a gin and tonic, "an actor and a Londoner, born of a long line of the same."

Then, leaning cross-legged against the tile sink counter, sipping at his drink, puffing at a battered meerschaum, while Ruby scrubbed pots and pans, he questioned her shrewdly until she confessed that she herself had hopes of an acting career.

"You know, Ruby, perseverance like yours is a rare and noble thing, and it ought not to go unrewarded," he said, after she had recounted her Hollywood misadventures, both real and invented: "An extra-role in *Teenage Zombies*, a place in line at the cattle call for *North by Northwest*, dumped from a supporting role in *Rawhide* at the last minute..."

"Oh my God!" exclaimed the Englishman. "Is there anything I can do to help?"

"That's very kind of you, Mr. Burnham," she said, smiling. "What is it you have in mind?"

"Well, I hadn't thought, really. Perhaps a job, just to tide you over. Something on the set of this 'shoot-'em-up' I'm doing. Running errands, pouring coffee, that sort of thing. I've some pull with the director, you see. He's English, and all that."

"I'm sorry, but I've already done that kind of thing, and it's not what I'm looking for."

"Why not take it, then?"

He seemed genuinely perplexed that she would turn down his offer so abruptly.

"Do you want to know the truth?"

"I should be unhappy with anything less."

"For me, Mr. Burnham, it's all or nothing."

"But my dear, you must have no illusions."

"About what?"

"Very frankly, Ruby, yours is not the kind of beauty that will translate to the screen," he said. And then, flattering her to soften the blow: "It's for connoisseurs, not crowds."

"But how do you know that, Mr. Burnham?" she demanded, banging a copper pot for emphasis. "How can you be so sure?"

"My dear, I've nearly forty years in the business," he said, very gently. "The camera loves some faces, others not. And I'd hate to see a lovely young girl like you waste all her time, energy, and emotion on something that is not to be. Now look, here's my card, and if you should ever change your mind..."

Later, as Ruby finished up the dishes, morosely reflecting on Miles Burnham's advice, a swart, fat, hairy little man in his late forties sidled up, puffing at a long cigar. Magnificently pompadoured and manicured, sporting dark glasses, a diamond pinky ring, a white knit polo shirt, white patent leather belt, shiny black slacks, and white dancing pumps, he projected the kind of oily charm and unearned prosperity that was bound to excite Ruby because it was so richly authentic. At last, she had found a recognizable Hollywood type, someone who met all her previous expectations.

"Couldn't help overhearing what Miles said a while ago," he said out of the side of his mouth. And I want you to know, he's full of shit."

"You really think so?"

"Sure," he said. "Need some help with the dishes?"

"I don't mind."

"Rickie Cooper," he said, picking up a towel and starting to dry. "And I tell you, I think you got what it takes to be a star."

"You wouldn't be kidding me, now. Would you, Mr. Cooper?"

"Naw," he said, revealing a pursed, fishy little grin. "But call me Rickie, okay?"

"You a friend of Mrs. Preminger's?"

"My folks are," he said. "I brought my mother."

"And your dad?"

"In Hong Kong, shooting a flick."

"What's his name? Maybe I've heard of him."

"Same as mine."

"Richard Cooper?"

"Uh-huh. I'm Richard Cooper, Jr."

"You in the same line?"

"Well, I spent years working with my dad," he said. "Now I'm kind of branching out on my own."

"No kidding?" Ruby said and regarded him more closely. Rickie's dark hair grew so luxuriantly it went all the way down his neck, met his eyebrows at the temples, sprouted in great clumps from his nostrils and ears. Yet his pale, squinty brown eyes, button nose, and smeary little mouth were remarkably ill-defined by comparison, projecting weakness and irresolution. In sum, there was something soft and sluggish and… endomorphic about Rickie that interested Ruby greatly in her present distress. Not to mention his father, whose name was of a household currency nearly equal to that of Otto Preminger.

"So," she continued, trying her best, "what part of this great big town do you live in, Rickie?"

"Me?" he said, sniffing, shaking his small head, as if the answer were so obvious it was barely worth conveying. "Where else? I live at the beach."

"The beach?"

"Yeah. You know, Venice?"

"I've heard of it."

"Who hasn't?"

"You show me around sometime?"

"If you want."

"Really?" she said laughing, fixing him with her patented grin. "When?"

"I tell you what," he said, enunciating every syllable as if he had just come to some momentous decision. "I can do even better than that. You like the beach? I got another place up in Carmel. Why don't you fly up for the weekend? My producer's gonna be there, and I got all my equipment set up. We do a screen test, and if it's any good you read for a part in a film called *Blue Desert* that I got in the development stage now... Very artsy, you know. Very European."

"Sounds interesting," Ruby said. But her experience with Michael had made her wary. "I'll think about it and give you a call tomorrow."

Later, she made it a point to consult Mrs. Preminger on the matter.

"Darling, number one on Rickie's agenda is certainly you-know-what," she said, woman to woman, while she counted out Ruby's generous wages for the evening's work. "But if you are asking what in your place I might do, or whether his movie is real, this I cannot tell you. It is your decision to take."

Ruby sold her old Chevy in a used car lot the next day for sixty dollars and flew to Monterey.

Rickie picked her up at the airport in his Jaguar and drove her through thick, swirling summer fog to his home near Point Lobos.

A small, boxy, unimposing place made of roughhewn redwood logs; it looked like an overgrown sauna. There were no windows, anywhere, though it was in a spectacular setting on a cliff above Shelter Cove.

"Views distract me from my work," he explained when Ruby looked puzzled.

"Where's your producer?"

"Got held up."

"Had a feeling he might."

"Hey, hey, hey," Rickie said, raising his hands, palms outward, as if to show they were empty of weapons. "Trust me."

"I'm trying, I'm trying."

"So," he said, letting his hands fall, and then briskly rubbing them together. "What do you say? Should we get right to work?"

"You mind if I set my bag down first?"

"No, no, go ahead."

"Where do you want me to put it?"

"Anywhere," he said, grabbing a small moving picture camera off the mantlepiece and starting for the door again. "There's only this one room."

"What?"

"Yeah. I mean, along with the kitchen and bath."

"I'm beginning to get the picture."

"What else you expect?" he said, grabbing her bag, dropping it on the day bed.

Out of the house he took her, across a field of soggy wild oats, through a grove of gnarled, wind bent cypress trees, over a patch of water plant, down a slippery wooden stairway to a gray, kelpy beach.

Somewhere, nearby surf was humping into rocks and sea caves, hollowing out, sending up fountains of spray, but the fog was so thick you could only hear it and smell it.

Leading her like a blind woman, Rickie brought her along the edge of the cove to where a massive phallic-shaped hunk of granite thrust out of the shallows, out of the mist.

"Here's what you do!" he said, shouting to make himself heard above the sound of the surf. "Take off your clothes and go fuck that rock!"

"What? You must be joking!"

"No, I'm not, no, come on!"

"How the hell you gonna film in this stuff?"

"What stuff?"

"The Fog!" she yelled, whipping it about with her hands.

"Hey, this is a Super 8, honey!" he shrieked, raising the camera up and pointing it at her like a gun. "It cuts through anything, even pea soup!"

Ruby thought this over for a minute, weighing the miniscule chances that he was on the up-and-up against some of the more bizarre scenes she had seen in recent Neo-Realistic European movies, and decided that it was at least worth a try, just to show him what she could do. She stripped off her clothes and laid them on the sand.

"Say, you got a little spare tire there, babe. Makes you look knocked-up."

She waded out and wrapped herself around the rock and fucked it just like he said, though the water was cold as ice, and she felt she might die of shame.

"You know, you wanna be in pictures, you gotta lose some weight!"

She fucked that fucking rock like her life depended on it, till she felt it would turn from stone to live warm flesh and sprout a great erection. Yet when she was done, and turned around to look for Rickie, he was gone.

Wending her way back up the cliffside stairway and through the ghostly cypress trees in the drifting, curling fog, Ruby imagined finding Rickie at the bottom of an *arroyo*, dead of a prurient middle-age heart attack, his tongue hanging out, his eyes rolled back in his head. She imagined driving his Jag into town, reporting his death to the police, and all the questions they would ask, the assumptions they would make, especially when they learned that the father of the deceased was a famous Hollywood director. She imagined the publicity, the notoriety, and thought it might not be such a bad thing for her career.

Back at the cabin, Rickie was preparing lunch in a long white apron, a red checkered scarf, and a tall chef's hat. He had it all set up near the fireplace, with wine and a fresh bouquet of flowers. His camera was lying on the mantlepiece. When he went out to the kitchen, Ruby was tempted to open it up and find out if there was any film inside. She'd have been willing to bet there was none.

"I don't like the kind of person I'm turning into," she said, when he reappeared. "Will you take me back to town?"

Rickie gave her not an instant's trouble, not even over the wasted lunch. He said little on the way to Monterey and left her off at the airport with nothing more than a shrug and a sheepish little grin. It was like he'd already got himself off and didn't really need her company anymore.

The plane for L.A arrived, but she had to let it go without her because she was short of money for the fare. It had never occurred to her that she might be required to pay for her return flight. Fortune would sweep her up, she had imagined, and carry her away on wings of gold.

Unsure of what to do, or where to go, she bought a *Los Angeles Times* and sat down to read it in the lounge. Incredibly, on page two of the regional section, she came across an item about Dr. Martin: PHONY TIJUANA ABORTIONIST REVEALED AS NUN. According to the article, which turned out to be a kind of exposé, Dr. Martin was no doctor at all, but a renegade Dominican named Sister Martin of Porres, whose self-imposed mission in life was to save as many limbo-bound fetuses as she could and plow all her considerable profits back into her cause.

After hesitating for the longest time, reading the *Times* from cover to cover, watching the fog clear off and the sun come out and ride across the airfield and into the sea, Ruby went into a phone booth and dialed Gold Hill.

"Max isn't home," his mother said. "Who's calling, please?"

The phone booth began to shake and rattle and rock back and forth, as if an earthquake had struck, while outside in the airport lobby she could see that everything was normal.

"Is this Ruby Rose?"

Now the booth was teetering, falling, spinning around like a top.

"Is there any message?"

Now it was lying on the marble floor like a coffin, with airport passengers peering down like mourners, Ruby looking up at them, a corpse. And the Black boy, the airman, swinging above her head in a pepper tree.

"Any message?"

Now the booth was flying through space.

"Any message? Any message?"

"Yes," she said, alighting at last, fixing on the number before her on the telephone dial. "Yes, this is Ruby. I wonder, could you have Max phone me at 517 889 0091?"

"Of course."

"Tell him I'll wait right here till he calls."

"Is there anything the matter, dear?"

"No," she said. "I think for a minute there it was just a bad connection."

Part II

Chapter Ten

The birth of the child, Ned Bauer, on December 17, 1960, was almost anticlimactic, for the first few months of his embryonic development were surely the most perilous and eventful of his entire life.

Looking back on it, years later, picturing his son as he was at the time, floating around in Ruby's over-agitated tummy, Max thought of him as so helpless and vulnerable, an endangered species, and he marveled at his ultimate survival.

Even so, Max's attitude toward the pregnancy was always colored by ambiguity. On the one hand, he was delighted that despite all the odds and omens arrayed against him the boy had miraculously succeeded in getting born. On the other, he sometimes caught himself feeling almost guilty, imagining Ned as a tiny, throbbing, barely human entity the size and shape of a fried prawn, yet potent, implacable, growing remorselessly inside his young wife's womb, malignant to all her hopes and dreams, to the talent that she had yet to fulfill.

Ruby herself seemed marvelously unconcerned about such matters. She even consented to calling herself Mrs. Max Bauer after their marriage and gave up her stage name Ruby Rose without a peep.

Ned was a healthy, happy child, with his mother's red hair and good looks, his father's solid build and steady temperament. And he gave her a new purpose in life, a new role to perform. She played it with gusto, redirecting all her energy, imagination, and sense of drama into his upbringing.

For the first few years of his life, she was obsessed with him. Only rarely would she let Max or Sybil get near him. She spent hours playing games with him on the floor, reading to him, pushing him on the little swing she'd had Reno rig up on the almond tree in the backyard, taking him on long stroller rides up Sand Canyon Road, never seeming to tire of it. And she made such a spectacle of his achievements: At his christening in the local Episcopal Church, she wept till she was ill. When he focused his eyes for the first time, she howled the news all over downtown Gold Hill. When he crawled, it was grounds for a local celebration. When he walked, all the friends and neighbors were invited in to observe the miracle child in action. And when he uttered his first word, it was the Christ Child preaching in the temple. Though Max kept his own counsel, as usual, he was of the private opinion that she was spoiling the kid rotten, making him a mama's boy. She had Reno build another room onto the house, a fanciful child's room shaped like a boat, with portholes and swinging lanterns, a double-decker ship's berth set into the wall, and a wrap-around charthouse window with a view of Sawmill Mountain. And she filled it with educational toys and doodads of every description, all with a nautical motif: teddy bears dressed in little French sailor suits, building blocks designed to be formed into paddlewheel steamers and ocean liners. She spent days painting his room (baby blue with puffy pink and white clouds hovering above a frothy Japanese-looking sea), weeks working on his little white sailcloth curtains, months acquiring his books and pictures, a whole year embroidering his magnificent anchor quilt. She gave up cigarettes to protect his little pink lungs and made all his food in a special baby blue grinder. She never spanked or punished him in any but the most cursory manner, forbade Max to do anything but the same, and raised him strictly according to Doctor Spock. Max was amazed the kid didn't turn out an insufferable brat, but in fact a lot of Ruby's compulsive care and pampering just went right over his head. Ned liked it well enough, except for the times when she got too cloying. He didn't seem to completely trust it, though, even as a small child, because Ruby was a bit of a ham, and she nearly always overplayed her roles. Yet there was no real harm done, as far as Max could see, and the boy never doubted that his mother loved him very deeply. The only problem was that Ruby required Ned to play roles as well, and she was constantly exhorting him to perform. "Look at Ned tap dance, you guys, watch him dance!" she would holler at visitors, hovering over him, clapping her hands, as the boy, a mere three or four years old, quickstepped, double-shuffled, windmilled his arms, showed his teeth, and strove mightily at a Scat Man Carruthers imitation. "Dance, Ned, dance!" She made him dance when he didn't want to dance, stoked him up when he was meant to remain quiescent, made his little heart beat madly, overexciting him, infuriating Sybil, who was not nearly as patient or forbearing as Max and held a very dim view of these antics.

Sybil disapproved of Ruby on other grounds too, and Ruby harbored grievances against Sybil as well. It was nothing more than a raised eyebrow from Sybil now and again, and then a quick parody of that raised eyebrow from Ruby. Yet, it was serious enough, and it worried Max at times, especially since everything had seemed so fine when Ruby first moved onto the ranch. Back then, Sybil had bent over backwards to make her feel at home. She had even presented her with her own wedding ring (three small diamonds set one on top of the other, surrounded by sapphire chips on a sort of Victorian shield), an heirloom handed down by her own mother on her deathbed. And Ruby had proclaimed to all who would listen that her misadventures in Hollywood were kismet, that by fate or fluke she had found what she had been looking for all her life... a family.

And in certain ways, Max supposed, they were like a small nuclear family. As newlyweds they lived in Max's old room—still cluttered with model cars and airplanes, motorcycle trophies and photographs, high school pennants and athletic paraphernalia—almost like brother and sister. Sybil presided at dinner like the mother Ruby had always dreamed of. And neither Ruby nor Max felt the least reservation about living under the maternal roof. On the contrary, they were delighted that someone else was willing to take responsibility and attend to all the details of homemaking. Max's garage was right on the ranch, so they were never far apart. Sometimes they even spent lunchtime together in bed, much to Sybil's discomfort. Always the lady, she tried to feign obliviousness, but her true feelings became increasingly clear. It was not that Sybil was a prude or an enemy of spontaneity. On the contrary, she was a champion of romance. But Sybil's idea of romance was becoming more and more subtle with the years. She had a horror of "pushiness and blatancy," and she could be insensitive at times to her social and intellectual inferiors. Unfailingly polite and well-spoken, never forgetting to display her lovely, wistful, thin-lipped smile, she would sometimes allow a bitchy little edge of impatience, disapproval, or superiority to creep into her voice, an arch double-message belaying her sweet words and looks.

Ruby, on the other hand, was brash and loud, craving excitement, while at the same time she was frightened and insecure, requiring constant reaffirmation. When slighted, she would try frantically to entertain Sybil into submission, tickle her into a recognition of her inherent adorability. The more Ruby pushed; the more Sybil disapproved. The more Sybil disapproved; the more Ruby pushed. Their relations were like a chain reaction, impelled entirely by negative feedback. In the end, it seemed, they would either consume each other or cancel each other out.

To make things worse, after the first year or so they were left much alone. Max and Charlie had rented an old garage in Lancaster, renovated it, and expanded their business to include motorcycle as well as auto repair. Their reputation as specialists in British machines had preceded them, and they were so immediately successful that they rarely found time to spend at home. Sybil passed the hours of her son's absence painting in her room, or outside if the weather was fine. She wasn't a bad watercolorist—if a bit pale and washed out for Max's taste—and she was beginning to sell her work to amateur collectors in Los

Angeles and Santa Barbara, where she had established a small reputation as a "High Desert Original."

In the beginning, Ruby had volunteered to keep house while Sybil painted. But Sybil would not hear of it and had a Mexican cleaning woman come three times a week instead. For a time, Ned was enough to occupy Ruby's attention, but eventually she grew bored and began asking her "girlfriends" over. Most of Ruby's old friends from high school had left town for college. Her only remaining acquaintances in Gold Hill were Gil's wife Sally, Charlie's wife Juanita, and his sister Preçiosa. They were all newly married, Preçiosa for the second time. Each of them had a baby or two, and they were very lively, fun-loving, and good-hearted. "The salt of the earth," as Ruby said of them. Sybil had always tolerated Max's friends, as she had his down-scale tastes, with a mixture of uneasy affection and good-humored condescension. But what she would tolerate in Max she could not in Ruby. The situation came to a head one day after Ruby had invited her three girlfriends over for lunch. All but Ruby were pregnant at the time, wearing lacquered beehive hairdos and mini-dresses too short to flatter their pot-bellied torsos and skinny legs. They had consumed far too much wine and were twisting around the room with each other to the music of Trini Lopez on American Bandstand, squealing and giggling and puffing on cigarettes while their neglected toddlers, Ned included, squalled, and gagged, and soiled their diapers in a playpen in the corner. And just when the party was at its height, with Trini twanging sleazily on the flickering black-and-white TV, and Ruby down on her haunches demonstrating a dance she called "The Duck Walk," Sybil slipped in from the ridge where she had been painting a landscape and put a stop to the proceedings with nothing more than the overweening hauteur of her presence.

After the girls had collected their babies, blankets, diapers, and bottles, bundled them all out to their pickup trucks, and sheepishly said their goodbyes, Ruby sought out Sybil again to apologize for having offended her.

"I always wondered what would happen when you got tired of your mother-of-the-year role," Sybil said, by way of reply. "But this has gone farther than I ever imagined. I simply cannot understand why you insist on hanging about with those women. They're so uncouth. I've a feeling you're fond of them because they're easy. They don't challenge you. They look up to you and laugh at your jokes. You can control them. But if this is what you call friendship..."

"Listen, Sybil, the only other female in Gold Hill I've got anything in common with is you, and we don't seem to be getting along very well, do we?"

"I'm afraid not," Sybil said, shaking her head, holding her long white hands poised together as if in prayer. "Why don't we, do you think?" Sybil asked, tilting her head to the left and spreading her hands suddenly, a rhetorical gesture of hers conveying discreet hesitation. "I mean, why must you be so relentlessly common?"

"Has it ever occurred to you, Sybil, that you could ask the same thing of Max?"

"Oh, Max!" Sybil laughed. "I gave up on him years ago. I was hoping you might instill a bit of class."

"I'm sorry," Ruby said. "But what you see is what you get."

Sybil had kept her council until this confrontation, but her disapproval now turned to anxiety, and she spoke to Max of her concerns about Ruby's attitude at the first opportunity.

Surprised and pained, Max went back to Ruby with a gentle but firm admonition to "cool it" around his mother, and to show a little more respect.

"But I do respect her," Ruby said. "The problem is, she doesn't show the same respect for me."

"Look," Max said, holding his hands up toward her, as if to push her away, and then slapping them together. "What do you want from me?"

"I want you to see my side."

"I can see your side, and I can see her side too."

"Your first loyalty is to your wife."

"I have no intention of being anything but even-handed in this," Max said. "I mean, we're living in her house, for Christ's sake."

A week or two later, Ruby read in the Antelope Valley Ledger-Gazette that an entire neighborhood of some twenty to thirty Victorian houses had been dislocated by a tract development for employees of the National Rocket Propulsion Laboratory. They were sitting up on blocks on the outskirts of Barstow, ready to be moved, and were to be put up for sale at public auction. Due to a lack of interest from the public, whose taste in these times of aerospace boom ran to ranch style tract homes and singles apartment complexes with swimming pools, the bidding was not expected to go over three thousand dollars. Without consulting Max or Sybil—and having no notion of where she might obtain the money to bid on a home or move it to Gold Hill—Ruby sneaked Ned off the ranch one Saturday morning and drove her old Nash Ambassador to Barstow. There she fell in love with a big, old, drafty Victorian of vaguely Italian Gothic inspiration.

Caught up in the excitement of the auction, unwilling to see the house go to anyone else, she bid for it, and won, and paid for it with a bad check.

Only on the way home did she think to stop at Eagle Field and consult her father on the feasibility of the project.

"Well, it's gonna be hard to move, all right," Reno said. "Barstow's seventy miles away. But I know a guy who can do it."

"What guy?"

"Norman Steel, over in Palmdale."

"How much?"

"Maybe two, three thousand."

"Now all I have to do," Ruby said, "is figure some way to cover it."

"Cover what?"

"The check I gave them for the house. I got about half the amount in the bank right now. All I need is to find the rest."

"The rest?" Reno said. "That's fifteen hundred dollars! Where're you going to get that kind of money?"

"I don't know, lemme think."

"What about Sybil?"

"Gotta hit her up for the mover's fee."

"The mover's fee!" Reno said, smacking his hand with his fist. He was up in his sixties now, set in his ways after years of living alone. And though he was well preserved for his age—still dapper, and quite the ladies' man—he'd grown cantankerous and impatient with young people. "You mean you don't have it already? That's no way to run your affairs!"

"Daddy, you're not being very helpful."

"All right then, how about Max? He ought to be rolling, with that new garage of his."

"Max went over his head to get that garage, and we'll have to use what little he's got left to fix the house up."

"Who're you going to get to do the work?"

"Why, *you*, Dad, if you can find the time."

"I'll tell you right now," Reno said. "I'm not going to work for peanuts, like the last time. I've got bills to pay like everyone else."

"Then it's a deal!"

"What deal?"

"You'll lend me the fifteen hundred if I let you renovate our home."

"I didn't say that!" he said.

But she had him, and he knew it. He had time on his hands. He was retired. Eagle Field had been vacated by the state and no one else had come along to replace it. His watchman's job was mostly honorary. He had little more to do than feed the half-wild tabbies that he'd inherited when the population of the dependents' housing area scattered to the winds. And nothing pleased him more than working on old Victorians. They reminded him of the old family manse near Provo, Utah, which he hadn't seen in over forty years.

That night, just before Max got home from work, Ruby gave Ned a bath, put him into his best pajamas, combed his hair into cute little curls, and rehearsed him for his role in the coming performance. Then, the minute Max was in the door, she sent the boy running toward him shouting, "Daddy, Daddy, we're gonna get our own house, gonna get our own house!"

"What's this?" Max said, sweeping up the little squealing, squirming, bundle in his arms, swinging him around, planting a smack on his fat rosy cheek. "What's this?"

Ruby followed Ned into his arms and kissed him passionately, throwing everything she had into it.

"Wow! What've I done to deserve this?"

"This is only for starters."

"I hate to guess how I'm gonna have to pay for this."

"It's free," she said, laughing, spinning him around. "Yours for the asking."

"Uh-huh," Max said, grinning down at her, delighted with her. "I bet."

"Come on, come on, quit smooching, you guys," Ned hollered, in his gruff little bear's voice, dancing about their flanks, pulling at their clothes. "Quit smooching!"

"Oh, Max," Ruby said, when Ned had finally succeeded in dragging them apart. "We've got such wonderful news!"

"Yeah, yeah, we're gonna get a house, gonna get a house!" Ned chanted, jumping up and down in time to the rhythm of his words.

"Sounds great, honey," Max said, after listening to Ruby's rendition of the day's events. "All I want to know is this. Where we going to get the money to move it seventy miles across the desert?"

"Well, quite frankly," Ruby said, grinning down at the boy conspiratorially, "we were kind of hoping your mother would lend it to us. Right Ned?"

"Right! Right!"

"My mother?" Max said. "She hasn't got anywhere near that kind of money."

"She could get a bank loan."

"Using what as collateral?"

"The ranch."

"She tried that before."

"Sure, honey, but now we've got your income," Ruby said, wheedling, clinging to Max's right hand while little Ned clung to the left. "And I'm going to get a job, soon as the house is set up."

"What about a piece of land to put it on?" Max wondered. How're we going to get that?"

"I thought we'd put it on the foundation of your mother's old place."

"What place?"

"Come on. Max! She's only got one other place. The one that went down in the earthquake."

"How you know it's gonna fit?"

"I measured it."

"Got it all figured out, huh?"

"Yep."

"All right, I'll talk to her about it," Max said. "But I'm not making any promises."

Just as Max had suspected, Sybil was dead set against the scheme from the first and thought it "cheeky" that Ruby had gone out and bought the place on her own.

"The whole thing is quixotic in the extreme," she said. "Better tell her to put a stop on that check."

Caught in the middle as usual, Max went back to Ruby with the bad news. But Ruby refused to budge on the issue, and the check went through anyway. Presented now with a *fait accompli*, Max felt he had no choice but to go back to his mother and try again.

"All right," she said at last. "But I feel as if I were doing this under duress."

"We'll pay you back, Mom, I promise."

"Oh, it's not that, darling. It's just that I feel as if I were consigning it to the wind."

Undaunted, Ruby threw herself into the project. She met with the flinty little moving man, Norman Steel, haggling over costs for weeks. She got him down to twenty-one hundred dollars, eventually, on the condition that she personally provide the crew members he could not afford to hire. Having agreed on price, she pored over maps with Norman for days, trying to discover the best moving route. They would have to take secondary roads, avoiding traffic, sharp turns, steep grades, power lines, and populated areas. They must travel only during off-peak hours and find a safe parking place each night. They would have to stay with the house every inch of the way, guarding against pilferage, vandalism, and accidents of nature. They would have to go the long way round, through Boron, Mojave, Willow Springs and Tropico, and the trip would come to over a hundred miles. With luck, it would take seven days: one to jack the house onto Norman's great wide-load sixteen-wheel trailer, five to cross the desert, and one to set it down on Sybil's old ranch house foundation in Sand Canyon.

It might take as long as ten days, depending on the weather, Norman said, but the news did nothing to diminish Ruby's excitement.

Having notified the State Department of Highways of her tentative dates of departure and arrival, furnished them with a copy of her projected route, and paid the requisite road tax, she talked Max into braving his partner Charlie's violent objections—they had just been granted the Triumph sportscar and motorcycle concession for the valley and were overloaded with work—and taking a few days off from the garage.

Up at five in the morning, they left Ned with Sybil, picked up Reno at Eagle Field, and drove to Barstow in Max's pickup.

It was Max's first day off in some time, and he enjoyed the trip across the desert. They drove by way of Lancaster, the weathered little pink and white stucco metropolis of Antelope Valley. Out Avenue G and Shadow Mountain Road past the south end of Edwards Air Force Base and the National Rocket Propulsion Laboratory. Around the hamlet of Movie Set Junction, with its views of mock nineteenth century frontier towns. Through Joshua Tree State Park and the Butte Valley Wildflower Sanctuary where the poppies would soon be in bloom. Then over the black volcanic Shadow Mountains to the National Trails Highway and the Mojave River.

None of them could take their eyes off that river. A mere trickle in a concrete culvert, shimmering in the bright, white, February sun, it was the only free running stream of fresh water between the Pacific Ocean and the Colorado River.

Barstow was a smokey, noisy little railroad town with shady, cottonwood-lined streets and bright sub-tropical shrubbery that stood out in vivid contrast to the brown, bone-dry mountains that loomed to the east. Driving down Main Street past the Spanish Colonial-style Santa Fe depot, Max crossed the Mojave River Flood Control Basin on a spanking new steel bridge painted bright orange. On the other side, on Fossil Bed Road, crowded in close by the white clay riverbed on a long embankment covered with yucca plants and tumbleweed, stood a line of old wooden houses perched on roller blocks.

"There's our house!" Ruby hollered. Excited as a child, she pointed at a tall Italian Gothic. It boasted a mansard roof, a turret with wraparound windows, a loggia terrace, a glass conservatory, and fanciful detail work, but its ornate woodwork was cracked and faded.

Norman Steel, a lean, anxious little man as weathered as the house, was standing on the front steps in a black ball cap, a denim shirt, and a pair of black Frisco jeans. Another fellow, a couple of years older and a little taller, in a straw fedora and a pair of striped, bibbed overalls, stood below him, sucking a wild oat stalk, kicking at dirt clods.

Ruby got out of the pickup, leaving Max to follow behind with Reno, and swaggered over toward them in cowboy boots, a pair of tight faded Levis, a purple sweater, and a fringed leather jacket. Tan, healthy, and almost peasant looking with her long sturdy legs, broad hips, small waist, hefty bosom and wild red hair, Ruby had an air of animal excitement about her that day, and it must have created a stir in old Norman because he dithered for a moment when she approached and forgot what he had to say.

"We all set, Norman?"

"Ready as we'll ever be," he managed at last, as Reno and Max sauntered up behind her. "This here's Hank, and he's all we got for help."

All that morning they labored—Ruby sweating and grunting right along beside the men. They set hydraulic jacks beneath the house. They raised it up to pull out the blocks. They backed Norman's huge flatbed trailer under, and slowly released the pressure until the house was resting on top. Then, after spending the entire afternoon securing it with cable, they hitched Norman's big old Mack diesel up and dragged the whole rig out to within a few yards of the road. By that time, it was 8 p.m., they had been at it twelve hours, and Norman decided to call it quits for the day. Leaving Ruby and Max to watch over the load, he headed for home with Hank and Reno.

Max lit a campfire, and they sat around it, bundled up together in blankets, drinking beer, eating cheese sandwiches and Campbell's Pork & Beans out of cans.

"My dad always promised to take me camping," Ruby said. "Makes me feel almost like a little girl again, snuggled up with you by the fire like this."

"Well, I ain't your daddy, so you can get that out of your head right now."

"Maybe not," she said, snuggling even closer. "But I sure would appreciate a bedtime story or two."

The beer and the campfire and the proximity of a warm, fragrant female having put him in the mood, Max obliged. Told her things he never had before. Told her about Fritz leaving in '56, and the earthquake, the trip to Santa Barbara.

Ruby gazed up at him, listening intently, smiling at him as he spoke, and he was struck very suddenly by a heightened awareness of her singularity as a human being, the things about her that were unlike anyone else on earth. When she laughed, he heard, as if for the first time, the exact quality of her voice, deep and throaty like her mother's, with a tendency to articulate in rapid bursts. He regarded her profile in the firelight, her mass of wavy red hair, her high-domed forehead, thick brows, large deep-set eyes, tipped-up English nose, fleshy lower lip and thin upper, strongly defined jaw and sharp chin. He smelled her breath, tart and cheddary, like the sandwich she was chewing, and her skin, musky and warm. He felt her large firm breast poking into his side, her strong tense arm around his waist, her pulse going much faster than his own. And the moment, the rich and unique reality of his young wife beside him, their life together, their love, he wished it could go on forever.

Just before they turned in for the night, Max went out behind a clump of sage to take a pee. Afterwards he lingered a while, smelling his own piss on the wind, listening to the coyotes' howl, gazing up at the sky. The moon and the stars were so bright they had turned the desert white, and they illuminated their tall old house in a portentous cinematic light. Max stood there looking at it for the longest time, imagining it as it would be in living color, rising loftily above the almond orchards. Imagined Ned growing up in it, himself and Ruby growing old in it. And a feeling of great shivery contentment ran through him again, as it had when he discovered Ruby Canyon.

He climbed up into the house over Norman's flatbed trailer, crawled into his sleeping bag, and cuddled up to Ruby on the floor, listening to the wind moaning through the cracked windows, the creaking of the walls.

"I could never make something like this happen," he murmured.

"What?"

"A house like this."

"You make other things happen."

"How do you do it, honey? How do you do it?"

"It's not done yet," she said.

And her words proved true, for by midnight the wind had reached a dangerous velocity, and the air was full of blowing snow.

Norman showed up with Reno and Hank at four in the morning and advised holding off for a few days, till the weather changed.

"What for?" Ruby said. "The snow's stopped. There's no more than an inch on the ground, and that's as hard as stone."

"What about the wind?"

"The wind's from the east. It's just going to help us along."

"What if it starts snowing again?"

"How many times have you seen it precipitate around here for more than two days in a row?"

"Couple of times."

"How long you been here, Norman?"

"Fifty-six years," he said. "I was born here."

"Then I figure I'll take the chance."

"Your funeral," he said, and climbed up into the cab of his big red Mack and dropped her in compound low. "Let's go."

Max rode ahead with Ruby in the pickup truck with a "Wide Load" sign hanging from his front end. Reno and Hank rode behind with a like rig hanging down from their tailgate.

Out on Fossil Bed Road, Max looked back. Ruby's tall old gray house, impelled by the strong east wind, was sailing along at a steady four miles an hour, surrounded by a great snowy desert basin as wide as the Bering Sea.

"Only in America," she observed with pride.

"Only in America," he agreed.

They made twelve miles that first morning, to the desolate, windswept corner of Old Highway 58 and Harper Lake Road.

"Not nearly enough," Ruby said.

"Just gettin' the kinks out," Norman replied.

"Why don't we cut down across the dry lake to Old Woman Road? That'd save us nearly fifty miles."

"What if it rains?"

"Too cold to rain."

"What if it changes?"

"Then we'll float it out."

"How about my truck and trailer?"

Ruby laughed: "Never thought of that."

"I'll bet you didn't."

"Thought you were a gambler, Norman."

"I am, but I ain't suicidal."

"I'll lay you odds."

"What kind?"

"It rains, I'll double your money."

"And if it don't?"

"Your fee stays the same, and you save three, four days of labor."

"Well, you put it that way..."

The next day they got an even earlier start, at 2 a.m., and turned southwest onto Harper Dry Lake. The cold weather held. The surface was smoother and harder than the state highway. And they sped across the thin crackling layer of snow at nearly ten miles an hour.

Harper Dry Lake cut into Edwards Air Force Base for about a half mile on its western edge. It was posted "MILITARY RESERVATION", but nobody paid it any mind, and the bed of the lake was crisscrossed with the tracks of off-road vehicles. Since it was still technically illegal, however, the hotshot Air Force pilots considered all trespassers fair game. And the local barrooms were full of stories about dune buggy drivers getting buzzed so low they had gone temporarily deaf, motorcycle riders getting blown off their bikes by jet exhaust.

Even so, Max was not at all prepared when at the crack of dawn a pair of camouflage-painted Phantoms screamed out of the sun at rabbitbrush level, threw in their afterburners just short of the Victorian's quaint turret, stood on their tails, spun off into the clouds like a raveling strand of genetic code and, trailing an ear-splitting sonic boom, dove back around for another run from opposite directions, missing each other—and the house—by inches as they rose belly to belly to the sky.

Crawling out from under the pickup after the planes had gone, brushing the snow off their jeans, and trying to get their heartbeats down to normal again, Max and Ruby went back to inspect the house. Reno and Hank arrived at about the same time, with the same thing in mind. But Norman had already gone over it and pronounced it fit as a fiddle.

"These old places are damn near indestructible," he said.

"How about yourself, Norman?" Ruby asked.

"Me, I'm the same way. How about yourselves?"

"We're all right."

"Damn!" he said grinning, swatting his dusty pantleg with his cap, looking up at the sky. "Wasn't that somethin', though?"

They reached Old Woman Road at eight in the morning, smoothed over the gentle flanks of Old Woman Butte and kept heading southwest until they hit Shadow Mountain Road where it turned into Avenue G.

That evening, after covering a formidable distance and reaching a point only twenty miles from home, Reno announced that he was too tuckered out to go back to Eagle Field.

"I got some blankets in the pickup," he said. "If you don't mind, I'll just tucker down right here."

"Make yourself at home anywhere you like," Max replied.

But that night, Max and Ruby got to cutting up around the campfire, laughing, tickling each other, and acting like kids.

"Ruby, you look so funny covered with that alkali dust," Max said. "You look like one of those New Guinea cargo cultists who's painted herself white to attract manna from the heavens."

"And I don't smell so good either, I bet."

"Smell good to me."

"Oh yeah? What're you gonna do about it?"

"Whatever it is," Reno said, rising to head over to the pickup truck. "I wish you'd wait till I clear out."

"Come on, Dad," Ruby said. "We were only fooling."

"Let me know when it's safe to come back."

"You know what, Max?" she said when he was gone. "I think he's jealous."

"Well, you got rid of him, anyhow."

"Uh-huh, I sure did."

"So?"

"So come on," she said, heaving him up to his feet. "Let's take a walk in the desert."

They strolled out to a clump of tall silver sage, threw their sleeping bags on the snow—hers on bottom, his on top—and lay together. They could hear Reno in the pickup, listening to the evening news on the radio, and later they could hear him stomping around on the wooden floor of the house, trying to find a place to flake out for the night. And they could hear the coyotes howling as usual, and the sound of the wind in the sagebrush. But until the moon came out, they could see nothing, not even each other's faces, and had to rely on touch.

On the way back, groping their way through the salt brush, creosote, and prickly pear, Max said, "Gee, that was nice, honey, but what exactly did it signify?"

"Well, let me put it this way, Max. I'd managed to get you involved. But I hadn't gotten you excited yet."

"Ruby," he said, "you underestimate yourself."

The hardest part of the whole trip was right at the end, when they had to negotiate narrow, winding Sand Canyon Road. By then even Sybil, even the Gonçalves family, were helping.

They had squeezed around the last bend and were just coming across Sand Creek Bridge with the ranch right in front of them when the sky, which had been black and threatening for twenty-four hours, suddenly spit fire, roared, burst, and poured down on them for twenty minutes—"like someone pulled the plug on the celestial swimming pool," as Ruby put it.

"Keep a look out!" Norman hollered. "That dam tops over and we're gonna have a flash flood on our hands."

"I hear you," said Max, and ran to escort little Ned and Sybil up the hill to safety.

Reno was shoving at the rear of the trailer with his pickup, spinning his wheels, screeching rubber. Ruby and the others were pushing with their bare hands, slipping, and falling in the torrents of water and mud. Meanwhile, Norman was straining forward with his diesel inch by inch, foot by foot, aided by a power winch on his front bumper and a double length of steel cable looped around the sentinel rock at the top of the hill.

Soon as Max left Ned and his mother off, he ran down the hill again to lend a hand. But before he'd gotten ten feet a mass of what looked like Scotch Broth Soup came seething around the bend, moving at incredible speed, knocking down everything in its path, carrying cottonwood trees, pieces of gold trestle, fence rails, farm animals, chicken coops, and the old Gonçalves outhouse along with it.

"Run, you guys," Max hollered. "Run, run!"

But they had no time for that, and he saw them scramble up into the Victorian only seconds before the flood hit.

It hit with tremendous force, swinging the house and trailer around violently and sweeping Reno's abandoned pickup truck clean away. Yet, Norman had managed to maneuver his big Mack diesel above the waterline somehow, and he stayed with it, gunning the engine in compound low, winching slowly forward on the cable, holding the rig in place till the worst was over.

Though it was probably only a matter of minutes before the water subsided, it seemed to Max long enough to live and die and go to hell. And when he saw Ruby and Reno and the others climbing down at last from their perches in the soggy old Victorian, laughing and cracking jokes and making light of their near disaster, he found that he was drenched in sweat, and his hands were clenched so hard he could barely pry them open.

But then the sun peeked out, the air grew warmer, Max went back down the hill again to help, and they bent their backs once again to their labor. Norman wound out his diesel and his electric winch, his clutch and gears protesting, and the house moved slowly up the driveway to Sand Canyon Ranch.

Max would never forget his vision of the Victorian that evening, after they had jacked and levered it down onto the old ranch house's foundation (not a perfect fit, of course, but still good enough) and it was standing near the ridge in all its glory. Framed darkly against the scudding cloud formations and the fiery sky, it seemed to be flying against the wind, its tall, archaic turret like a Jules Verne rocket ship, aimed for the stars.

It was then that Sybil came up beside Max on the ridge, folded her hand in his, looked up at him with tears in her eyes and said, as if he were still a small child and she were instructing him on something of immense importance to his future, "I want you to remember this, Lucky. I was wrong about Ruby. I was wrong about this house."

Chapter Eleven

Five, six years went by, and the Victorian seemed to fit more and more into its implausible surroundings. Rising majestically above the almond orchards and the meandering dry creek canyon, surrounded by lawns, rose gardens, a white picket fence and giant spreading cottonwood trees planted during the construction of the original ranch house in 1907, it began to look as if it had been there forever, or at least since horse and buggy days. Its mistress grew prouder and prouder of it, and of all the work she had done on it, all the good things it had brought her way since she impetuously bid for it at the Barstow auction.

Renovations on the place had not been completed a month before articles were being written about it in the *San Bernardino Sun*, the *Pomona Progress Bulletin*, and the *Bakersfield Bee*. Then the *Los Angeles Times Sunday Magazine* picked up on it and did a four-page photographic piece on the house, and on "the remarkable young woman who discovered it, moved it a hundred miles across the desert, set it on a barren hillside, and lovingly restored it."

Locally, the story was even bigger news. Ruby and her home were featured prominently in every publication in the region including the *Barstow Beagle* and the *Antelope Valley Ledger Gazette*. She was interviewed on radio and television and invited to give talks at service clubs all over the valley. On stage for the first time in years, Ruby outdid herself, and audiences responded warmly to her humorous and convincing recitation of the pleasures and old-fashioned comforts of her wonderful Victorian. Inspired by the favorable public response, Ruby took a real estate course, got her state license, enrolled in the Creative Writing program at Antelope Valley Community College, and began writing feature articles about her place, with the intention of eventually doing a "How To" book on Victorian restoration. After accumulating twenty or thirty rejection slips, she got one of her pieces published in *Sunset Magazine*. The article, accompanied by photos and watercolors by Sybil, raised considerable interest. Ruby received approving letters on it from all over the West Coast, and soon she found herself conducting guided tours.

Generally, she started her tours with a swing around the tall and imposing Italian Gothic exterior, pointing out the clever and elaborate structural details—turret, loggia, mansard roof, scrolls, fretwork, stringcourses, balusters, dentils, lion heads and rosettes—all beautifully refurbished by Reno's masterful carpentry work, Ruby's gray enamel paint job, and Sybil's black and white trim. Then into her spacious, domed entrance hall, and on to the parlor, the study, the glassed conservatory, the circular dining room, the kitchen and pantry, pointing out her antique furnishings along the way: the grandfather clock, hat stand, chandelier, piano, rocking chairs, wicker chairs, daybed, lounge chair, loveseat, the marble washstand where she kept her stereo (all of which, as she proudly informed anyone who would listen, she had picked up cheap at antique furniture warehouses and garage sales on weekend jaunts to the San Joaquin Valley and the Mother Lode Country). Then upstairs to the bedrooms and bathrooms, calling attention to additional details: the authentic Victorian pottery that contained her hanging plants, the stained-glass door panels, the leaded glass side windows and bathroom windows, the burnished redwood wall paneling and wainscoting that ran all the way through the house, the handprinted flower pattern wallpaper that she had sent for all the way to England.

In the evenings sometimes, when Ruby showed her visitors out, the Victorian's great bay and bow windows would suddenly catch fire in the desert sun and the entire facade would be transformed into a shimmering mirage, a fantasy of glass and changing color and baroque form, chiaroscuro and reflection, and the tourists would thank her profusely, as if she had summoned the display just for them.

More than anything else in her wonderful home, Ruby loved the narrow, stretched-out, high-ceilinged old bathroom in the master bedroom. She had decorated it herself, right down to the smallest detail: the light green Liberty print of the wallpaper, the antique porcelain tub standing on satyr's hooves, the polyurethaned hardwood floor, the beveled mirror above the sink, the tall stripped-pine linen closet, the stained-glass skylight, the hanging ferns.

Every morning, after getting Max off to work, walking Ned down to the school bus, having a coffee and chat with Sybil, Ruby liked to go upstairs and run herself a nice, hot, herbal bath. With a busy schedule—juggling family, housework, gardening, a part-time job at a local real estate firm, and a weekly Home Section column in the *Antelope Valley Ledger Gazette*—Ruby considered this morning ritual her one self-indulgence, and she would often lie soaking in the tub, sipping a second cup of coffee, till her skin puckered up and the water went tepid and cold.

Soaking in her bath one morning in the fall of 1970, replenishing the hot water whenever it grew cold, filling the tub so deeply that the water lapped at her chin, pouring herself a third and fourth cup of coffee from the pot she'd brought in and set down on the floor beside her, Ruby had time, as she would note later in a published account, to think of many things. She thought of Ned, she said, and his touching desire to please her, the wildflowers he picked on the hillside behind the house and presented to her formally, ringing the front doorbell and hiding them behind his back. She thought of Sybil and their troubled past, the friendship they reestablished as they worked together on the renovations. She thought of Max, her man, her rock, her anchor in the storm.

Assessing her life, Ruby knew that she had little to complain of. Nevertheless, here in the solitude of her bath, she had to admit that despite all her blessings there was still something missing. For a long time, she had thought it was simply more children to fill up this huge old house. But she was just fooling herself about that, she thought, because even now, three years after the miscarriage she had suffered in this very bathroom, she had not seen fit to give up on birth control. And in any case, she and Max did not make love all that much, anymore. How it happened, Ruby didn't know. But for some reason they had settled into a once-a-week routine. Still, they loved each other very deeply. She was sure of that. It was just that they had such busy, conflicting schedules, so much on their minds.

The other day at the supermarket she had run into Michael Marczaly. He had a good job now, she knew, running the drama department at Antelope Valley Community College. Yet, since his wife Veronika died last year—breast cancer, it was said—he had gone all gray and put on weight. His skin had begun to sag, he shuffled when he walked, and his face, once so mobile, seemed vacant, bereft of life, as if he had already concluded that he would join his wife soon. Michael seemed so innocuous, so pitiful now, that Ruby might have passed him by with nothing more than a sympathetic glance. Instead, she hid herself behind the cookie counter, cringing in shame. And not only for what he had done to her in Hollywood.

More than anything, Ruby had wanted to be a star, wanted Michael and the whole world to know that she could make it. And she had thrown it over at eighteen. She could have given it another shot. Some stuck it out for years, despite all the knocks, then went on to the big time when they were approaching middle age. But she had taken the easy way out, coming home to Max and giving to love what she might have given to art.

Sure, she had done her best since she got back to Gold Hill to stay in the public light. She had launched a local film society, a summer stock theater, and Max had always been there to cheer her on. And yet...

Ruby stood up and soaped herself vigorously from head to toe, carefully checking for evidence of cellulite deposits, weight increase, sagging breasts, cancerous lumps, while simultaneously looking out her small, oval, leaded-glass window at old Pete Gonçalves as he supervised a gang of Mexican laborers knocking almonds on the sunny slope of the canyon. Max hired Pete every year to do the almond work at the ranch, and he wasn't bad. The passions and rancor of the past were all but forgotten now, and even Sybil had a good word for Pete from time to time.

Feeling something between thankfulness and regret, Ruby rinsed herself off with a special spray attachment. Then she washed her thick, wavy, red hair, which she kept shorter now, and conditioned it with a special balsam solution.

Just as she was about to step out of the tub, she felt something—something less than a twinge, no more than a soft, pliant friction—in the shadowy, secret hollow between her left upper thigh and pubis, and found with trembling fingers the small, hard, painless lump that she was sure could never be. And she instantly discounted the discovery as a figment of her imagination suggested by Veronika's recent death, or hypochondria inherited from her mother, or a minor cyst that would soon disappear.

Later that same morning, infused with energy and purpose, and mindful suddenly of her long-neglected promise to get a better-paying job, Ruby placed a phone call to her father, and another to Norman Steel, asking them to lunch the next day.

At the lunch, she served a lavish *Cassoulet de Campagne*, plied them with French wine, and proposed that they form a partnership and go into business together.

"What kind of business?" they wanted to know.

"The home restoration business," she replied, and went on to describe in rather convincing detail, she thought, her plan to seek out and discover wonderful old Victorian houses in remote desert communities, in ghost towns, and derelict gold camps. She would buy them for a song, she said, move them, if necessary, restore them, and then—with the resurgence of interest in older homes that she would inspire through her personal appearances and written magazine and newspaper descriptions—sell them for a huge profit.

"So, what do you think, boys?" she asked, as they rose—Norman still in his greasy work clothes—from the table.

"Not a bad idea," Reno said, admiring the view of canyon, mountain and desert out her great curving dining room windows.

"But just remember, this time we're going to need some competent help."

"And you, Norman?" Ruby asked, as she saw them out. "What do you think?"

"Well," he said, grinning rakishly up at her from the bottom of the steps, with his black ball cap pulled down to shade his eyes from the sun, "if you can do business like you cook, honey, you're gonna make us a million bucks."

Ruby went to work on the project that week, and right away she came upon a likely little Queen Ann in Gold Hill that was going for a fraction of its real worth. But the Viet Nam War had lately given an added impetus to the local aerospace boom, and skilled construction labor, as Reno had suggested, was either unavailable or impossibly overpriced. Combing the want ads, traveling the valley from end to end, putting up help wanted signs in supermarkets and laundromats, Ruby failed to come up with even a single candidate for her building crew, and a month after she started—a month during which she continued to ignore the lump in her secret place and avoid sex with Max—she was already on the point of packing it in, trying some other line of work.

Then, out of the blue, she got a letter from her brother Lonnie, the first in many years. He was stationed at Howard Air Force Base, in the Panama Canal Zone. He had "tied the knot with a local gal," as he put it, and enclosed a snapshot of his dark and pretty wife, Dominica, and their two-year-old son, Lonnie Jr. The reason he was writing, he said, was that he had decided to leave the Service. He would be heading back up to California with his family and his Air Force buddy Bill MacDougal in a few weeks and she wondered if Ruby had any ideas about jobs and a place to live.

Ruby's first reaction was pity. She recalled Lonnie's disappearance, and the extraordinary measures he had taken to convince the world that he was dead at eighteen. She imagined the secret agonies that must have driven him to such an extreme, and her heart went out to him. Her next reaction was suspicion.

"What's he writing now for, after all these years?" she asked Max at the dinner table one night, after recounting Lonnie's childhood cruelties.

"Damned if I know," said Max. "Maybe he read about the house somewhere, and figures you got it made."

She showed the letter to Reno, and he seemed only a little less favorably disposed.

Yet, the more Ruby thought about it, the more she thought her brother's decision might be a stroke of fate. Lonnie had learned carpentry from Reno when he was a kid. In the Air Force, he had spent most of his time in a construction battalion. He was just the man for her new business, and his buddy, Bill, was probably cut from the same mold. Meanwhile she would be doing him a huge favor, for he would surely need help getting started again and settling in with his little family.

Browbeating Max and her father, nagging and wheedling them for days on end, and ignoring all their protestations, "I mean, Jesus, he's our own flesh and blood!" she convinced them at last that Lonnie deserved another chance.

She found a little house for rent in Gold Hill, put a deposit on it, and wrote her brother in Panama.

A few weeks later Lonnie showed up at Eagle Field alone, towing a decrepit little trailer behind an old, pink, mud-splattered Cadillac Coupe de Ville with Canal Zone plates.

Ruby happened to be visiting her dad at the time and ran out to greet him as soon as he pulled up in front of the Rose Quonset hut.

"Ruby? Ruby? Ruby?" he called, leaping out from behind the wheel, grabbing her under the bared arms of her mini-dress and swinging her about the tiny front yard as effortlessly as he had in the past. "Wow, have *you* changed!"

"And *you*, Lonnie," she said, breathlessly, after he put her down on the grass, "you've stayed exactly the same."

And it was no mere compliment.

Grinning his same old mocking, teasing grin, sporting his same old pomaded pompadour haircut, dressed almost as he had been dressed on the morning before he disappeared—in black engineer's boots, dirty faded jeans and a greasy T-shirt with the left sleeve rolled up to accommodate his pack of Lucky Strikes—Lonnie appeared to have stepped out of a time warp, a dimension where the world still existed as it had before the Korean War. At thirty-seven, and despite all his problems, all his adventures around the world, his eyes still seemed as wide and blue and evasive, his hair as fine and full and unlikely blond, his face as handsome, strong-jawed and unmarked by experience, his body as trim, tan and athletic, as that of the boy who had "drowned" in Sand Canyon Reservoir nearly two decades before.

Reno was standing just outside the front door watching them, waiting for them, dressed very carefully in brown zip-up boots, tan summer-weight slacks, and safari jacket, surrounded by four or five sleek purring cats. Yet, looking at him through Lonnie's eyes, Ruby was struck by how gray and old and shrunken he seemed. At sixty-eight, their dad had finally begun to age.

"Tell me one thing, son," he called out, as Ruby led Lonnie up to the porch. "Why in hell did you quit the Air Force?"

"Long story," Lonnie said, reaching out to shake his father's hand.

"I'll bet it is," Reno said, pushing the door open behind him, holding it while they squeezed by him into the Quonset hut, then slamming it shut quickly so as not to permit any of the water-cooled air to escape. "You only had a year to go for your retirement."

"I know that, Dad, but believe me I had my reasons."

"And how come you drove?" Reno wanted to know, following them into his metallic, aerodynamic living room, shoving a pair of big black and white tabbies away and settling cross-legged, almost primly, in the same old leather easy chair that Alma used to lounge in while she watched soap operas on TV. "All the way up the Pan-American Highway! You'd think at least they'd fly you home."

"Well, between Bill's stuff, my stuff, the baby's stuff, Dominica's stuff," Lonnie said, "we had so much to carry we'd have probably been a half ton overweight."

"I thought the military sent dependents' stuff home free of charge," Ruby put in, settling down beside her brother and a yellow tiger-striped tom on the worn blue sofa.

"They do, usually," Lonnie said, blinking, switching his eyes rapidly back and forth from one of them to the other, reaching out absent-mindedly to stroke the cat. "But you see, Dominica and me, actually they don't consider us legally married."

"Why not?"

"Hey, what is this, you guys? The third degree? We just never got around to signing all the forms and sending them into the military registrar, that's all."

"So where are they now?" Reno wondered.

"Who's that?"

"Your *family*, Lonnie."

"Well, Bill—he's almost like part of the family now, seems like—I left him off at his mother's place in Berdoo," Lonnie said, flinging a leg and a dirty boot over the arm of the sofa, leaning on the back rest with his hands folded under his head, for all the world as if he had just left home an hour or two before. "And Dominica and the baby, they're still down in Mexicali."

"Mexicali?" Ruby said. "What're they doing in that hellhole?"

"US Customs wouldn't let 'em in. Said they needed an entry visa."

"But why didn't you attend to all that down in Panama?" Reno wanted to know.

"Never got around to it," Lonnie sighed, avoiding their eyes. Then he smiled, looked up at the ceiling, and shook his head. "We left in a kind of hurry. And now they say we gotta go all the way back down there to apply."

"So, what're you doing up *here?*" Ruby demanded, in exasperation.

"Sis, I got an idea of how we might get 'em in," Lonnie said, swinging his foot off the sofa arm, sitting up straight, flashing a grin in her direction, but still avoiding her eyes. "And I thought maybe you could help."

"Well, that depends," she answered, warily. She was already beginning to have doubts as to the wisdom of inviting her brother back to Gold Hill, and she knew that Max would thoroughly disapprove of him. Was it military life that had frozen Lonnie in late adolescence? And why was he suddenly calling her 'Sis'?"

"What kind of help did you have in mind?"

"I tell you, Sis, what I need is . . . rent receipts, bank books, credit cards, social security cards, birth certificates, anything that would validate U.S. residence, made out to a Hispanic woman and her kid."

"I don't know."

"I know it's asking a lot."

"Oh, not at all!" Reno scoffed. "Just let anybody have your credit cards, use them any way they want."

"Okay, I'm not promising anything, Lonnie," Ruby said at last, after she had thought the matter over for a long, long moment and convinced herself that blood is thicker than water. "And I'm probably crazy to do this. But I'll talk to a few people I know and get back to you this afternoon."

Then, leaving her brother sprawled on the sofa beside the purring yellow tomcat, already drifting to sleep, and her father in the easy chair, shaking his head, she went out and got in her Nash Ambassador and drove straight to Juanita Gonçalves' little flat-top tract home on Sancroft Avenue in Lancaster.

"Charlie's gonna kill me for this," Juanita whined, as she handed over the documents.

"Charlie's not gonna find out," Ruby said. "Not unless you tell him."

Driving the six miles back across the desert to Reno's place, Ruby thought of Juanita's situation in life, and she couldn't help but compare it with her own. She was much better off than Juanita, she decided. She had a nicer home. She didn't have four little screaming brats to contend with. She hadn't gone to fat. And her husband, unlike Charlie, was faithful and temperate by nature. Yet, if you compared Ruby and Juanita in terms of happiness, or which of them was closer to obtaining what she really wanted from life, who would come out on top? Ruby wondered about that for a mile or two, and then thought again of the lump, the forbidden fruit, ripening slowly in its dark, secret place. She yearned to confide in someone about it. To Juanita, or Sybil, perhaps. But a confidence of that kind, and the advice it would provoke, would lead inevitably to a medical examination. And Ruby still clung to the notion that the whole thing was simply a result of her hyperactive imagination.

"That oughta do it," Lonnie said, after she had dumped all the documents out on the coffee table and roused him from his nap. "Now all I need is someone to go down and bring them across the border for me."

"Why the hell can't *you* do it?" Reno wanted to know.

"Dad, if you don't mind, that is just something I'd rather not talk about right now."

But later—after Reno had gone off grumbling, followed by a dozen mewing cats, on his watchman's rounds—Lonnie confided that he had been in trouble in Panama, "and the government might have my name on some kind of list."

"Then how'd you get through the border the first time?" Ruby wanted to know.

"Just lucky, I guess. They didn't check."

"What kind of trouble were you in down there, Lonnie?"

"They claim we stole some shit from the government and sold it on the black market."

"Who's 'we'?"

"Bill and me."

"What kind of shit?"

"Construction material. You know, drywall, roofing, vinyl flooring, finished lumber, insulation. They have to import it down there, so it's worth a lot."

"Did you?"

"Did we what?"

"Steal it."

"We skimmed some off the top," he said. "Everybody was into it. We're just the ones that got burnt."

"So, that's why you guys had to quit the Service?"

"Quit? We didn't quit," Lonnie said, winking extravagantly, making a lopsided triangle of his mouth, showing his long tobacco-stained teeth, the only part of him, apparently, that had aged in the least. "We split."

"You *split?*" Ruby said. "What does that mean? You're AWOL? You escaped from custody? The FBI's after you?"

"Hey, cool it, will you? It's no big deal. I mean, they were even offering us immunity. We said no way, we're not gonna rat on our buddies, so the other guys got the immunity, and we got the shaft. But anyway, like I say, it's no big thing. We were on loan to the Canal Zone Administration when it happened, so there was no court martial. Only thing the Air Force did was discharge us 'under less than honorable conditions.' We were tried in a civilian court. They even let us out on bail. Then when it looked like they were actually gonna put us away, we walked. Hey look, Sis, we're talking nickels and dimes here, from the government's point of view. It'll all be over and done with if we can just kind of lay low for a while."

"Lay low?" Ruby said. "You call this 'laying low?' You're staying in your father's *home,* for God's sake, right where they'll look first."

"Yeah," he said, sniffing apologetically, "Bill and me, we thought of that. Got any ideas?"

"Well, I don't know about Bill, but you're gonna have to get out of here, that's for sure. I had this nice little house all lined up for you. But you can't go there now. I know a trailer for rent in Gold Hill. I'll put a deposit on it, under another name."

"What name?"

"I don't know. How about Mom's name, Stroud?"

"Naw."

"Well then, Lonnie, what name would you like?"

"How about Johnny, Johnny Brunetti?"

"Brunetti? You don't look like any Brunetti."

"Okay, okay, let's make it Bruno."

"Bruno what?"

"Bruno Von Braun."

"Fine," Ruby said. "A nice plain name. Nobody will ever remember that."

"Hey, don't get snotty, Ruby."

"I'm trying, Lonnie, honestly, I'm trying. Now what're we gonna do about your wife?"

"I was hoping that you'd run down and bring her and the kid across, Sis, if you don't mind."

"I was afraid of that," she said, wondering why she took so much trouble with him, when he had never troubled himself with her. "Okay, Lonnie, but it's against my better judgement;

my husband is going to be furious with me, and I'll only do it on one condition."

"What's that?"

"You keep your nose clean, and you and your friend give Dad and me a year of honest carpentry work."

"What's the wages?"

"Union."

"That oughta be alright," he said. "But I'm warning you right now, Bill and me, we're no good for overtime."

Ruby got home just in time to see, a quarter mile down the road, the Gold Hill Elementary School bus pulling up at Sand Canyon Ranch, and Ned jumping out onto the dirt shoulder. He was a tough, solid-looking little guy, Ruby thought, in his high-top sneakers, Levis and T-shirt, a budding athlete. Yet, he was by no means the replica of his father that she sometimes imagined him to be. For one thing, his legs were longer; he would be taller when he was grown. And he was lighter on his feet, quicker and more graceful at things. Also, he was fairer than Max, with reddish hair. And there was something of Ruby in his face, which was oval rather than square in shape, and in his mouth, fuller and more expressive than his father's.

The bus geared off, leaving the boy behind in a cloud of dust, looking bewildered. He stared toward the tall Victorian for a long moment and then started slowly trudging up the hill.

"Mom where *are* you?", she could imagine him complaining, for she rarely failed to meet him at the bus.

Though her son's posture indicated his disappointment, his crankiness after a long day at school and a hot forty-minute ride on the bus, Ruby made no attempt to increase her speed.

On the contrary, she took her foot off the accelerator and even applied a slight pressure to the brakes. She wanted to prolong this moment, to admire him from this perspective, this objective distance, for as long as possible.

In the mornings, she remembered, she often wanted the same kind of thing.

Her favorite time was the morning, walking down the driveway with him in the sunshine, holding hands, he with his school bag over his shoulder, she with his lunch pail under her arm. Then waiting by the mailbox, smelling dewy almond trees, purple sage, crested wheatgrass, mustard weed, goldenrod, till the school bus arrived, full of shouting children. Then Ned climbing up inside with his backpack slung over his shoulder and his lunch pail in his hand, finding a seat by a window, slinging his stuff down beside him, looking down to where she stood beside the mailbox, catching her eye. Then his morning ritual, mugging at her through the window, thumbing his nose at her and sticking out his tongue, laughing at the faces that she made back at him, till the bus started to pull off and he suddenly went solemn with the prospect of parting from her for the day. Ruby would never forget her son's rapt little face in the window (changing a little year by year: kindergarten, first grade, second grade, third grade, fourth grade, fifth grade), his small hand waving at her, waving and waving as she waved back at him until she must have seemed to him a tiny speck on the far horizon.

This morning, however, just at that bittersweet moment when the bus went around the bend at the bottom of the canyon, she had thought of the lump again, and it had broken her heart.

"Hey there, handsome, want a ride?"

"Mom! Where were you?" Ned said. His voice was deep and husky for his age, a voice—she was convinced—that would one day command.

"Come on, big boy," she said roughly. He liked her to treat him roughly. "Hop in and I'll tell you all about it."

He got in beside her, slinging his backpack down on the seat between them, slamming the door shut.

She leaned over and, overwhelming his token resistance, planted a fat, lip-sticky kiss on his forehead, and another on his smudged cheek. Hot and sweaty, he reeked of little boy.

"All right, Mom," he said, in an ironic tone that she recognized as her own. "Tell me about it."

"It's kind of a long story, honey."

"I don't mind," he said, anticipating a good tall one, his crankiness forgotten for the moment.

"Well, all right," Ruby said, watching her son's huge, innocent blue eyes light up with pleasure. "Here's what happened..."

And so, as they drove up the driveway, parked the Nash Ambassador in front of the house, went inside, and had their daily tea-time snack together at the kitchen table, she told him the story of his Uncle Lonnie, his Aunt Domenica and his baby cousin, Lonnie Jr., their epic overland journey from Panama, their adventures with snakes, wild beasts, savage Indians, mounted *bandidos*, and roving bands of anti-American guerillas in the tropical jungles, trackless mountains and impenetrable mangrove swamps of deepest Central America, their crossing of Mexico and the great Sonoran Desert, their troubles at the US border, their painful separation, Uncle Lonnie's dash in his battered pink Cadillac to seek help from his devoted sister.

"Aw, come on, Mom," he said, when she was done."Is that really true?"

"True as I'm sitting here now," she said. "And if you don't believe me, you can ask your Uncle Lonnie."

"I bet he's just as big a liar as you are."

"A liar? My brother a liar?" she shrieked, chasing him into the living room, catching him, getting him down on her braided Victorian carpet and tickling him under the arms while he squealed with laughter. "Why, how dare you cast aspersions on that pillar of the community, that marvel of piety and probity, Lonnie B. Rose!"

Ruby just could not lay her hands off Ned that day. She helped him with every stitch of his homework and sat with him all through his piano practice, though Sybil had said she preferred him to work alone and without distractions. She cooked him up his favorite dinner—lamb chops and corn on the cob with a raspberry sherbet dessert—and read him stories from his favorite book, *The Children's Bible*, until Max came in from work at eight-thirty. Then, while Ned got quizzed about the day's events at school and put to bed by his father, Ruby cooked her second dinner of the evening: Chicken cacciatore with zucchini squash and garlic bread. She served it with Valpolicella, and not until she had uncorked the second bottle did she dare broach the subject of Lonnie.

"Well, Max, my brother finally showed up. And I swear, it's amazing, he hasn't aged a day."

"Oh yeah? Is he ready to go to work?"

"Says so."

"So, what's all the excitement about?"

"What do you mean?"

"You look like you're about ready to jump right up out of that chair."

"Oh, I don't know, honey. I just got a glimmer that it's not gonna be too easy with him."

"Well, I hate to say I told you so."

"See, he had to leave his wife and kid down in Mexicali because Immigration wouldn't let them in. So, I got some ID from Juanita and now he wants me to go down and bring them across."

"Not if I have anything to say about it."

"Now, wait a minute..."

"I mean, what do you owe this guy, anyway? After the way he treated you."

"You never had a brother, Max, so you don't know how I feel."

"I know you when you're in this mood," he said. "And I don't like it."

That night in bed, Ruby tried to contact Max again by getting him to give her a rubdown. For weeks she had used the excuse of a painful lower back as her reason for not making love, when in fact she was afraid he would... He would what? Discover, or confirm, what she had no desire to know?

"This time I want you to sit on me," she said, rolling over on her tummy. "And press down hard."

Max, who always slept in the nude, pulled her nightie up around her shoulders and sat on her thighs, kneading her lower back with his hands. His penis lay naturally in the groove of her buttocks, and the friction of his rough hairy ass on her soft smooth thighs turned her on. Turned him on as well. Got him hard. She wanted him hard. She wanted him from behind, where he would never know.

After a time, Max stopped his kneading, pulled her nightie off over her head, leaned forward, and started kissing and biting her lightly about the ears, neck and shoulders while continuing to gently undulate against her rear. She opened to him then and he slipped inside. She was wet and he went in very deep. He came in a minute, spurting a great strong gob of the stuff against the wall of her cervix.

Then right away he had to have it again. She let him have it. He was even bigger this time and took longer. He filled her completely and fucked her as she fucked the sheets until she was sated.

"I guess that was all just to get your way with me, right?" he said, when they were done.

"Naw, Max, I could've got that anyway."

"Then what for, all of a sudden, after all this time?"

"For love," she said, and started to cry. "For love!"

"Ruby, sometimes with you I don't know what's acting and what's real."

"I understand exactly what you mean," she said, laughing through her tears. "Because I don't know that either."

The best day to go down to Mexicali was on Sunday, Lonnie said. The best time to come back across the border was at 7 P.M. The bullfights let out then, and the customs agents had their hands so full they couldn't check but a tenth of the cars that came through.

Dominica's motel, Lonnie said, was located six kilometers east of Mexicali, in the industrial suburb of Abasolo, across the street from a cement factory. And though it had no name, it could be recognized by its two-story cinderblock construction, its Kelly green and red trim paint job, its pink doors, its chicken-plucked dirt yard, its fringe of organ cactus windbreak, and a sign in English on its rock and gravel roof boasting of AIR CONDITIONING! COLOR TV! ADULT MOVIES!

Crossing the salt marshes of the Colorado River Delta and pulling into Abasolo at siesta time on a hot, chalk-white Sunday in early November, Ruby found the motel and parked in front of Unit 37. Switching off her overheated engine, sitting behind the wheel of her beloved old Nash Ambassador with the windows rolled up till the dust settled, feeling the sweat start to prickle and chafe under her shaved and deodorized arms, under her breasts, between her legs, she was reminded of her last trip to Mexico, to the phony abortionist in Tijuana, and became heir again to disquieting intimations.

Then someone, someone with a mass of long curly black hair caught up in a white bath towel, peeked out through the yellow plastic curtains, smiling, waving enthusiastically, recognizing her.

Ruby got out of the car and went for the door. But before she could knock, it opened, and a tall, voluptuous, mixed-blood

Latina in a long white terrycloth dressing gown stepped forth. She was young, at least sixteen or seventeen years younger than Lonnie, and so exotic that she looked to Ruby as if she ought to be wearing a sarong, or a Carmen Miranda outfit with a turban of fruit and flowers on her head. Her skin was dark, darker than in pictures, mocha brown, and her smile was very white. She was prettier than her pictures too, with high cheekbones, great slanting yellow eyes, a curved nose, lush plumy lips, and the neck and carriage of an Ethiopian queen. Her expression conveyed warmth, good humor, alertness and sincerity, qualities conspicuously lacking in Lonnie. And Ruby's first impression was that she thoroughly outclassed him. At the same time, however, she could not help but wonder what folks in Gold Hill, especially Reno, would make of such a tropical specimen. Mexican blood, as that in the veins of the Sanchez family, was hard enough to deal with, yet here there was obviously an even darker strain. And it occurred to her that it was for precisely this reason—for the reaction of his family and community—that Lonnie had tied up with her in the first place.

"Dominica?"

"Yes."

"Hi, I'm Lonnie's sister."

"I know, I know, he just ring me up about it," she said, in an accent that sounded almost Jamaican. "Come in, Ruby dear, come in! Lonnie always telling me so much about you, I feel like I know you already."

"Lonnie said you were Panamanian," Ruby said, following her into the motel room, glancing at the peeling yellow walls, the single hanging lightbulb, the baby stroller beneath the rattling air conditioner. "But you don't sound like it to me."

"Well, you see now," Dominica said, still smiling broadly, motioning her to sit down beside her on the bed, "in Panama they a lot like me. Great grandpa, he come over from Jamaica to build the canal, and we down there ever since, mixing it up with the natives."

"And you never lost your English?"

"No, no, never lose it, never lose it, if you want to call it 'English.' Because, you know, in the *barrio* where I come up, and in Balboa where my mama from, we the majority."

Mahjoreetee, she pronounced it.

"And your dad?" Ruby asked, smiling back. She found the girl's simplicity appealing.

"Dad, he Spanish, they say, but he run Venezuela before I so much as get a peep at him. So, sometimes I wonder, you see, is this man for real at all?" Dominica said, laughing at the thought, rolling her eyes, and shaking her head in mock disbelief, jangling her long silver earrings.

"Mama, Mama, Mama!" Lonnie Jr. cried, waking from his sleep, and Dominica went over to the stroller to pick him up.

He was bigger than Ruby had expected, plump and lusty looking, two and a half at least, with tawny brown skin, green eyes, and swirls of fine blond hair. Rocking him gently in her arms, cooing and crooning to him in a husky, mellifluous Caribbean tone, Dominica brought him over to the bed, sat down beside Ruby again, opened her robe and put him to breast. Ruby found herself mildly shocked by the action, despite herself. This child, this dark little foreign nephew of hers, seemed awfully large and well-developed to be feeding so. She had weened little Ned at nine months, she remembered. And this one suckled so greedily, it seemed, squinting, puckering, making great slurping sounds, cupping his mother's dusky breast with his lighter brown hand almost erotically. And indeed, Ruby thought, what male would not? For it was surely the ripest and most succulent breast she had ever seen, high and smooth and flawless, with a purplish areola and a large erect nipple.

Unaffected by Ruby's presence, Dominica gave the child her full attention for a moment, humming, swaying, and smiling serenely down at him.

Watching them, feeling their warm sweating bodies beside her, smelling them (baby smell, mother smell, milk smell), Ruby built a case for flesh, intimacy, instinct, and started to envy Dominica. And asked herself again why she had held off having a child for so long. Was it fear of another miscarriage? Or was it to leave herself unfettered for another lunge at stardom? Now maybe it was too late.

That evening, just about the time the bullfights were letting out, they packed the car, paid the motel bill, and made for the border. Very soon, just as Lonnie had predicted, they were caught in a four-mile-long traffic jam. Waiting her turn in line, easing the station wagon forward, Ruby spent a few minutes halfheartedly attempting to train the Island lilt out of Dominica's voice, so she would not arouse suspicion at the crossing. But the effort proved futile, because Dominica was preoccupied with the needs of Lonnie Jr., and she was far too open and direct by nature to have any gift for mimicry or dissimulation.

To relieve some of the nervous tension that was building in the car, and to assuage some of Dominica's natural curiosity about the Rose family, Ruby gave a capsulized version of her life. She told it as farce, as black humor (including her childhood feud with Lonnie, Alma's death, and the Hollywood debacle), making grotesque and horrendous jokes at her own expense, giving them both a giggling fit, getting even little Lonnie Junior—who had become fretful in the car—to reel with laughter.

Later, with still a mile to go, and the baby finally asleep in back, Ruby could not help but pry a bit more into Dominica's past as well.

She was the youngest of seven, she said, and the only girl. Her mother was a maid in the home of a Canal Zone doctor. They were very poor and lived in a shanty town called Barrio Norte. But Dominica was smart in school. Her brothers, having gone to work at an early age, made sure that she never dropped out. Later, with her knowledge of English, and the good offices of her mother's American employer, she was able to secure a position as a practical nurse at the Canal Zone Hospital. One night, Lonnie came into her ward to visit his friend Bill, who was suffering from a liver complaint, and on his way out he made it a point to chat her up.

"That man, he lie through his teeth when we meet," Dominica said, smiling almost fondly at the memory. "Say he a Major, pilot at Howard Field, Viet Nam ace. Flash a lot of money as well, and this big pink Cadillac that he drive about. By the time I get wise to his games, I's pregnant with Lonnie Jr.

And then I s'pose it just doan't matter that much anymore, you know?"

"What I can't figure out is this," Ruby said. "Why'd you allow yourself to get involved with my brother in the first place? I mean, let's be frank. He does have his failings. And he's nearly old enough to be your father."

"Well, you know, Ruby, down where I come from, they probably laugh at your question. The gringo, they say, he treat you right. Not like our macho man. And the high class in my country, you see, they only one thing: White. Besides, tell me what girl from Panama not dying to get in the States?"

"So," Ruby said, keeping her tone perfectly neutral, "you just used Lonnie, then. That's it?"

"No," Dominica said, laughing like a child, "no!" And then, skipping a beat, she added, "Perhaps a bit at first."

"And now?"

"Now, like I say, we got the little one to contend with. And, you know," she said, leaning closer to Ruby across the seat, lowering her voice, as if to utter something shameful, and then grinning with self-awareness, "my daddy run away when I's only four. I got this thing for older men."

And for some reason, they both laughed uproariously.

They reached the checkpoint at nine o'clock that night. Harried and overworked by the heavy traffic, the customs men took a quick look at Dominica's documents, another at Ruby's red hair and freckles, and waved them over the border.

Drained by the crossing, they decided to get a motel for the night. They felt they deserved a good one, so they checked into the Ramada Inn, on the freeway just outside Calexico, California.

Then, having showered, phoned home, and put the baby to bed, they sent for a bottle of Vodka and some orange juice and sat around in their panties drinking screwdrivers, watching the Late Show, and doing their nails. After a couple of drinks, they took turns brushing each other's hair. After a couple more, Ruby leaned back in her chair, took a deep drag on her cigarette, her first in years, and found herself confessing to Nurse Dominica what she had admitted to no one else, not even herself.

"There's this lump I've got growing on me," she said. "I don't know what it is, and it's scaring me to death."

"Probably nothing," Dominica said, after she had examined her on the bed. "Probably just a swollen gland. Best see a doctor though, just to set yo' mind at ease."

Dr. Silverman, a tall, sober, muscular young man with a Pancho Villa moustache, intense brown eyes, a shiny pate, and a fringe of jet-black hair, enjoyed a reputation as Antelope Valley's most eminent gynecologist. He was not married, and despite his hulking appearance there was something slightly effeminate about him, especially in the way he used his eyes and hands. Ruby had always suspected that he was a secret homosexual and pictured him cavorting in Hollywood bathhouses on weekends. Perhaps for that reason, she had never taken his dour, humorless demeanor very seriously. But today for some reason it frightened her.

"I... I'm so sorry," she said, after she had removed her clothes and gotten herself into an open-backed hospital gown.

"I phoned your secretary from down in Calexico and said it was an emergency and fouled up your whole schedule and rushed all the way up here with my sister-in-law and her baby and the whole reason I guess is probably just a swollen gland."

"I see," said Dr. Silverman, impassively. "Why don't you just get up on the table and we'll have a look."

On the table, though, Ruby could not stretch out full length. Her skull, her arms, the muscles in her stomach and thighs all tightened up, and she began to tremble and palpitate. Sweat ran into the corners of her eyes, into her cleavage and the creases beneath her breasts. And she could smell herself. She was glad Max knew nothing of this. She expected even the doctor to recoil from her, and was grateful when he said, "Here, let me help you, Ruby."

Firmly but gently, he guided her down. Then, without an instant's hesitation, he ran his rubber-gloved hand under her gown and found the lump.

"It's bigger than you said," he observed, probing her groin with his fingers. "And harder. Is it painful when I push down on it?"

"No."

"It's not a swollen lymph node, that's for sure. It might be a hernia or a rupture of some kind, but I doubt it. I believe it may be affixed to the pelvic bone. I tell you what," he said. And she could see that all over his bald white head and behind his ears little beads of perspiration had suddenly oozed forth. "What I'd like to do, Ruby, I'd like to do a biopsy on this."

"When?"

"As soon as possible.

"Why?" she asked.

But she already knew the answer.

She read it in his eyes.

Thus revealed, the truth pierced, struck home, carved out a great, yawning chasm in Ruby's heart, filled it with something beyond fear, beyond description, something awesome, infinite, distinct from all else.

"Why?" she said again. "Why me?"

Chapter Twelve

The room was small and white, with shiny black linoleum floors, and a window looking out onto the parking lot. Ruby was sitting up in bed, pale and heavy-lidded, with her hands resting on her thighs.

"Hey," Max called from the doorway. "How you doing?"

"Not so bad. Considering. How about yourself?"

"I'll be a lot better when you get out of here."

"Yeah, me too. How's Ned?"

"Fine. He's over at Juanita's, along with little Lonnie. We'll pick 'em up on the way home."

"How much does he know?"

"Not much. Hell, how much do *we* know?"

Passing by the foot of her bed, Max glanced at the nurse's chart.

Mrs. Ruby Bauer
Exploratory Surgery
7 p.m., Monday, November 10, 1970
Dr. Silverman, Dr. Metcalf

"I brought you some flowers," he said, setting a bouquet of large white roses in her lap, kissing her on the cheek.

"Nice." She sniffed the air perfunctorily.

"You seem pretty calm."

"I'm heavily sedated."

"So, what exactly are they gonna do? You were so vague on the phone."

"I'm, I'm not really sure," she responded, in a tiny, childish voice. "Just have a look, I guess. Try to figure out what it is."

"Which side is it on?"

"Does it matter?"

"I guess not," he said, and he had a hard time holding her glance. Her eyes, inexplicably, seemed hurt and reproachful. He managed a smile, and went on, "Ruby, how long have you known about this?"

"I just found out."

"I mean, how long have you suspected?"

"A while."

"How come you never told me?"

"I thought... I thought you wouldn't love me anymore," she sighed, and suddenly reached for his hand, held it against her lips. They both sniffed out a laugh, then the nurse came in with a gurney to wheel her away.

He went out to the waiting room where Sybil, Reno, Lonnie, and Dominica—whom Max had met for the first time only an hour before—sat their armchairs as if mounted on uneasy horses, everyone but Sybil talking in whispers, very fast.

Max met Sybil's eyes and saw that she was suffering Ruby's relatives with difficulty. She had not been able to sleep for the last couple of nights and looked completely worn out.

"Please," he said, raising a hand, as Reno and Lonnie both started to question him at once. "I don't know any more than you do."

"But Max!" Dominica piped up. Despite her color, her alien accent, her dubious relationship with Lonnie, and her very recent arrival, Dominica had already appropriated for herself the status of family member. "Doan't they say nothing of her condition, then?"

"No, I'm sorry," he said, more gently than he had intended. "We're just gonna have to wait and see.

Two hours later, Dr. Silverman appeared at the door with the surgeon, Dr. Metcalf, a stout, red-faced fellow with a yellow Van Dyke whom Max knew as a regular Jaguar customer at his garage. Dr. Silverman, looking even grimmer than usual, headed straight inside toward the family. But Dr. Metcalf skulked in the doorway, shuffling his feet, wringing his plump pink hands, and flitting his puffy little eyes about the room in a fat man's panic. Then, seeing Max rise from his place beside Sybil and start to move toward him, he snapped his fingers as if he had just forgotten something terribly important, spun on his toes, and scuttled around the corner, leaving Dr. Silverman to approach alone.

Having immediately apprehended the grave implications of Dr. Metcalf's cowardice, Max suffered a moment of stopped time, an instant when his heart, his lungs, his mind, his entire world and all its systems went down and the problems and preoccupations that had lately consumed his waking hours—his unsatisfactory sex life with Ruby, his disagreement with Charlie over whether to get into used cars, the new Jap bikes and cars that were rapidly taking over Triumph's markets, the backlog of major repair work at the garage, his heavy indebtedness, Ned's growing disinterest in hunting, fishing, team sports, and all the other manly arts—faded into insignificance.

Even so, Max did not blame Dr. Metcalf, the steady easy customer with whom he had laughed and joked a dozen times at the garage and thought he knew so well, did not resent him for his failure to confront him man to man. He sympathized with his predicament, in fact, and thought he might have done something of the same, had he been in his place.

"Mr. Bauer, I'm afraid we have bad news," Dr. Silverman said, while Sybil, Reno, Lonnie, and Dominica all strained to hear from across the room. Sybil stood and started toward Max, but he motioned her away. He felt a need to protect her from this. "Your wife has developed a small, hard, immovable mass on the left side of the pelvis. It's fixed to the bone, and it could be bone cancer, but we can't be sure until we get the results of the biopsy and the other tests."

Max kept looking at him, trying to get him to say what he couldn't ask.

"The prognosis?" the doctor said at last, shaking his head. "I'm afraid it's not very good."

"What's he say?" Reno shouted from across the room.

"Yeah, what's he say?" Lonnie parroted.

"Excuse me, Doctor," Max said.

Reeling out onto the floodlit parking lot, ducking behind cars to elude Ruby's pursuing father and brother, Max tried to think. But he couldn't think. It was like contemplating the end of the world, or his own death sentence.

"Get out of here!" he shouted at them when they finally caught up with him. "There's nothing you can do now. So, just get the fuck out of here and leave me alone!"

"What a thing to come home to," Lonnie said.

Max sat by Ruby's side all night, holding her hand. She looked so peaceful lying there, so young, and robust, with the light from the bedside lamp glowing pink against her skin, red in her hair. Watching her, listening to her deep steady breathing, he tried to conceive of a lifetime without her, to picture himself and Ned alone in the big house, to imagine another woman coming along someday to take her place. It wasn't painful, exactly. It was hollow. As if they had cut out the part of him that felt.

Later, he dozed and dreamed that it was his mother who was ill. She must have a hysterectomy, and he had to break the news to her. "Hell, Mom, a little plumbing job," he said, a way he never would in life. "It can't be such a big thing."

Then he woke to see Dr. Silverman in the doorway, and his heart stopped.

By the time Ruby came to, they were standing together by her bed. She woke with a start, sitting straight up. And then, with wide suspicious eyes, she looked each of them over very carefully.

"I'm going to die," she said.

"Now calm down, Ruby," Dr. Silverman warned, taking her by the wrist, feeling her pulse. "Actually, we just got the results from the x-rays and they're pretty encouraging. It's not bone cancer, thank God. What we've got here, I think, is a cartilaginous tumor."

Ruby took a breath.

"Is that good or bad?"

"Well, a little of both. What it is—it's a tumorous mass composed mostly of cartilage. We have the biopsy report and the malignancy on it is low level, which is usually the case on this type. The problem is, it's a notorious seeder. We've got to be extra sure that we get it all out at once."

"So, what do we do now?" she wanted to know, turning from one of them to the other.

"We're not equipped to handle an operation of this kind," Dr. Silverman said. "We're going to have to transfer you to someplace where they specialize in this sort of thing—the Mayo Clinic in Minnesota, perhaps, or the Sloan-Kettering Institute in New York."

"Max, what's he trying to tell me?"

"Honey," he said, in a firm, manly voice that was not quite his own. "What you've got, it's very, very serious. And I wish it was me who had it, instead of you. I really do. But it's growing fast, and it's gonna have to come out."

"How, Doctor? How are they going to get it out?"

"Because of the tumor's location, Ruby, so close to all of your vital organs, I believe that radical surgery is indicated."

"Which means?" she said, angrily. Apparently, she already knew the answer, and was trying to bully him into not telling her. But if such was her ploy, it did not work, because Dr. Silverman came straight to the point.

"Ruby, I'm afraid your left leg and part of your pelvis will have to be surgically removed. The operation is called a hemipelvectomy, and it's a very arduous procedure. But it's our best and probably our only solution."

"And if you do get it, what are my chances?"

"I'm not going to fool you, they're only fair, but if we sit around and do nothing, they're virtually nil."

"Isn't there some way," Ruby said, calm now, as if she were discussing another case entirely, "isn't there some way to extract it without taking everything else along with it?"

"No, not really, because it's so hard to get to. Some of it would almost inevitably spill and seed."

"But couldn't someone try? I mean, what have I got to lose?"

"I'm sorry, Ruby, but I doubt you'd find anybody in this country who would perform an operation of that kind. The procedure would be so unorthodox, and so risky to the patient, there's probably no insurance company that would pay for it."

"Well then, we'll go to some other country!" she cried, flinging herself back down on the bed. "Won't we, Max?"

Max nodded, though he was not sure why. He felt that he should go to her, that she was beckoning to him. Yet he was reluctant to approach her, to touch her, or even speak to her, as if she were under some terrible enchantment.

"Ruby, I know how hard it must be to accept this," Dr. Silverman said, "especially with so little time to prepare yourself psychologically. But you still have a lot to live for—a husband, a son who needs you very much—and you cannot hesitate too long."

"We won't hesitate, will we, Max?" she said, and he knew that he must go to her now. He stepped forward and sat uncertainly on the edge of her bed. She patted him on the knee, as if he were the one deserving sympathy. "Max and I know exactly what we're going to do."

The Instituto Cabo-Arco, Panama's most prestigious cancer clinic, was situated on a wooded knoll just off the Boyd Roosevelt Highway in suburban Ancon, with a view of the Culebra Cut and the Isle of Taboga. A rambling Spanish Colonial mansion surrounded by exotic trees and plants, reflecting pools and manicured lawns, it had been bequeathed to the institute's founders—Doctor Francisco Cabo, Central America's most renowned pathologist, and Doctor Miguel Arco, its most distinguished surgeon—by a sugarcane heiress who had died of Hodgkin's Disease in the early 1960s.

Yet, despite its gorgeous setting, its handsome facade, graceful porticos and fancy grillwork, Max found the place oppressive, unpleasantly reminiscent of his ancestral mansion in Santa Barbara. And, pulling up in an airport taxi from Panama City on a sultry evening in mid-November, he felt increasingly doubtful as to the outcome of their business here. Not that the feeling was new. He had been assailed by doubts ever since they placed the call to Doctor Arco the week before, at the behest of his former employee, Dominica. And Max wondered how

Ruby could sit beside him now so calm and cool while he sweat rivulets in the tropical humidity, worrying about her.

The trip was madness, of course, as all their friends, relations, and medical advisors had told them. Ruby ought to be at Sloan-Kettering right now doing whatever was necessary to save her life. Max had kicked his ass a hundred times for giving in to her, accompanying her down here despite all his reservations.

"I'm too proud to just sit back and let myself become captive to the whims of fate," she had told their family and friends this morning, in an oddly rehearsed little speech, out on the tarmac at Palmdale Airport. "I'm gonna fight this thing. And I'm gonna beat it, on my own terms. And I thank you, Dominica, for helping me find Dr. Arco."

Though Max disagreed with her decision, thought it selfish and illogical and vainglorious, and had fought as hard as all the others, with Dominica's exception, to change her mind, he was full of admiration now for her courage, her strength of will, and wondered what he would have done in her place.

He would have played it safe, he thought, and felt diminished as a consequence.

Paying the driver, Max helped Ruby out of the cab and saw to their bags. A *mestizo* boy appeared from around a corner of the white stucco mansion, pushing a little baggage cart. "*A sus ordenes, señor,*" he said, smiling and bowing.

Max stuttered for a moment, trying to remember his high school Spanish, but just then a tall, portly Black man in grey gabardine trousers and a white waiter's jacket came puffing out from behind one of the porticos.

"Hello, hello! Can I help you? Can I help you, please?" he said, in the same curious, lilting accent that Dominica had brought with her from Panama.

"We're here for a consultation with Doctor Arco," Ruby said.

"Ah," he said, nodding enthusiastically, showing a row of large white teeth. "Then you is Mr. and Mrs. Bauer! I am a friend of Dominica. Used to work with her. Dr. Arco expecting you."

Their rooms were apart from the main house, in a quaint little tile-roofed, white-washed adobe cottage surrounded by banana trees, with pots full of red and blue flowers in all the windows. Inside, it was cool, dark, and fragrant, with gleaming red tile floors, a magnificent hand-stitched white linen counterpane on a great dark-oak matrimonial bed, and a sunken marble bath.

Ruby only spent a moment freshening up before hastening over to the main house to try and see Dr. Arco. But he was performing surgery at the Canal Zone Hospital this afternoon, she was told, and in any case, there were no consultations after 6 p.m..

Exhausted from their flight, she returned to their lodgings and—with the aid of one of Dr. Silverman's powerful sedatives—was asleep by nine o'clock.

Sitting up alone, trying to read a *Time Magazine*, listening to Ruby's steady, even, breathing in the next room, Max marveled again at how she held herself together, as if her world were not about to fall apart. When they stepped inside the cottage that afternoon, its charm had turned her giddy for a moment, and she had danced about the room, picking up objects of native craftsmanship and exclaiming over them—"Oh, Max, how lovely! Look at this, and this!"—as if she had just arrived on her honeymoon at some first-class hotel. Yet, she seemed to him at that instant more fragile and vulnerable, more feminine, and ephemeral, than he ever remembered her. And for the first time since her illness began, he felt that he might lose his composure. It was as if she were seventeen again, and not quite his yet, too exciting, too beautiful for him, likely to slip away forever.

The reception room at the clinic, where they appeared the next morning at eight, was wide and airy, with the same polished red tile floors, whitewashed walls, and high beamed ceilings as their cottage. It was full of patients, even at this early hour, some of them in wheelchairs and hospital gurneys, attended by relatives, others seated in armchairs that were grouped together around throw rugs and coffee tables to give the illusion of home. All the patients were seriously ill. Some were misshapen. Some had missing limbs. Others were bald from the effects of chemotherapy. Though there must have been over thirty people in the reception room, it was curiously odorless, and quiet as the grave.

The place gave Max the willies. All his life, he'd had a horror of death, disease, and disfigurement. But Ruby strode straight to the reception desk as if she were exposed to such spectacles every day of her life. The receptionist, an elderly, frizzy-haired white man in a gray business suit who spoke English with only a slight, soft Spanish accent, asked politely for Ruby's name, looked it up in a file catalogue behind the counter, and pulled her card out. It was a red card, marked "URGENCIA" at the top. The sight of it there, amid all those pale green cards, left

Max feeling dizzy and faint, but again Ruby seemed completely unfazed.

While she filled out a long medical form, the receptionist informed Max about clinical costs and doctor's fees. Though not exorbitant by American standards, they were still vastly expensive, and payable in advance.

Signing travelers' checks, waiting for the receptionist to write out an elaborate receipt in Spanish, Max thought of all the blood they'd had to sweat to come up with this money that now slipped so easily from their hands...

"You know," Sybil had said, after Ruby won her over—with threats, as she'd won Max—"if it were me, I think I would rather die than go beg for money from my Santa Barbara family again. But since it's for you, Ruby, I feel I have no choice."

"No, Sybil," Ruby said. "I'm afraid you haven't."

Wheeling up the palm-lined driveway of the Prince Estate the following Sunday in the battered family station wagon, catching sight of his cousins, in white ducks, straw hats, and pastel dresses, playing croquet on the lawn by the pool, Max experienced that same doubtful, doleful feeling he'd had when he was a kid. And, unable to prevent himself, he brought the car to a screeching halt, dropped it in reverse, and started backing swiftly, perilously down the long winding hill.

"What're you doing? Stop!" Ruby shrieked, smacking him about the ribs and shoulders.

"No!" he hollered back, staring out the back window over Ned's frightened little face, trying to keep the car on the road. "No, listen, honey, I got an idea. What if it's not just the old lady who's holding out? What if it's somebody else? So, let's sneak around the back. Then you and Mom can go up and talk to her alone."

"He's right! He's right!" Sybil shouted at Ruby, who appeared to be gathering steam for another onslaught. "It's probably the only way we'll ever be able to get through to her."

Later, creeping up through the eucalyptus woods behind the house, in danger of being caught and arrested as trespassers at any moment, Sybil and Ruby laughed and cut up together like schoolgirls, they said later, as if it were not a life and death enterprise they had embarked upon, as if so much did not depend on the will of a senile old woman. Yet, when they entered the house, through a secret way that Sybil remembered from when she was a child, they were both petrified with fear, and tiptoed up the stairs to the old lady's room past her ancient, somnolent butler like burglars in the night.

"Mrs. Prince was tall, fashionably gaunt, and amazingly well-preserved, with the aid of some deep auburn hair-dye and several face-lifts," Ruby said later, "but her coloring was like that of the dead."

She was reclining on her bed in a long, black dressing gown from another era, and appeared to be asleep, barely breathing. But she opened her eyes and recognized Sybil as soon as she bent to touch her shoulder.

"Well, Sybil dear, I'm glad you've finally come to your senses," the old woman said, sitting up smartly and shaking a finger in her face, as if their quarrel were only of an hour's duration, as if Sybil were still a rebellious girl. "I can't tell you how angry I've been with you."

"Mother," Sybil whispered back. And, in a moment of supreme inspiration, she threw herself on her knees beside the bed and bowed her head. "I've come to beg your forgiveness."

"That's all I've asked, my dear," said Mrs. Prince, a smile like the smile of a burn victim cracking her long, lacquered face. "That's all I've ever asked. Is it so much?"

"No, Mother, it isn't."

"There, then, you're forgiven!" the old lady said. "See how easy that was?"

Whereupon Sybil found herself suddenly overcome with genuine emotion, shedding real tears.

"I've brought my daughter," she said, inspired again, dabbing at her eyes with a hanky, rising and leading Ruby to the bed. "She's had a spot of bad luck in the past few weeks, and . . ."

In short, it was walk. After hearing Ruby's tale of woe, the old lady wrote out a check for twenty thousand dollars on the spot.

Touched by her stepmother's unprecedented generosity, Sybil promised to phone soon and visit often. Then she hustled Ruby downstairs and out the back door before anyone *compos mentis* appeared.

As an urgent case, Ruby only had to wait a few minutes the next morning before being admitted into the clinic.

"She'll be given tests all day long, Mr. Bauer," the receptionist said. "Relatives are not permitted inside, so why don't you come back around six?"

With plenty of time on his hands, Max hiked into town and caught a bus. It was an ancient, creaking, yellow bus with fanciful figures and pessimistic proverbs painted on the side in gay colors, and a sign on the windshield proclaiming its destination as Colon. Colon was forty miles north of Ancon, at the Caribbean end of the Canal. Dominica's mother lived there, with her eldest son and his family.

Sitting back in his seat near the *mestizo* driver, scanning the narrow, pot-holed, highway ahead, bombarded from a half dozen blaring transistors with the monotonous rhythms of Panamanian folk music—high trilling female voices backed by concertinas and guitars—Max thought of Dominica, at whose behest he was making this trip: "Now you go say hello to my mama, you hear? You pass up the chance, I doan't forgive you." Dominica, the hothouse flower. And he tried to contemplate the odds against her survival with Lonnie B. Rose in the California desert. Not much better than Ruby's, he thought.

It was gently rolling country, out Max's window, sparsely settled, with wave upon wave of low jungle hills and long wisps of clouds in the valleys. The primeval green of the rain forest, the angry red swath of the road, the blue of the tropical sky, the white of the cumulous clouds, the cocoa brown of the lakes and streams, the pink of the flamingos in the shallows, the yellow of the parrots in the trees, the new penny hue of the *mestizos* walking by the road, the purple-black of the Afro-Panamanians, were colors that appeared to Max incredibly intense and primary even when viewed through his dark polaroid glasses, and as diverse from the grays and duns of Antelope Valley as he could imagine.

In a jungle settlement called Gamboa, a little redheaded, freckle-faced peasant girl of about twelve—a dead ringer for Ruby at the same age—got onto the bus with her little brother, a blond, handsome little lout of about three, and chose a seat on the opposite side of the aisle from Max, behind an old Indian woman with a sack full of live chickens at her feet. The children were not Americans, evidently, because they spoke rapid, staccato, Panamanian Spanish together. Max couldn't figure what they were doing out here in the middle of nowhere, among all these darker races, unless they were the result of some casual liaison between a gringo canal worker and a light-skinned countrywoman.

The girl played mother to her little brother, wiping his nose, shushing him down. Yet she was such a thin and frail little thing on that bus full of bean bellies, so small and undeveloped for her age.

A rough *mestizo* boy of about thirteen was sitting across the aisle from her. And he started laughing at her, calling her "*Flacita*" and "*Pelo Rojo*," poking at the little pods partially visible through the tattered sleeveless dress she wore. She struck him off, fire in her eyes, and thereafter he left her alone. Soon, the little, Black conductor came around, collecting fares. Fifty centavos per person. Babes in arms included. But all she had was forty. "*Lo siento, señor, pero no tengo mas que cuarenta,*" she said, haggling like an adult over her deficit. "*No es possible, no es posible,*" the conductor kept repeating, and apparently, he had every intention of putting her off. Max would have happily paid for her, if it had come to that, but he wanted to see what would happen. She fought like a little vixen to stay on that bus, just as

Ruby would have done, befuddling the poor little bespectacled man, who went forward to question the driver. The driver merely shrugged in response, and nothing further was said of the matter.

In the jungle, near Chilibre, the bus stopped, and everyone got out to relieve themselves, men on one side of the road, women on the other. Max went behind a palmetto tree and was peeing up against it when he saw the girl not fifty feet away, with her brother in hand, calmly staring at him. And those eyes, those bright, inquisitive, blue eyes, Ruby's eyes, with something in them that Max would never know, moved him to somewhere beyond tears.

Then it was back on the bus, the driver wheeling wildly around the curves above Lake Madden, everyone crossing themselves piously at the dangerous places. The girl sat nearer Max, this time. She liked him, maybe, or felt a racial kinship to him. He wanted to speak to her but found himself strangely shy of her. She was such a quick, excitable little thing. With that same delightful habit of biting her lower lip. All the other faces on the bus were blank, chewing gum. But, like Ruby, this one was thinking, thinking, all the time.

Rounding a bend in the road just outside New Providence, Max saw a black and white spotted pig drag a laughing, barefoot, Indian boy fifty meters down a green grassy hill. The girl saw it too, saw it for only an instant before the bus was around the next bend. And they laughed and laughed, just the two of them, and no one else.

She got off with her little brother at the bus station in Santa Rita. Max followed, but she disappeared in the crowd before he could hand her the twenty-dollar bill he had clasped in his hand, and so he never learned her name.

In Colon, he went to the address that Dominica had provided him with, a sugarcane shack by the side of a banana warehouse. And he reflected that, on second thought, even Lonnie B. Rose and the California desert might not look so bad in comparison.

Jangling the strung bottlecaps that served for a door, he roused a red-eyed, young, Black man, buck naked, and asked for Dominica's mother, Dolly Sloan.

"Dolly go Chiriquí," he said, shaking his dreadlocks, blowing ganja smoke at him through the bottlecaps. "Go with her boy for to cut cane. Doan't know when she be back."

And so much for Dominica's family.

Dr. Arco, to whom Max and Ruby were introduced the next morning, was a squat and coppery brown, with a low forehead, slanting black eyes, a curved Indian nose, and a mop of black hair. If you took away his long, narrow, fine-looking hands and put him in a loincloth, Max reflected, he would look like he just crawled out of the Darien rain forest. Yet Dominica's former employer at the Canal Zone Hospital had described him as "a brilliant, inspired surgeon, one of the two or three best I've ever known," and the United States Consul in Panama City had confirmed him as a graduate of an American medical school. Such a man, Max thought, having come so far in life, could only have succeeded through excellence.

Dressed for comfort in leather sandals, suntan slacks and a white, hand-embroidered guayabera shirt, he ambled out from behind his desk and approached them with a warm smile and an extended hand.

"Hello, I'm Dr. Arco," he drawled. "Please, won't you sit down?"

"Your accent in English is almost perfect, Dr. Arco," Ruby said, holding to Max's hand very tightly. "I think I even detect a slight regional accent."

"I don't doubt it," he said laughing. "Did my pre-med at Baylor and my internship at Houston Presbyterian."

"No kidding?" Ruby said, but she was clearly not interested in small talk, and as soon as they were decently acquainted, she asked him to explain the surgical procedure to her.

"Why, surely, Ma'am," he said, "but I'd be remiss if I didn't warn you again about the dangers. Now, I don't want to mislead you. I've examined all the records and x-rays you sent down and I'm convinced that your doctors in the United States recommended the proper procedure in this case. However..."

"Doctor, I thought we settled this on the phone!" Ruby interrupted.

"However," the doctor repeated, holding up his hand, smiling at her, "as a *Latino,* as a man with a wife and daughters of his own, believe me, I can understand the fear and reluctance of a beautiful young woman such as yourself."

"Thank you, Doctor Arco, I appreciate your understanding."

"Tell you what. Why don't y'all call me Miguel, and I'll call you Ruby and Max? Okay? Now, all I'm asking, Ruby, is that you understand what we're up against here. The tumor's located in an almost inaccessible place. I'm going to have to go in there and remove it without spilling cancerous tissue, without damaging the bone, or the arteries, or the muscles and tendons that surround it..."

Listening to this, Max began to feel lightheaded, nauseous. He'd heard it all a dozen times since Dr. Silverman broke the news, had read volumes about it, yet only now was it sinking in.

"So, what I'm saying is this, Ruby," Dr. Arco continued. "I've set myself a nearly impossible task. Now, I'll do my best, and I'll get as much of it as I can, but I can't promise anything."

"I'm not afraid," Ruby said. "But I must start thinking about the future of my little boy. I want you to tell me right now, straight out, what you think my long run chances are going to be."

"I'll tell you frankly, Ruby, and I wish I didn't have to say it, but I doubt if they're more than one in ten."

"And the other way?" Ruby said, tightening her grip on Max's hand. "With the radical surgery? Amputating my leg?"

"Maybe one in five."

"Then I'll take my chances."

"There's just one thing I'd like to know, Doctor," Max said, as they were preparing to go. "How come you're willing to do this operation, when no one in the States would touch it?"

"Well, y'all so scared of getting sued up there, you only want to do the sure things. Down here we're not afraid to take a calculated risk, if we feel it's warranted. And you'd be surprised, Max. Some of the recoveries we've had, up there in the States you'd probably call them 'miraculous.'"

"That's what's gonna happen to me," Ruby said, "something miraculous."

But the minute he got her back to their cabin she collapsed in tears.

"I know, I know," Max said, holding her tight, and the little redheaded girl on the bus came to his mind again.

The thing of it was, she was just the age that Ruby had been, the age when they first met, when she used to help him with his paper route, when she took him into her house and they found her mother, still alive, yet reeking of death.

"Don't worry, honey, I'm not crying because I'm scared," Ruby said. "It's because I'm so happy!"

"Happy?" he said. Suddenly, he was almost furious with her. "What the hell have you got to be happy about?"

"Max, for the first time in weeks," she said, slipping out of his arms, out of her lavender summer frock and into her robe, "I feel like I've actually got an outside chance, a shot in the dark."

Then she went into the bathroom, murmuring something about "having a nice soak."

But she stayed in there too long and remained too still.

After an hour, he went in to check up on her. He found her floating in the bath, her body limp and ghostly white under the water, her fiery red hair spread out around her head like that of a drowned woman, an Ophelia.

"Ruby?" he gasped. "Ruby, are you alright?"

"You wouldn't want to touch it," she said, keeping her eyes shut tight. "Would you?"

"Touch what?"

"My lump."

"No," he said. "When it's gone, I want to pretend it was never there."

Ruby's surgery was scheduled for 8 a.m. AT 7 a.m. they wheeled her into pre-surgery and gave her a mood elevator shot, but the operation was put off for an hour because Dr. Arco was called to an emergency. Ruby's euphoria wore off, yet she bore it quietly, stoically. She even had the presence of mind to take her mother's gold locket from her neck, and Sybil's diamond and sapphire wedding ring from her finger and give them to Max for safekeeping. He tried again to talk about the little girl on the bus, and how much she reminded him of herself, of the daughter they might still have, but he found it impossible to comfort Ruby in any way save by staring into her eyes and repeating, "I love you; I love you."

There were six patients crammed into the small pre-surgery room, including Ruby, all of them strapped to gurneys, all grievously ill, some of them smiling at each other vaguely, trying to reassure each other with their eyes. To Max they seemed incredibly brave, for surely some would not come out of this alive. Yet, in every case but one, he felt more revulsion than pity.

"Honey, if this doesn't work out," Ruby said, shaking her head apologetically, as they came to wheel her away, "tell Ned, tell him I'll always be watching over him. And I want you to know how much I love you. I love you more than anyone in the world, even more than . . ."

"Ned?" he said to himself, after her voice was lost in the bustle of the corridor. His own voice was lost as well, for he barely knew what he said, and couldn't bear to know.

"Your wife is in recovery now," Dr. Arco said, moving toward him nearly eight hours later, smiling tautly, wearily, still in his hospital green surgical outfit and paper shoes. "But the procedure wasn't easy. There's some damage to the muscles and tendons, I'm afraid, and there'll be a deep scar, an indentation in the skin, similar to a war wound. She'll probably have a slight limp, and she'll have to use a cane, possibly for the rest of her life. On the other hand, I think we did pretty damn well, under the circumstances. There was some distortion of major vessels, but I don't think they were invaded by the tumor. There might've been some spillage during the surgery, but I doubt it. Now, we won't be sure about any of this for another few months, maybe even years. And she's going to have to be monitored very closely. But all in all, Max, I'd say there's a better than even chance her bet paid off."

Fleeing outside with the news, into the pinkish tropical light and the heavy-laden air, smelling flowers too sweet, grass too green, fruit too ripe in the trees, Max carried his wife's good fortune like a burden of guilt. An hour ago, he had been scared half to death that he was going to lose her. And yet, somewhere deep inside, a little part of him had already begun to prepare for that eventuality.

Part III

Chapter Thirteen

The night after Max went back to California, Ruby threw a lavish champagne party for herself and Dr. Miguel. Wearing a lacy peignoir, she held court at her bedside, serenaded by a marimba band and the entire off-duty staff of the Instituto Cabo-Arco.

"Esperanza," they sang, at her request, and *"Cuando Caliente al Sol,* smiling down at her and swaying like Latins from the silver screen.

Later she drank too much, flirted shamelessly with Miguel's handsome associate, Francisco, and ended the evening with a sentimental speech in which she described her astonishment at having survived the operation, her growing wonder at the simple joys and sorrows of existence, and her deep feeling of gratitude to the brilliant man of vision who had saved her life.

"We've beaten all the odds," she told Dr. Arco's cheering staff a few days later, as they trundled her, and her wheelchair, onto the airport minivan, "and made fools of the *Yanqui* medical profession!"

And she felt much the same during all her month-long period of convalescence in Gold Hill, where she threw more bedside parties for herself and granted interviews to excited local reporters.

VALLEY CELEB CHEATS DEATH IN PANAMA

But once she was up on her feet again, in the early months of 1971, and life at Sand Canyon Ranch slowly returned to normal, her 60/40 odds against living the year out began to look less and less miraculous.

Then, as a precaution against addiction, Dr. Silverman made her cut back on her medication, and she began to experience pain.

Pain that weighed on her, wore her down, drained her body of energy.

And all the while she burned with a mental anguish that fed off itself: that the operation had failed, that the spots she saw before her eyes now would multiply until they blotted out the universe, that she would die, and leave her child without a mother.

She said nothing of this to her family or friends and managed with some difficulty to sustain her optimistic pose. Yet secretly, she began taking unnatural care of her left leg, pampering it, rubbing it down, shaving it, coating it with balms, as if it needed more attention than her right leg, as if it might suddenly go "poof!" and disappear.

At the same time, she had become fixated on the scar in her groin. Dr. Arco had said that it would resemble a war wound. But his description was understated. To Ruby it looked more like she had been skewered with a medieval pike dipped in human feces, shredded by shrapnel from an exploding cannonball, hit with a dum-dum shell from an AK-47. The scar seemed to her almost volcanic in its textures, colors, and contours, from the soft, damp, blue-black of its deep furrowed crater to the angry red and yellow of its cracked and peeling ridges. She could not leave off touching it, probing it, running her fingers over it.

Frightened, she confided in Dr. Silverman.

"Perfectly normal reactions," he said. "You've suffered deep trauma, both physical and mental. And these are the psychological aftereffects, the price you have to pay."

As the weeks went by, and summer came, some of the symptoms began to disappear, but they were almost immediately replaced by others. She feared that she would limp forever, that people would pity her, that the pain would never go away. She feared sex with Max, feared that it would hurt, that he would be repelled.

And always there was death. Not death in the abstract, but death as a palpable human presence, a figure in her dreams. *"Señor Mañana,"* she called him.

"It's best to try and keep active," Dr. Silverman said, at their next consultation. "You're letting it prey on your mind."

Reflecting on his advice, Ruby decided that perhaps it was time to get back into the home restoration business.

During her illness, Reno and Norman had allowed their partnership to lapse in all but name. Lonnie had failed to find another job, and Dominica was supporting him and the baby by working as a weekend cocktail waitress and Wednesday lunchtime fashion model at the Calico Inn. A renewal of interest in their common enterprise, Ruby surmised, would set everyone back on the right track.

Later, searching for bargains in the *Antelope Valley Ledger Gazette,* she came upon a headline: HILLARY BENNETT DIES. FILM STAR ONCE ADORED BY MILLIONS ALONE AT DEATH. HOME BEING AUCTIONED OFF FOR BACK TAXES.

At first, the news struck Ruby as merely poignant. "The actress' mansion, which fell into a state of disrepair in the last years of her life," the article said, "is not expected to go for more than a few thousand dollars." But the more she thought of it, the more fortuitous and symbolic it all seemed. She recalled Miss Bennett's advice to her, just before she left for Hollywood: "Keep your mouth shut, your eyes open, a price tag on everything including your privates, and don't take any wooden nickels."

From Ruby's present perspective, it seemed amazingly prescient and wise, and she wished she had listened better. And how fitting, somehow, that Miss Bennett's wonderful, fanciful old home, which had loomed so long and glamorously over Ruby's life, could now be purchased for a song.

She got her father on the phone at once. Intrigued by her idea, Reno called Norman. Norman rang his friend the auctioneer, who said the house would be open for inspection until the auction, and since nothing of value remained, its key was available to perspective bidders.

First thing next morning, just after she had seen eleven-year-old Ned off on the school bus, Ruby drove her old Nash Ambassador to the auctioneer's house in Lancaster, got the key, headed up Gold Hill Road to Anaverde Ridge, and pulled up at the same old rusting mailbox that she had noticed years ago. "Bennett," it still said on the side, though the stencil had faded almost past recognition.

The last time Ruby had stopped here she was with Max. She was eighteen years old, and they were on their way back from the motorcycle races in Newhall. Max did not ride motorcycles anymore, it occurred to her as she bounced up the overgrown driveway toward the decrepit mansion. He just fixed them at his garage. He was different in other ways as well. He had not touched her with those magic hands of his since the day she got back from Panama.

Ruby got out of her station wagon and slammed the door. The sound carried far on that cold, gray, February day, on that high, windy ridge with the valley spread out below her all smooth and ashen white.

Slogging around the wide, six-acre yard on her cane, she discovered that the house was in even worse condition than the newspaper reported. The fake thatch roof had caved in over the garage. Someone had practiced target shooting on the front bay window. Across the rear of the place, the white mortar had fallen away between the supporting timbers, exposing its wallboard innards. And the garden had been invaded by sand and sage.

Rapping at the back door with the metal handle of her cane, receiving no reply, Ruby let herself in quietly. Trying the light switch, she found the electricity off, and had to wait an anxious moment until her eyes adjusted to the gloom. She made her way into the kitchen stealthily as if she might disturb the spirits of the place. And she found that it had been left just as it was at the time of Miss Bennett's death, reeking of rancid cooking oil, with dirty dishes moldering in the sink. Avoiding the rear bathroom—Miss Bennett had died in the bath, the newspaper said, and had not been discovered until after she had begun to decompose—Ruby hastened into the dining room. There she found a rickety card table set for two, with an empty Dannon Blueberry Yoghurt carton centered on one white paper plate, and an empty green plastic bowl marked "Purina Gourmet Dogfood" on the other. The living room was unchanged from her last visit. Yellowing newspapers, old *LIFE* magazines and piles of clothing cluttered the corners, and dust had drifted thick on the tattered, antique furniture, the stained and moth-eaten Persian carpets.

In Miss Bennett's enormous timbered boudoir, the four-poster bed was unmade; its blue velvet canopy hung down from a jagged tear across the center, and it listed steeply toward the headboard. Old shoes, unclean panties and bras, empty yoghurt cartons, and beer bottles lay strewn about the warped parquet floor. The fireplace was full of ancient ashes, soggy dogshit, and last week's rainwater. A ripped and discolored Art Deco print of Hillary in a black Egyptian wig, with movie set pyramids in the background, hung off-kilter on the wall.

Yet, snooping about in the bedroom's voluminous walk-in closet by the light of a candle stub, looking in places a county sheriff's deputy would never think of—behind a suspiciously neat stack of old shoe boxes, for instance—Ruby was thrilled to discover a small door that opened onto a musty storage space that contained a treasure trove of the old lady's personal effects.

There were boxes of legal documents: She was born—wouldn't you know it?—Velma Schwartz, in Williamsburg, Brooklyn, on January 21, 1897, to Abraham and Shulamite, naturalized American citizens from Szczebrzeszyn, Poland.

There were dozens of diaries, all of them brutally frank, some with graphic accounts of affairs with Rudolph Valentino and Douglas Fairbanks. There were stacks of personal mementos from movies she appeared in (a lock of Johnny Mack Brown's hair, the buckle off Tom Mix's cowboy belt, a gold slave bracelet from *Cleopatra*). There were studio publicity shots of a beautiful young Hillary at the peak of her form. There was a partially completed autobiographical manuscript that she had started with a ghost writer named Marvin Stanley back in 1952. And there were albums and albums full of browning snapshots, each scrupulously numbered, arranged in chronological order, and described or commented upon later in Miss Bennett's crimped but rather elegant handwriting.

> *"My debut on Broadway with the Gibson Girls. The costume is borrowed from a (considerably larger) ex-dancer and doesn't fit, so I've stuffed the bra and top hat with cotton and pinned the black tails and shorts all around and I'm terrified of suddenly finding myself exposed naked on stage."*

Ruby spent hours in the Tudor that morning, and found out many other marvelous things, not only about Miss Bennett, but about the house as well. Caught up in the romance of the place, she set her cane aside and sat stiffly, painfully, on the floor. Surrounded by dust, cobwebs, dying candlelight and the dead woman's most precious possessions, she began jotting down her thoughts on a yellow legal pad she had brought along. They came quickly, categorizing and outlining themselves automatically in her head, and before she knew it, she had written a clean page of second draft:

> *"The Bennett house was designed by one of America's foremost architects for his mistress, a famous ballerina named Nadia Alexandrovna. Anna Pavlova and Isadora Duncan spent weekends there and, it is said, danced together before the magnificent stone fireplace in its elegant Tudor living room. The garden of the home was laid out by Leyland Spence, one of the greatest landscape architects of the era, its trees and shrubbery imported at great expense from every corner of the world. Pheasants and peacocks roamed free in the yard. Doves roosted in the trees. Then, only two years after taking possession, Nadia Alexandrovna died of the consumption that had brought her to the high desert country in the first place. And Hillary Bennett, who was apparently yet another of the architect's mistresses, was given title to the property. Though Miss Bennett lived in the Tudor house for the remaining forty years of her life, and rarely if ever left its immediate environs,*

> she was never happy there, and claimed until the end of her life to be haunted by the ghost of the ballerina."

Reading it over, Ruby thought it damned good copy for a former Home & Real Estate columnist on the *Antelope Valley Ledger-Gazette*. And it came to her—like a ray of sunlight piercing the dark timbered ceiling, the leaky thatched roof, like an illumination from the heavens—that no one else knew about this wealth of biographical material, that she could write it up herself. Then, it occurred to her that anyone with a key could do the same, could rifle through Miss Bennett's private records, taking notes, and put them all together as a "definitive biography." The notion seemed to her grossly unfair because no other writer would have her own deep sympathy for Hillary Bennett, her understanding as a fellow actress, her feeling for the desert where the actress chose to spend the last forty years of her life.

It was then that Ruby decided to remove Miss Bennett's papers, folders, and important personal books, so that they might remain in safe hands no matter what happened at the auction.

She got her brother to help her, and they looted it that very afternoon, hauled two great loads of it to Sand Canyon Ranch, carried it down to the cellar, and hid it behind a pile of old unwanted drawings that Max's father had left behind when he went back to Germany.

After she had paid Lonnie for his help and sent him on his way, she could not resist going back down again to her treasure trove in the cellar. In the envelope where Hillary kept her birth certificate, she found a gold ring that she had overlooked before. It was a tiny ring, with the scrolled initials V.S., and to Ruby it seemed extraordinarily precious. She slipped it on the gold chain around her neck, where she also wore her mother's locket.

For a week after that, Ruby worked alone, organizing, cataloguing, hauling out stuff she would not need and burning it in the incinerator. And all the time that she was working, she was thinking about how she was going to write her book. The research part would be easy, she thought. Aside from diaries, journals, photo albums, and bound correspondence, the old lady had kept copies of every gossip column, newspaper article, movie review, or book ever written about her. So, it wasn't the meat of the story that bothered her so much, it was how to approach her subject, how to get into it. For days, she agonized over the question. Eventually she concluded that she must bring *herself* into it. She must begin the book with a preface, she thought, a description of the lonely little girl that she herself once was, her dreams of Hollywood, the house of the old movie star that loomed above the insane asylum where she was raised. That would lead her smoothly into Hillary Bennett's story. And Hillary Bennett's story would virtually tell itself:

"As a starstruck teenager I used to look up at the mountains above my desert home and see the Tudor mansion of Hillary Bennett, splendidly alone and unassailable, on barren Anaverde Ridge. In the dog days of August one year, I borrowed my father's pickup truck, drove up the ridge and into Miss Bennett's yard.

"'Go away,' she shouted from behind her blinds. 'I don't want to see anyone.'

"'Oh please,' I said, 'I want to be an actress too, and I'd like you to tell me about Hollywood.'

"For some reason, perhaps my youth and naivete, Miss Bennett gave in eventually and treated me to a tour of her dilapidated mansion. Having gotten my foot in the door, I patiently cultivated this pathologically shy and reclusive former queen of the silent screen. Driving up to visit her almost daily, bearing gifts of food and drink, magazines, and newspapers, I gained her trust, and encouraged her to tell me stories of her life. Our secret friendship blossomed and grew through the summer and fall and on into the following year. In time, she informally 'adopted' me by slipping her gold baby ring on a chain around my neck, and thereafter she made me call her 'Mother.'

"I never became the actress that I'd dreamed of being, but our very close familial relationship continued for many years, with Miss Bennett aiding and advising me on all my major life choices, until I was married and had a child and was stricken with cancer. Then, near the end of her life, when I had to go abroad for treatment, and it appeared that we might never see each other again, Miss Bennett presented me—'in recompense for your years of devotion'—with her diaries, albums, and mementos, charging me to write her story someday, so that the truth might be told. Now, having survived my bout with cancer just as Miss Bennett promised I would, after taking her advice and refusing to have my leg amputated, I am fulfilling my obligation to her. This is her story. This is how she told it to me. This is the way she saw herself."

Polishing up her handiwork after her first day's work, Ruby was quite pleased. She liked this approach to her subject. Even if it wasn't literally true, it was true in spirit. Sybil would surely appreciate it, though Max was probably too literal-minded. But she wouldn't bother with Max now, she thought. First, she would write the book, and worry about explaining when it was done.

The auction in February 1972 was livelier than Ruby had anticipated. Attracted by the legend of Hillary Bennett, a great crowd of people gathered at the house on Anaverde Ridge, many from Los Angeles, and the bidding rose swiftly beyond the means of all but a few big spenders.

In the end, a group of Pasadena real estate investors placed the highest bid. Yet, by this time Ruby was not so interested in Miss Bennett's house as in her biography, and the loss only troubled her on her brother Lonnie's account, for he still had no job prospects.

Later that same week, Ruby surprised Max at the job and invited him out to lunch.

"What's the occasion?" he hollered from under the car he was working on.

"Oh, nothing special," she said. "Go on, clean yourself up."

Awaiting her spouse, Ruby ignored Charlie and Gil—who were too busy to care—and went snooping about the garage. It really wasn't much to look at when you thought about it. Just this big, old, former Chevron station sitting on a corner in a cotton-woody residential neighborhood, with a couple of vacant lots alongside where they parked their merchandise. They'd had some trouble with their neighbors when they first moved in, as there was a good deal of fear about noise and the "motorcycle element." But it turned out that the boys who rode Triumphs were a completely different breed from those who rode Harley-Davidsons, and the drivers of British sportscars happened to be some of the most respectable professional people in the valley. Max and Charlie had defused any further talk by contributing regularly to the neighborhood beautification campaign.

"Bauer & Gonçalves, Experts in fine British Road Cars and Motorcycles" said the elegant little sign hanging outside the garage. And though it sounded rather grand, it was still basically just a three-man operation, with an easy division of labor. Gil, who had a fast mouth and wasn't much with his hands, ran the sales office, Charlie repaired bikes, Max worked on sportscars, and when they got busy in any particular area, they all pitched in to help. They hired an elderly lady named Mrs. Cheney to come around every couple of weeks and handle the books, and they used to have a Black kid named Rufus clean the place up, but he had joined the Navy and hadn't been replaced. As a result, Ruby could see, the office was a mess, the garage floor was cluttered with tools and rags, the bathrooms were a disgrace, the cars and bikes could do with a good wash and wax, and the place was hurting for an employee to handle the maintenance end. Ruby figured it might as well be Lonnie as anyone else.

"So, where you taking me?" Max wanted to know when he met her out front. He had tried to straighten himself up, and his corduroy pants, turtleneck sweater, and leather jacket were clean, but his fingernails were a sight, and his hair was sticking straight out on end.

"To the Calico Inn," she said, reaching up to smooth his hair.

The Calico Inn was once the Gold Hill City Hall. Before that it had been the administration building of the old Calico Mine. Red brick, three stories high, with wide ornamental green gables and a green tarpaper roof that recalled an old railroad station, it was perched at the top of the conical hills which had given the town its name, on narrow Surgener Street, and looked quaint to Southern Californians raised on modern ranch-style stuff. So, a couple of years before, perhaps inspired by Ruby's success with her Italian Gothic, a group of local businessmen had bought the place and fixed it up inside. They sanded and polyurethaned the scuffed hardwood floors and the ceiling beams, exposed the brick walls, dug out the fireplace from behind the gas stove, brought in a prefabricated Victorian style bar from Carson City, Nevada, and re-did all the rooms with calico curtains, bundling beds, patchwork quilts and other frontier paraphernalia. They set red and white checkered tables out in the dining room, put in a modern stainless-steel kitchen, imported a chef from Santa Barbara, and within a month of its opening the inn had become a brilliant success, the destination of tour buses from Los Angeles and San Bernardino, the vibrant heart of Gold Hill. The Lion's Club held its meetings there. The Jaycees had their dances there. And every Wednesday, the ladies' dress shop merchants of the area put on a lunchtime fashion show.

The show was extraordinarily well-attended, particularly by middle-aged men, who came to partake of the generous luncheon specials and ogle the lovely young amateur models.

The hostess saw Ruby and Max to a table near the fireplace. They ordered ribs and salad, with a beer for Max and a glass of red wine for Ruby. Max seemed uneasy, so she tried to loosen him up with small talk about Ned. Max was still bridling because Ned had quit the Little League last summer.

"I mean, shit, sport is the one thing we got in common. Hell, he'd rather bang on that piano of his than toss a ball around with me."

"Maybe you ought to spend more time with him, Max."

"What time have I got? That damn garage takes all my time."

"Look at it this way," Ruby said, and tried to make him see that Ned's emerging artistic talents—he was a promising watercolorist as well as a musician—would be far more meaningful to him in the long run. "Anyway, you should be delighted," she added. "He takes after your side of the family."

"What makes you think that would delight me?" he asked.

The fashion show began, and the models started parading across the floor in bathing suits and sport clothes. Dominica walked out, not a particularly graceful model, not even in comparison to the local junior college girls who had preceded her. She seemed awkward, unsure of herself, almost rustic, as she strutted her stuff across the room to the Rolling Stones' "Satisfaction." Her long, curly, black hair had been layered and permed to a frizz. She wore a tacky, fluorescent-pink, beach dress with the mid-section cut out. The thing was so short it cut across her uppermost thigh, so flimsy her purple nipples showed clearly through the fabric. Ruby was embarrassed for her, and immediately began planning to make her over.

But then she noticed her effect on the men: Long after Dominica had made her way back to the dressing room, they were still in a state of distraction, coughing nervously, wiping their sweaty brows with their napkins.

Only Max seemed oblivious.

"Honey, the reason I wanted to talk to you," Ruby said, when the fashion show was over, "I feel kind of guilty about my brother. I brought him up here on the promise of a job, and now I've lost the Bennett place."

"That's not your fault."

"I know, but I still feel kind of responsible."

"Lonnie's a grown man. He can look out for himself."

"And, to tell the truth, Max, I don't like Dominica working in this place."

"Why not?"

"It can only lead to trouble."

"Well, I can see that," he said, with only the tiniest trace of irony. "So, where do I fit in?"

"I was hoping that you could offer him something at the garage."

"At the garage?" Jesus Christ, honey, your brother is a complete fuck-up."

"I know, I know, but I was hoping that you could find something... Cleanup. Anything."

"Well, I guess I could, if I really had to. But Charlie's not gonna like it."

"I'll get Juanita to work on him."

"You do that," Max said. "I'll need all the help I can get."

Ruby spoke to Juanita, as she'd promised, and Max was able to talk Charlie into giving Lonnie a job on a trial basis.

Yet, almost as soon as Lonnie went to work, he started calling Ruby to complain. He was being given only the most menial tasks, he said. He was not allowed to deal with customers or do mechanical work. He was not trusted to handle the cash register...

By then, however, Ruby was too busy to do anything more than hold his hand, for her book had taken all her energy and imagination.

It had become symbolic to her, on a very deep level.

It was her talisman against death.

One morning, just after she had fed Ned and Max breakfast and seen them off, she went down and cleared a little place for herself in the corner of the cellar. Struggling with her gimpy leg, she rigged up a table with a pair of sawhorses and an old door, carried down her typewriter, and switched on the hanging overhead lightbulb.

Then she started writing.

It didn't bother her that she seemed to be writing more about herself than Hillary Bennett. She just let the words flow. They came fast and easy, and she did not stop until it was time to pick Ned up at the bus.

"I've decided to write a book," she said to Max, over dinner that night.

"Oh really?" he said. He thought she was joking. "What about?"

"I'm not exactly sure yet. I'll let you know when I'm finished."

Chapter Fourteen

In the dream that Max had a few weeks later, he lived alone with Ruby on the ranch. She got sick again and lost one leg, then the other. She died and he had to dig a grave for her on the ridge above the house, had to tear down the old chicken coop for wood and build her a coffin, drag it up all by himself, and deliver her funeral oration to the wind. Then, just as he was about ready to lower her into the ground, a faint rumbling came from inside the coffin, as if from a distant storm. Louder and louder, it got. The coffin started to shake, rattle, jump up and down. Cracks appeared on the surface, from which smoke and tongues of yellow flame escaped. Straining upward, as if from some superhuman force, the hinges shattered with a sound like a double-barreled shotgun blast and burst open. The coffin lid flew around and hit the ground, raising a great storm of dust that swirled into the air and settled on Max's black mourning clothes, coating them white as flour. Inside the coffin, on a bed of cushioned blue satin, Ruby lay pink and warm and round, her arms folded on her naked breasts, a single white rose in her red hair. Miraculously, her amputated legs had regenerated while she was sleeping, and her form was again immensely pleasing.

Her pale lashes fluttered open. Her eyes, reflecting the sky, focused slowly, and then locked with his own. She licked her lips as if from thirst. She smiled, raised her arms, and beckoned to him seductively.

"Come," she said. "You promised you'd never leave me."

And he woke with a start.

Judging by the quality of light—a watery blue playing upon the ceiling, a single moted shaft of fluorescent white piercing the Italian blue drapery—it was still early morning. Yet, feeling for Ruby beside him, he found the bed smooth and unrumpled. Thinking back, trying to discover a reason why this should be, he recalled that last night over dinner, over wine, she had given out certain subtle, unmistakable signals. And he had wanted to respond but found that nearly five months after her surgery it was still not easy. So, he looked for a second bottle of wine and when he couldn't find one, he stretched, and yawned, made a great pretense of sleepiness, and headed guiltily for bed.

Ruby was by no means out of danger yet, he told himself on his way up the stairs. She still hobbled around painfully on a cane. As soon as the doctors gave her a clean bill of health, he would start responding normally again. But he was kidding himself and he knew it. And in bed alone, he asked himself how it had happened. Not overnight, he knew, and not just since the operation. It was nobody's "fault." In fact, it was the result of a surprising paradox in their natures: Max, the quiet, careful, plodding one, had a much stronger sex drive than his volatile wife. It was as if, in reaction to the example of her mother, Ruby feared becoming a tramp, and the fear grew worse as she got older. On the other hand, Max was not vain enough to suppose that with another man, another marriage, Ruby might have responded more frequently and ardently. Perhaps it was because they had grown up together, almost. They were too close, like brother and sister.

Back when their sex life had begun to show the first signs of abatement, Max was very hurt. He looked at this wife, whom he loved with all his heart, and he deeply regretted it. But he felt there was nothing he could do or say. It wouldn't do to beg for more, since he only wanted what she freely gave. Watching her, loving her, desiring her, he saw in her eyes that she did not crave him in the same way that he craved her, that her strongest energies were elsewhere, focused on other things. And it broke his heart that he could not have her as she could have him, body and soul. Yet he would never dream of leaving her. He couldn't. She was his life.

So, in the end, only one solution presented itself: He began to seek outside what he did not get at home. He assumed that Ruby, knowing his physical wants, would understand his need to compensate, and took her silence on the matter—when, holed up with some hot little barmaid or divorcee in a Palmdale motel, he would phone with feeble late-night excuses—as tacit approval. And all through that first year of his wandering, right up until the operation, he had believed that in her most secret heart she preferred things that way. They still loved each other, he told himself, but it was not really about sex anymore. It was about their son and their home and their life together.

Then, not long after she got back from Panama, Ruby changed. Suddenly she was the aggressor, she was the one who could not get enough, and she could not figure out why Max wasn't always ready for it. But the truth was, he had kind of gotten used to things the way they were.

Rising naked from the bed, preceded by a stiff piss hard-on, Max strode to the window, smelling his own stale sweat, tasting his own bad breath. Then he flung open the drapes, as if to open his eyes after sleep, as if to clear his head of bad dreams, as if to discover on that vast panorama of canyon, desert, and mountains before him the whereabouts of his missing wife.

It was a Sunday morning in mid-March, about 8 a.m., judging by the height of the sun. A heavy storm had blown in off the North Pacific during the night. And though it had dropped only an inch or so of rain on the desert, it had soaked the hills all around, topping the flood control dam, filling the dry creek bottom, preparing the ground for a rich crop of wildflowers in the month ahead. Snow had fallen on the San Francisquitos, but it quit abruptly at 4000 feet, on a line as straight and true as a county road, just above Max's blossoming almond orchards. Wispy bright clouds, milked of moisture, still clung about the peaks. And the sky was so clear, the mountains so white, the shadows so deep and long, that you could pick out an individual ponderosa pine tree on a ridge seventeen miles away.

Leaving the window, throwing on an old flannel bathrobe, he hastened down the hall to Ned's room. The boy was asleep, but frowning fiercely, clutching a book that Ruby had given him for his birthday, *The Yearling*. The reading light was still on above his head, he was shivering under a single flannel blanket, and it was clear that no one had thought to tuck him in last night. Max rarely concerned himself with such matters, but it was unlike Ruby to forget. Ned often slept restlessly at night, rising at odd hours, padding into their room, swearing that someone was peeking in his window, someone was hiding in his closet, someone was under his bed. And he would settle down only after Ruby had put him to bed, several times, with songs and stories and endless reassurances. Recalling his own childhood, when a delicious dreamless sleep had descended upon him the instant he hit the pillow, Max was heartsick to think that Ned had so little peace. Basically, he was such a smart, lively, good-looking kid for his age, with natural physical coordination. But under it all, he was the sensitive type, and it would not be easy for him. A loner by nature, he had trouble making friends and keeping them. So, he spent whole days locked up in his room, reading books, writing in his diary. If the truth be known, Max thought tenderly, the kid is a little weird. Ruby had taught him to dance, and he used to hate it when he was little, but now he would twirl about his room for hours, with no radio on, keeping time to a rhythm of his own.

Gently pulling another blanket over his son, Max went downstairs, where he found the dining table spotted with wine and specked with garlic breadcrumbs, the kitchen floor slick with spilled olive oil, the cooking range splattered with red spaghetti sauce, and last night's dirty dishes piled high on the kitchen counter.

At this point he began to grow alarmed, for Ruby was normally the most fastidious of housekeepers. And he went calling her name, unavailingly, from room to room. Then he thought of the cellar.

The cellar was the oldest part of the house, the only portion of the original house that had survived the earthquake, yet they had rarely used it in the past, and he wasn't even sure what was down there anymore.

Thrusting his cold bare feet into a pair of rubber 'zories' that he found in the kitchen closet, Max headed out the back door and gingerly picked his way down the puddled garden path. Rounding the corner of the house, he noticed that the weathered old cellar door had been pulled open, and he could hear the hollow echoing clatter of Ruby's Smith-Corona coming from deep inside. Relieved, he tiptoed down the stairs, pushed open the squeaky inner door and halted for a moment while his eyes grew used to the dim light.

Across the bare cement floor, under a single hanging hundred watt bulb, surrounded by diaries, photo albums, yellowing hand-written notes, mounds of crumpled paper, and a little portable electric heater, Ruby—in a pair of Max's heavy work socks, the same blue woolen dress she had worn last night at dinner, an old Toluca sweater, and one of Ned's stocking caps—was seated at a door-and-sawhorse desk, pounding away at her battered typewriter as if her life depended on it. Chin up, neck stiff, eyes narrowed, she seemed to be focusing on some object high above her, and infinitely far away, as if it were there that she found the words that flew from her fingers so fast they were only a blur on the moving page.

Watching her—skin mottled blue with the cold, hair sticking out every which way from beneath her cap, brow furrowed, teeth clenched, jaw grinding, back rigid, feet wrapped tightly around the legs of her fold-up chair—Max was struck by her intensity, an intensity so concentrated, so ferocious, so all-consuming that she had apparently not even noticed his arrival. And he felt the same ambivalence he always felt when he discovered a new dimension to his wife. On the one hand, he was proud of Ruby, amazed by her ability to summon pages from the void, while on the other he found himself more than a little distrustful of her sudden involvement and absorption in something so remote from him and Ned.

"So, *there* you are!" he called cheerily from the doorway, and he half-expected her to jump at the sound of his voice. Instead, she kept right on typing, with no perceptible change in her expression. "You been down here all night, honey?"

"Uh-huh."

"How come?" he asked, approaching her across the littered floor, smelling her before he reached her- first her perfume, *"Shalimar,"* which he'd always loved, then a faint whiff of nervous sweat in the chill air.

Reaching her side, laying a hand gently on her shoulder, he noticed the heavy, brass-tipped cane that she had leaned against the desk, and glanced surreptitiously at her last written line: *"To know suffering is to know death: to know death is to understand the meaning of life."*

"How come?" he asked again, thinking, *Now where in hell'd she come up with that?*

"I'm on a roll," she explained, resting her fingers on the keys for a moment, looking up at him over her shoulder.

"Say, that's great, but what're all these old papers and stuff?"

Her expression, at first almost radiant, turned hurt and reproving.

"Max," she sighed, stretching, arching her back, craning her neck so the white tassel of her green and white stocking cap rested on his heart, "you wouldn't believe me if I told you."

"How about giving it a try?"

"I'd rather keep it to myself for now," she said, shaking her head, covering the typescript with her hand. "Then, it'll be a surprise."

"Whatever's right," he said. "When you coming up?"

"Not for a while."

As they were chatting, Max noticed some wooden packing crates in the corner. The sides were stenciled FRITZ BAUER, and they were full of his father's old unwanted drawings. One of the boxes had fallen from the stack and overturned, spilling its contents onto the rough cement floor. Only a single drawing was facing upwards. It was a pen-and-ink of an amiable German Expressionist lion, wooly as an angora goat, that Max had hated ever since he discovered it there shortly after his father's departure for Europe. It occurred to him now that the reason he had always hated this lion was not because his father's astrological sign happened to be Leo, nor because the smile on its clever feline face bore a faint resemblance to that of its creator, but that Fritz, in his attempt at self-caricature, had been too kind. He had seen only the affable front that he sometimes affected but captured none of the cold self-absorption beneath. The truth was, Max had rarely been impressed by his father's work, and even the mild enthusiasm he felt for some of his early, more colorful, oil paintings, had diminished with time. The world of art, conversely, had come to appreciate Fritz Bauer more through the years. Not a month ago, Sybil had received invitations to a retrospective of his work at a prestigious New York gallery. Later, she had read in ART WORLD that the show was acclaimed a *"succes d'estime."*

Fritz had attended, apparently, but he hadn't bothered to fly out to California.

"Ruby, what're we gonna do about breakfast?" Max asked, redirecting his attention from the packing crates.

"Breakfast?"

"Food, food!" he said, clutching his stomach, rolling his eyes, parodying a famine-stricken native. But comedy did not come natural to Max, and his effort fell flat.

"Can't you fix it yourself? I mean, it's no big thing."

"Well, I guess. But who's gonna walk Ned to the bus?"

"The bus? It's Sunday, Max. Why don't you take him for a ride or something?"

"Oh, all right," he agreed at last, quite generously, he felt. "I'll take him up to the snow."

"You're a sweetheart!" she called after him as he went out the door. And then he could hear her typewriter start up again.

Upstairs, Max had a brainstorm. Since he was not much for cooking and wouldn't dream of starting the day without a hot and hearty meal, he phoned his mother and asked if he and Ned could come over and discuss an important financial matter.

Sybil took the hint and invited them for breakfast.

She came to the door wearing paint-splattered tennis shoes, faded Levis, a pearl-gray artist's smock, turquoise earrings, and a long-toothed grin. She was up in her mid-fifties now, and as she got older, she got leaner and taller, her stride longer and looser. Well-weathered, with a dark, desert tan and a nose that grew fiercer and more hawklike with the years, she left an impression of hard-earned wisdom, and the cool, dry self-possession that comes after a woman of her class and profession has opted out of the social and sexual wars. A few weeks before, when she learned that her stepmother had died, leaving her out of the will, she had taken to wearing her hair done up in braids again, German-style, the way Fritz used to like it.

"Come in, fellows," she said, leading them through to her kitchen, "I've made something you're going to like." And sat them down to a feast of sausage and eggs, buckwheat pancakes and maple syrup, hot chocolate, and *cafe au lait*.

"What I came to talk about, Mom," Max said, after Sybil had served up a mountain of flapjacks and was able to sit down with them at last, "I was down in the cellar talking to Ruby this morning—boy, you oughta see the way she's been writing, got her mind completely off that other thing—and I saw some of dad's old drawings. And I got to wondering. You think they'll ever be worth anything?"

"I doubt it, dear. You have to be super well-known before your throwaways are valuable."

"Too bad," he said. "We're always so damn short around here."

"Yes, darling, we are," Sybil said, glancing at Ned. She didn't like to discuss finances around children. "But who knows? Ruby may bring in something with this book of hers."

"You really think so, Mom?"

"It's just this feeling I've got. She's putting so much energy into it, and she's got such a terrific imagination."

"You know what it's about?"

She hesitated, shrugged.

"Me neither," he said.

"I know!" Ned chirped, polishing off the remainder of his hotcakes, licking his lips of maple syrup.

"You know what?"

"I know what it's about."

"So why don't you tell us?"

"It's a secret."

"But you can tell Grandma and me, can't you?"

"*Don't* Max," Sybil said. "Don't encourage the child to divulge a confidence."

Max yielded to his mother as a matter of course, but on the way back to his own place he began to suspect that she was in on the secret too, and the only outsider was himself.

Diligently fulfilling his new role as Sunday parent, Max saw to it that his son was dressed in woolen socks, rubber boots, jeans, turtleneck sweater, quilted jacket, mittens, and a fur-lined hunting cap. Then he loaded his little, green, plastic, supermarket sled into the pickup truck and drove him up Sand Canyon Road. They hit the snow just below the dam, and by the time they had labored up around the switchback curves and reached the pass, it was nearly knee deep. But the temperature was already ten degrees above freezing, the sun was nearly halfway up the sky, and the snow had begun to melt. At the summit, at the base of a high, gently rolling slope, Max pulled off the blacktop and parked at the end of a long line of cars, pickups, and RV vehicles. Above them, the white smooth hills were crawling with sledders, skiers, and tobogganists, smeared with the vivid reds and blues and yellows of their nylon parkas. Max noticed his partner,

Charlie Gonçalves, among them, towing a pair of orange plastic sleds up the hill, followed by his two oldest boys, Buddy, and Mike.

Giggling with excitement, Ned ran out into the snowbank by the side of the road, grabbed up a handful of dirty snow, and packed it into a hard solid ball.

"Watch out, Daddy, watch out!" he yelled, feinting with it, laughing to see his father duck and dodge snowballs that had not been thrown yet.

When Ned finally decided to launch his missile, he did it with astonishing power and accuracy, timing it to catch his quarry completely by surprise. And Max thought bitterly again, as he scrambled desperately to avoid it, what a magnificent Little League pitcher the kid had made, and what a crying shame it was that he had quit.

"Wham!" the snowball hit him square between the shoulder blades, and some of it went down his neck.

"Okay, boy," he hollered, scooping snow on the run, chasing his son down the culvert. "Now you're in for it!"

But Ned was fast and strong for his age. He hit the opposite bank of the culvert at a dead run, scrambled up the icy wall on his hands and knees, squirmed nimbly out of his father's grip, and came up barreling full tilt across the snowy flats on the other side, hurdling obstacles, weaving like a broken-field runner. Huffing and puffing, regretting his five cigars a day, Max doggedly pursued him, and it was all he could do to catch him. Finally, he managed to get a foot in between the boy's legs and trip him up. Ned landed rolling and laughing, and effortlessly regained his feet. He eluded his father again, but immediately stumbled over a snow-covered boulder and fell on his face. Max caught him with his last gasp and, while the boy squealed and kicked and trembled in delight, plastered his face with snow.

Later, on the ridge where the snow dazzled, the shadows lay dark, and the air was tart and chill as cider, they stood for a moment beside a pack of Cub Scouts and their leader, squinting into the wind. Off to the right and some fifteen hundred feet below them, Sand Canyon Reservoir lay flat and bright as a mirror. To the left, above and beyond jagged San Francisquito Gorge, the spiny Sierra Pelona shone, shaggy with frosted evergreens, steamy with melting snow. Across the ridge behind them, Charlie and his boys hollered and waved, and made their way over the saddle to join them.

Charlie had put on a good deal of weight in the past few years, mostly in the gut, and he came blowing like an ox through the snow, towing the sleds. But his fleshy aquiline face had retained something of its old, rugged charm, and he was still a success with the ladies. His boys were fraternal twins, very dark and curly-haired and Latin-looking. But they resembled each other only in their instincts, which were incredibly well-developed for kids their age, and largely anti-social. Buddy was short and fat, a crybaby and cunning teacher's pet. Mike was big and dumb, a loudmouth and bully. A symbiosis of brains and brawn, tirelessly warlike and venal, they were virtually unassailable as a pair, and Ned avoided them whenever he could.

"Hey, you boys are extending your range!" Max said heartily, clapping his partner on the back. "Haven't seen you up this way, Charlie, since you used to run goats up Portal Ridge."

Charlie joined in Max's banter only tepidly at first.

They'd had their disagreements lately, sometimes over the issue of Japanese products versus British, and whether to switch or not (Max for the Brits, Charlie for the Japs), but mostly over Lonnie's presence on the job. Ruby's bro never did anything right, couldn't take orders, and had a smart mouth. To make things worse, he was always barbing at Charlie. Taunted by a stranger in his own garage, Charlie had warned Max more than once that Lonnie had to go.

But today, thank God, Charlie had no intention of spoiling the fun with warmed-over talk from the job, and after he got over his initial wariness, he turned positively garrulous.

"All right, boys!" he cried, smacking his hands together and rubbing them vigorously. "You ready for the hill?"

"Yeah! Yeah!"

"You betcha! You betcha!"

"So, what're you waitin' for?"

"Yeah, come on!" Max joined in. "Line those sleds up. Last one down's a rotten egg!"

"Awwwwwright! On your marks, get set, go!" Charlie yelled, and the boys shoved off as fast as they could, Ned and Mike neck-and-neck, fat little Buddy lagging.

The snow was soft and wet, and it hindered them at first. Only slowly did they build up momentum. Then, about fifteen yards out, the incline dropped off suddenly, and soon they were flying.

"Wheeeeee!" Max could hear them yell and felt a vicarious thrill. Fritz had never bothered taking him up to the snow, and this was something he had missed.

Halfway down the slope, slicing through the slush at a furious clip, Ned and Mike hit a hump. They flew up, smacked into each other in mid-air, and went tumbling head-over-heels into a snowbank, while Buddy succeeded in maneuvering around them and guiding his sled to the finish.

Max and Charlie slogged down the hill, fearing an injury. But by the time they reached the boys, they had already managed to extract themselves from the drift.

"You all right, kids?"

"Yeah, we're all right," Ned said, giggling, shaking the snow off himself.

But Mike didn't seem nearly so happy.

"You stupid shit," he said to Ned, while their fathers, silently agreeing to let the boys settle their own differences, maintained a neutral distance. "How come you run into me?"

"I didn't run into you. You ran into me."

"Bullshit!"

"You did!"

"Wanna make something out of it?"

"Naw," said Ned, and started for his dad.

Embarrassed, and conscious that this was his business partner, his oldest friend, and sometime enemy, who was standing beside him on the hill, Max shook his head and said, "Don't come to me, Ned. You gotta learn to fight your own battles."

"Don't wanna fight," Ned said, sullenly, and started down toward the car.

"Let me tell you something, son," Max said, catching up to him, grabbing him by the arm, marching him back up the hill. "Sometimes you have to fight whether you like it or not."

"Why?" Ned asked, as if it were the most sensible question in the world.

"You gotta be a man," Max intoned, repeating things that he had heard when he was young, not from his own father, who called himself a pacifist, but from Pete Gonçalves and the dads of other kids he had grown up with around Gold Hill. "You gotta learn how to defend yourself."

They were facing Mike now. He wasn't over an inch or two taller than Ned, but he was far too stupid for a moment's self-doubt.

"You still want to fight, Mike?" Max asked.

"Never known him to pass one up," said Charlie.

"That right, Mike?"

"You betcha."

"Okay," said Max. His blood was rising. He wanted to hurt someone himself. He hadn't felt this way since he was a kid. "Go get him, Ned!"

"Dad, can't you see? I just don't want to fight."

"Get over there and fight, kid, or I swear I'll never respect you again."

Reluctantly, Ned walked up to the bigger boy.

"What if I apologize?"

"I'll apologize your ass, you stupid little fuck," Mike said, to his father's everlasting delight, and swung, catching Ned upside the ear with a tremendous roundhouse right.

Ned went down in the snow, his ear bleeding, but he was up again in a flash and bounding down the hill, wild-eyed, quick as a deer.

"Chickenshit! Chickenshit!"

Following his son down through the soggy snow, recalling the smirk on Charlie's face when Ned had run, Max felt almost as if the cowardice were his own. He recovered the sled and slammed it into the bed of the pickup truck. Then, climbing into the cab, he found the boy curled up on the seat in the fetal position, whimpering like a baby.

"Get up! Sit up straight!" he snarled, whacking him hard on the buttock with the backside of his hand. "You ever run from a fight again, boy, and you're gonna have me to fight next."

Partway down Sand Canyon Road, though, Max began to look at the episode from his wife and mother's point of view. Began to feel like a villain. And he hated to be the villain.

"I tell you what, Ned. Let's just forget it for now," he said, patting him awkwardly on the arm. "Let's just shake and be friends, okay? I don't think we been spending enough time together, here lately. You been around the women too much. Your mom gives you stuff to read, your grandma gives you drawing lessons and piano lessons, but nobody teaches you how to fight. So, you know... What if I start giving you boxing lessons? What about that?"

Ned sniffed, wiped a tear off his cheek with the back of his hand, and shrugged his shoulders.

"Yeah, every evening when I come home from work, son, we'll go out in the yard and have a little sparring practice. How about that? Just you and me," Max said. He sounded silly, even to himself, but he kept carrying on. "I'll teach you how to jab and hook and block. And footwork. How to bob your head back and forth. How to hold a bigger guy off with your left until you tire him out and then cop a Sunday on him with your right. Then, the next time Mike gives you any shit, you'll be ready for him. All right?"

"Sure, Dad. Okay."

"Ned, don't sound so miserable," Max said. "Even if I get mad at you sometimes, you know I still love you."

But that only made the kid start sniffling again. And he crept in too close, clung to Max in a way he didn't like. Maybe from a daughter he would've liked it. But not from a son, already eleven years old.

"I love you too, Daddy," he said. And the way he said it, in this trembly little voice too young for his age, it gave Max a chill.

It's a quandary, he decided the next morning on his way to work. Whether to force the kid into your own mold, and make him hate you in the process, or let him go his own way, the way his genes are marching, the way of Fritz and Sybil and Ruby, and probably starve. Yet by the time he pulled up out in front of BAUER & GONÇALVES TRIUMPH at Avenue J and Leatherwood Street in Lancaster, he had decided that the exercise was futile anyway. Ned, most likely, was already the person he was going to be, and nobody was going to change him one way or the other.

Max climbed down from the cab and unlocked the ribbed, aluminum garage door. Squatting, grunting, he heaved it up, listening to the loud metallic clatter as it wound onto the spool. He stepped into the garage, smelling the familiar, pleasant odor of floor gunk, sawdust, motor oil, high octane gas, greasy engine parts, new leather seats and new rubber tires. Then he switched on the overhead fluorescent light and discovered that Ruby's asshole brother, who was supposed to be first at work in the morning, had not arrived yet.

And he thought, *Look at Lonnie and his old man. Look at me and mine. Is that the way it's gonna be with Ned and me?* Thinking this, he searched his mind for a reason why it might be so. And, recalling the events of yesterday—coming downstairs to find the house a mess and Ruby in the cellar, driving Ned up to the pass, the confrontation in the snow—he was struck by the impossible notion that some crucial knot had just slipped, the knot that bound them together as a family.

Lonnie came dragging in a half hour later—red-eyed, unshaven, wearing the same ripped t-shirt, greasy Levis, and down-at-heel motorcycle boots he had worn on Friday—and did a double take when he saw Max.

"Jesus, you scared me there for a minute," he said, grinning brazenly. "Didn't expect you in so early."

"Early? Hell, it's past eight o'clock."

"Is it? Well, damned if it ain't."

"Lonnie, what I want to know, is this gonna be a habit, or what?"

"Sorry, Max, but I got this dose of the flu, I think. Couldn't hardly get out of bed this morning."

"Flu? Smells more like a hangover to me."

"Feels like it too. But it ain't."

"Oh yeah? Well tell me one thing. If you're so sick, how come you weren't home all weekend?"

"How you know that?"

"Your wife phoned last night. Wanted to know if we knew where you were."

"Aw, shucks, Max," Lonnie said, smacking his palm with his fist, grinning unrepentantly. "I guess you got me."

"Hey, your private life is none of my business, man, as long as it doesn't interfere with your work."

"It won't anymore, Max, and that's a promise."

"Okay, fine. Then here's what I want you to do. I want you to roll those used bikes out on the lot. I want you to sweep this place up, and I want you to clean the bathrooms. Looks like a pigsty in here."

So, what Lonnie did, he went in and started firing up the motorcycles and riding them out on the lot without warming them up first. Although Max had warned him a hundred times, if he'd warned him once, that to spare their spark plugs—not to mention the neighbors' ears—he was supposed to roll them out.

"Gee, I'm sorry," Lonnie said casually, after Max had taken the trouble to lay down his tools, crawl out from under the old Daimler he was working on, walk out to the lot, and confront him again. "I forgot."

"Forget again, Lonnie, and you and me are gonna have a little talk about your future."

Next time Max saw him, he was sweeping out the garage, but he was beginning to look a little green around the gills. Then, an hour or so later, when Max went to the bathroom, he found the hand basin splattered with red wine puke, the commode stuffed up with paper towels, and the floor a half inch deep in toilet water. He found Lonnie in the parts loft, curled up asleep on a pile of knobby dirt-bike tires. And he looked so innocent lying there, like this towheaded kid instead of a grown man pushing forty, that for a second Max almost felt sorry for him. He tried to put himself in Lonnie's place, tried to imagine what had caused him to stage his own death at seventeen. You couldn't blame it on his home life, he thought, because Ruby had surely coped with more. It was sheer perversity, he decided at last, a twisted desire for notoriety.

"Lonnie? Lonnie?" he said. But Lonnie just kept snoring away, dead to the world. "Goddamnit, Lonnie, wake up!"

"Wha? Wha?"

"What the hell you doing up here? Now, get your ass down there and clean that fuckin' bathroom out!"

Sullen, complaining of his "flu," Lonnie struggled to his feet, climbed down the ladder from the parts loft, and disappeared for another hour or so. Leaving off work on his transmission job for the third time, Max went looking for him again and found him steam cleaning the engine on his own bike, a little Beezer one-banger that he had bought from them used and was behind payments on.

"What the goddamn hell you think you're doing?" Max hollered. "Get the fuck out there on that lot and clean that Jaguar Mark IV inside and out. Gil's got a customer coming over to see it at four this afternoon."

"You want me to paint the tires too?"

"Yeah."

"What color?"

"What color you figure?"

"Black?"

"Now you're thinking, Lonnie."

"And the floorboard mat?"

"Paint that black too.

"You want me to do it before or after lunch?" Lonnie asked, consulting his watch.

"I don't give a shit, but do it, Lonnie, just do it."

Lonnie left for lunch right then and there, a half hour early, and got back a half hour late, with whiskey on his breath.

Let's face it, it's in the genes, Max thought; thank God Ruby didn't turn out a lush.

Then he started to worry about Ned again.

About four that afternoon, when Gil brought his customer around to see the Mark IV, he found Lonnie sleeping in the back seat. The car was filthy, inside and out; it smelled like a Wild Turkey distillery, and an empty whiskey bottle was lying on the floor. Ignoring Lonnie, Gil apologized to the customer and told him to come back tomorrow. Then he came looking for Max.

Gil was a squat, tough little Mexican dude. Real excitable. And he had a mean temper. But out of respect for Max, he just came up and calmly laid it out like it happened.

"I mean like I know he's your *cuñado,* bro, but the fucker gotta go, you know?"

Max walked out to the Mark IV and found Lonnie leaning on it, half-heartedly spraying the roof with a hose.

"Lonnie," he said, wearily. "I'm afraid this isn't going to work out."

"What're you trying to say, Max?" Lonnie retorted, adjusting the hose nozzle, shooting such a strong stream of water on the Jaguar that it made a rainbow all around.

"Well, it seems like I'm spending all my time checking up on you, and I can't do any work of my own."

"Maybe if you tended to your own business for a change, and quit spying on me all the time, you wouldn't have so much trouble."

"You see? It's your attitude, Lonnie. Nobody around here can stand you. So, I just want to tell you, today's your last day. Stop at the office on the way out and I'll give you your paycheck."

"Whatever you say, Max. I mean, it ain't no big deal," he said. "You only keep me around as your house nigger anyway."

Just before quitting time that night, while Max and Charlie were finishing up a valve job on a Triumph T-6 and Gil was busy out on the lot with a motorcycle customer, Max heard someone kick-start a 500cc one-banger and burn rubber out of the garage. Suspicious, he rolled out from under the car and ran into the sales office to check the cash register. The till, which had contained about six hundred dollars in cash the last time he looked, was empty, except for a little note. "*I'm taking a hundred and fifty. Which is what you owe me. Plus, what I think is fair. A one-month severance fee.*"

Leaping on the first bike at hand, a big Triumph Thunderbird, Max kicked it over, popped the clutch, and within ten blocks he was already on Lonnie's tail, neck and neck with him on the corners.

Lonnie apparently thought of it as a game and grinned maniacally at Max whenever he got up close. But Max wasn't having any fun at all. The T-bird was over-powered. The front wheel tended to come up off the ground when you gave her the gas, and he hadn't ridden much in the past few years. He was nervous on the high-speed turns, especially in loose gravel, and nearly burnt the soles off his work boots trying to keep her from sliding out from under him. Also, he felt like he had more to lose, nowadays, and he was not inclined to take the kind of chances he once had. Lonnie, on the other hand, suffered from no such compunctions. He kamikazed all the way across town and lost Max for good when he ran up the Southern Pacific Freight Depot ramp at seventy-five miles an hour, hurtled off the end, landed in the marshalling yard, and bounced over thirty-seven lines of track, dodging humped boxcars and tankers, scattering switchmen and brakemen every which way.

By the time Max got back to the garage, Charlie had called the sheriff with the license number of Lonnie's bike, and it wasn't but another hour before he was in custody. Somewhere along his escape route, he had apparently run down an old Mexican lady, who was now hovering between life and death in Antelope Valley Community Hospital.

At first, it looked like Lonnie was going to be charged with manslaughter as well as grand theft, and the op-ed pages of the local papers were full of letters clamoring for his neck. Even Dominica, when interviewed on television, said, "That man, I wash my hand of him." But then the old lady pulled through, the DA let Lonnie cop a plea, and the whole thing was reduced to felony hit & run.

A couple of days later, when it looked like Lonnie was going to be released on bail and probably do no more than six months in jail, either Gil or Charlie—Max didn't care which—phoned the sheriff anonymously and tipped him to the Panama scam. The sheriff ran a check, which he should have done in the first place, and found out Lonnie was wanted by the FBI.

After his local trial, in which he received a sentence of one to five years in the state penitentiary, Lonnie was indicted in Federal Court in Los Angeles for Falsifying Government Records, Grand Larceny, Theft of Government Property, and Fleeing Across a State Line to Avoid Arrest. And even though he had turned state's evidence, denouncing his Air Force buddy and crime partner, Bill, in hopes of a lighter sentence, he was speedily tried, convicted, and sentenced to three years in federal prison, to be served upon completion of his state term.

At the garage, they gave an after-work beer party when they heard the news, but when Max got home that night, he discovered he would probably be better off with Lonnie still on the loose.

Ruby announced to him over dinner that she was taking Dominica and the baby in, till Lonnie got out of prison. When Max objected, citing the proverbial dangers and discomforts of living under the same roof with in-laws, she countered with the argument that the poor girl was all alone now and had no one else to turn to. And besides, she said, she was going to need someone to help with Ned and do the housework and cooking now that she had decided to write full time.

Chapter Fifteen

Pacing the cellar, eight steps up and back, searching the rough, flagstone floor for cookie crumbs or a stray crumpled paper, Ruby was gratified to see that everything was perfectly in order. But she kept pacing anyway, sipping at a cold cup of coffee, clouding the air with cigarette smoke, hearing but not hearing her family stomping around and moving chairs and talking in the kitchen above her head.

Particles of sand sifted in with the afternoon wind, lighting on the desk, the typewriter, the manuscript, on ledges in the gritty stone walls. A shaft of sheer, white light veered in through the high slit window and crept across the room with the sun, while the packing crates in the corners, with their musty family secrets, stayed deep in shadow, and the single, hanging lightbulb, under its dusty cone of bone brown lampshade, tinted everything the color of an old photograph.

Cell... cellar, how aptly named, she thought, and remembered how it had depressed her when she first came down. With its floor an inch deep in dust, strewn with old papers and upturned boxes, its rafters bedaubed with cobwebs and exposed electrical wiring, it was like a picture of the inside of her head at the time.

Then as the months slid by, and her work progressed, she had acquired a salutary habit. Whenever she was stumped for an idea, she would go around nervously sweeping, dusting, and tidying things up until she arrived at a solution. So, willy-nilly, she had made the place her own.

She found that she enjoyed coming down in the dark every morning with her thermos of coffee, her jar of water and her sack lunch, enjoyed spending the day alone with herself, letting her imagination run free, then coming out in the dark again, so late at times that everyone in the house was sound asleep. By now, three months after she had put the finishing touches on her book, she had grown so fond of the cellar, with its atmosphere close and stale, smelling of herself, that she was reluctant to give it up.

Even in the beginning, she recalled, she had been jealous of her space, and had fought to defend it. "Go on, get out of here!" she would shrill at Ned or Max, when they came pounding down the flagstone stairs to visit. "Can't you see I'm working?"

Yet, it broke her heart when she had to run them off because neither of them could get it through his head how vitally important her work was, how essential to her recovery. Ned whined that he hated Dominica's spicy food, that Lonnie Junior's crying kept him awake at night, that he missed his mom walking him to the bus every morning, that Max was always picking on him. And Max grumbled that he had no more privacy, that Dominica was always putting his things in places where he couldn't find them, that Ned was not taking well to his mother's absence and was becoming sullen and insolent. But little by little, with her sunny disposition, and heroic efforts in the kitchen and around the house, Dominica had won them over, to the point that now Ruby sometimes wondered if they missed her at all.

Working up to sixteen hours a day, seven days a week, breaking stride only for her monthly physical exam with Dr. Silverman and an occasional visit to her brother, Lonnie, in Santa Maria State Prison, Ruby had worked for more than a year and a half on her book. For weeks at a time, she had become obsessed with her work. Whole lines and scenes would leap into her consciousness, flashing before her eyes at the breakfast table, the dinner table, cutting into the middle of conversations.

"Mom! Mom! Are you listening? You never listen anymore."

It was like an embryo, a parasite. It consumed her from the inside, fed off her life. And now she felt very much as she had when she gave birth to Ned, with her moods swinging wildly back and forth from elation to depression. One minute she was delighted with her story, certain of her bright prospects as a writer, proud of her sacrifice, while the next she was overcome with self-doubts and remorse that she had neglected her family for such a flimsy and pathetic hope.

Seating herself at the desk again, Ruby took a deep breath, blew the accumulated sand particles off, and opened her manuscript. Leafing through it for the hundredth time, hoping to find some typo or trifling grammatical error, she marveled at how alive and real this thing of mere ink and paper had become, and how intimately connected to herself. The act of writing made her feel quite literally fantastic, like a goddess creating a world in her image. At the same time, her work seemed to have a will of its own. It had constantly surprised and delighted her with its unpredictable new directions. And the manuscript that lay before her in four hundred and fifty double-spaced pages had almost nothing to do with her original intention to write a biography of Hillary Bennett.

It was an autobiography of Ruby Rose, with the old movie star and her looming desert mansion as little more than a pervasive metaphor, an allegorical reference point by which Ruby guided herself through the past, came to terms with her fears and failures, and sought a meaning to her life. Hillary's life had been grander than Ruby's, its canvas broader, its characters larger. But ultimately, it was a sadder and more sordid life, confirming in all its depressingly familiar details the popular notion that Hollywood leads inevitably to sex, drugs, divorce, and disaster, and it helped put things in perspective.

Paging through her book, Ruby picked a passage at random and read it aloud in the natural, un-enunciated "Method" style she had learned from her tutor, Michael Marczaly:

> "Halfway home and my mom started limping on her high heels and complaining that her ankles were all swollen up, so we plopped down on a flood control embankment under a cottonwood tree. Out in front of us, Caterpillar tractors were gouging a gigantic hole in the dry lake bottom, shoveling huge, tangled masses of rusting jeeps and fighter planes down inside, raising up great billowing white clouds of alkali dust. Then this enormous, silver bomber came

thundering overhead, so low and loud it was like the mother of all machines. It had six big pusher engines and twelve four-bladed counter-revolving propellors and absolutely no fuselage that I could see. 'The Flying Wing! The Flying Wing!' my father shouted. To a five-year-old like me at the time the picture seemed unreal, like a movie in Technicolor, and I wanted to slow it down. It was going too fast. So, I exerted all my will and suddenly it was like the electricity went out, or the projector went on the blink: All twelve propellors quit spinning at once. It froze in the sky. Everything and everyone around me went dead still. The very earth seemed to halt in its orbit. A moment later and I let myself relax. Things started up again. The plane droned on, and it flew over the movie star mansion on the horizon as if nothing had happened. 'Wow,' I said to myself, 'I can make anything happen that I want.'"

It was not such bad writing, Ruby thought. If her prose style was sometimes homely, her grammar and punctuation unsure, her vocabulary limited, there was a rhythmic, lyrical quality to her sentences that seemed quite original. She had managed to characterize her mother and father in a couple of strokes. Her evocation of time and place was competent, as well. And she had neatly foreshadowed the crash of the Flying Wing. She had also brought in Hillary's mansion, which had deep symbolic meaning later in the book. But the best part was how she had particularized in a few words her own character, which she felt to be fiercely ambitious and recklessly optimistic, while at the same time conveying a sense of the loss and dislocation in which her character was rooted.

Still, Ruby had no illusions. She'd had to sweat over every word she wrote, every sentence and paragraph. She had exhausted all her ideas and anecdotes, expended what meager talent she had. And she doubted very seriously if she would ever write another book. The way she figured, it was a mere steppingstone. In her most secret heart—incorrigible as Hillary Bennett's—she dreamed of a movie sale, with herself as part of the deal: the star.

Considering her work in more general terms, Ruby decided that its major triumph was what it had taught her about herself. Having sought a meaning to her life, something beyond her bonds of blood and marriage, she had discovered that the act of writing itself gave it meaning. Now for the first time she was defined not by others, but by herself, by her own unflinching self-appraisal. And this was something that she believed she had imparted—with an eye to future book sales—to her audience, which she assumed would be largely female.

Ruby had spent days, after she finished the book in October 1974, agonizing over how to exploit its commercial possibilities, how to find the right agent and publisher. Then one night she was sitting in bed with Max, sharing the newspaper. Finishing up with the Home Section and setting it aside, she reached for the *Writers' Digest* she had bought on her last visit to town, and an article entitled "Getting Published" caught her eye.

"Hey, listen to this, honey," she said. "'No use sending your manuscript directly to the publishers,' it says. You gotta go through a literary agent, and it gives a list of the hundred best."

"No kidding," he said, feigning interest, anxious to get back to his sports page.

"Yeah, and you know what? I bet everyone starts at the top of the list, with the A's."

"Yeah, I bet they do."

"So, you know what I'm gonna do? I'm gonna start at the bottom, with the Z's, and work my way up."

"Good idea," he said, returning to the baseball scores.

Undeterred by Max's tepid signs of approval, Ruby drove into town the next morning, had her manuscript xeroxed, and airmailed a copy to Mr. Sid Zyskin, 344 Park Avenue South, New York, New York.

All the rest of that day, and the next and the next, she paced her basement office, puffing cigarettes, drinking cup after cup of coffee. She worried that she hadn't put enough postage on her manuscript, that she'd not wrapped it carefully enough. She imagined it splitting open, spilling all over the cargo bay of the plane it was traveling in. She wondered how long it would take to get to New York, how long it would sit in Sid Zyskin's office before he got a chance to read it.

Then near the end of the week she began expecting word from New York. She imagined Mr. Zyskin, a distinguished Jewish gentleman in a pair of pin-striped pants, white shirt, and vest, sitting down to read her book in his overstuffed Greenwich Village apartment and suddenly leaping up, dialing California, shouting excitedly into the receiver, "Young lady, you have real writing talent!"

She had Pacific Bell come out and put a phone in the cellar and sat by it for hours, certain that it would ring any minute. She waited at the mailbox every morning until the mailman arrived. She haunted the Gold Hill post office, bombarding the elderly post mistress with arcane questions on air mail routes, arrival times and delivery hours.

Finally, she could not take it any longer and phoned New York.

"Sorry, but we've received no such manuscript," Mr. Zyskin's secretary said.

Feeling almost relieved, for she had begun to believe the agent had rejected her book and was embarrassed to tell her so, Ruby xeroxed another copy that day. Upbraiding the astonished post mistress for "careless handling," she sent it off Special Delivery and settled down again to wait. But this time it was even worse. She couldn't eat, couldn't sleep. She paced the cellar all day and half the night, coming out red-eyed, slack-jawed, sleepwalking from room to room, looking straight through her family, hearing nothing they said. A week later, she phoned New York again. The secretary said yes, she had received the manuscript, and she had found the other copy as well. It had been misplaced rather than lost. But Mr. Zyskin was now on vacation in Florida and would not be back for ten days.

In a state of the most extreme nervous anxiety, Ruby waited eleven and a half days and phoned again. Mr. Zyskin still hadn't gotten to it, the secretary said. He was working his way through a tremendous backlog. Ruby screamed at her and demanded an immediate reading.

"Hey, sweetie, if that's the way you feel," the secretary said, in her Brooklyn accent, "I'll send it back to you. I mean, we didn't *solicit* that manuscript, you know."

Pouring out tearful apologies, Ruby begged her to reconsider.

"Alright," she said, "but please don't call me again."

A month later, Ruby got both copies back, along with a form rejection letter.

Consulting her list of agents again, she sent her manuscript off to Victor Zellerdorf & Associates, of 439 E. 57th Street, New York City. This time she received her rejection notice in only three weeks. Disappointed, but not defeated, she continued up the alphabet through the Y's, W's, and V's, collecting rejection slips and pasting them to her cellar wall all through the year 1975. She would have reached the A's by the year 1985, she figured, if Sybil had not come across an article in the Los *Angeles Times Literary Supplement* about "New Age Publishing." An alternative publishing industry had recently sprung up in the Bay Area, it said, with some astonishing results. Several books had sold over a million copies. Most prominent of these new publishers was a Marin County outfit called *Good Times Press.*

"Sounds like right up my alley," Ruby said, when Sybil brought her the article, and together they shot off a letter and a copy of her manuscript.

Now, a week later, and already anxiously awaiting an answer, Ruby could hear Sybil's cool, dipthongy voice again, from upstairs in the dining room, along with Max's slow, measured baritone, Reno's low rasp, and Dominica's higher, more melodic tones, while Ned giggled nervously and Lonnie Junior squealed in delight.

It was dinner time, she concluded. Sunday dinner. And she had promised to attend.

Packing her manuscript in an old typing paper box and slipping it under her arm, she turned off the light and hobbled up the stairs on her cane. As always, she was caught off guard by the profusion of color, sights, sounds, smells, and feelings that assailed her when she came out of the cellar.

Stepping onto the lawn, adjusting her eyes to the sudden light, she found herself in a bright mid-afternoon in early August. The sun beat fiercely on her head, her bare arms, and shoulders. The wind came hot and dry, smelling of distant forest fires. The sky, summer white, with a thin stratospheric layer of cirrus clouds, seemed to go on forever. The yellow hills, the blue mountains, the green and white canyon, the burnt brown desert beyond, through shimmering waves of radiated heat, seemed mirage-like, chimerical, yet—by some trick of the prism—closer and more vividly colored than usual. A crow cawed up the ridge. A woodpecker went to work on an almond tree. A pickup truck labored up Sand Canyon Road in first gear. Wild oats rustled by the side of the house. Grasshoppers buzzed on the lawn. And from inside the tall, gray-faced Victorian came the sound of her family, talking all at once.

Slipping in through the screen porch, Ruby lingered in the kitchen a moment, looking around, sniffing the air, letting herself adjust. She had given Dominica full reign in the house for the past months, and the kitchen had inevitably changed under her dominion. It had a more colorful look now, yet it seemed to Ruby a bit stuffy and humid—a miniature reproduction of Dominica's torrid native isthmus, full of baby banana trees, hanging plants, and cloying tropical flowers in rattan baskets. There was even a pair of love birds in a cage.

Moving out of the kitchen, into the carpeted hallway, hesitating outside the dining room door to listen to the conversation on the other side of the wall, Ruby felt, as she often felt when she first came up from the cellar, half-conscious, unreal as if she were merely going through the motions of participating in the life of the house.

Amid the clicking of forks, the creaking of wooden chairs, the sounds of chewing and swallowing and Dominica's motherly clucking—"Eat dem peas now, Lonnie Junior, you hear? Why I never get you to drink milk, Ned, a growin' boy like you?"—Max could be heard, kidding Lonnie Junior about something that happened this morning.

"Halfway to the Gonçalves Ranch," he was saying, "with Ned's old schoolbag on your back. Now, where you think you were headed, boy?"

"Long Beach," the child said, in a poised, adult tone that Max and everyone else found richly amusing.

"Long Beach? What'd you want to go there for?"

"Wanna be a sailor, 'Ax," Lonnie said, gravely. He still had trouble pronouncing Max's name. "Wanna go on a submarine."

"Uh-huh, I see. And why is that, son?"

"Won't tell!" Lonnie Jr. said, laughing, dinging a spoon on his glass. "Won't tell!"

"Wants to go live underwater, I guess," Reno teased. "Wants to be with the fish."

"No, I don't! No, I don't!"

"Where was the last place we found him, Dominica, when he ran off?"

"Find him up to his ears in a pile of almonds. And you know, Max, I walk by there a dozen times 'fore I see that child. He never let out a peep."

"Before that, it was over in Grandma's dryer," Ned volunteered. "Turned the ranch upside down and we never found him."

"Not at least until I threw in a load and switched it on," Sybil put in.

"Don't know what we're gonna do with that boy," Max said.

His voice was gruff and ironic, yet unmistakably paternal.

"Gon' have to tie him up on a leash, I s'pose," said Dominica, "like a little dog."

"Woof woof!" Lonnie Jr. said, and everyone laughed.

Ruby was struck by the familiarity and affection in their tone, the easiness of their laughter, and by the fact that they had apparently not remarked her absence. She asked herself how they would act when she suddenly appeared. They would act just as they had the last time she came upon them like this, at Lonnie Jr.'s fourth birthday party. They would cut the horseplay and get all sheepish with her and treat her like a stranger, an honored guest.

And if I never came back, she mused, they'd probably go on the same way.

It was an oddly ambiguous thought, disturbing and comforting at once. And it led her back to her manuscript again. She remembered an awkward transition in the concluding scene that she had forgotten to revise. Smooth transitions were vital to her work, she knew, because she was always skittering shamelessly back and forth from the tragic to the comic, the obscene to the exalted, the real to the surreal. In this scene, she had her principal character, who was not exactly herself, sneak into the dark, Tudor mansion that had haunted her all her life, confront the witchy old movie star, and emerge from the experience a new woman, healthy and whole, free at last. She had meant it to symbolize a belated acceptance of her failure as an actress, a coming to terms with her fears of death, disease, and marital rejection. But she had never been perfectly satisfied with it, because it was so different in spirit from the rest of her book. Ruby had always been faithful at least to the fictional reality of her life and, taking Hillary's diaries as her model, she had told her story in the most graphic, even shocking detail, changing no names, making no compromises, leaving nothing out. This upbeat ending was the one real departure she had taken from the truth. There was a solid aesthetic reason for this: Her character had been through so much that she deserved a triumph. Not to mention the commercial advantages of a happy ending. Yet Ruby's current real-life prognosis was nowhere near so rosy as that of her heroine. Her relationship with Max was still unresolved, after all these many months, and Dr. Silverman had warned her not a week ago that her disease was merely in remission; it could show up again at any time.

When you fudge on the truth like that, she thought, there is always a danger of sentimentality. And she was tempted to just turn around, trusting that she would not be missed at Sunday dinner, tiptoe back down to the cellar, and work on that last scene again. At the same time, she had a strong counterimpulse to join this very warm and live little family scene just on the other side of the wall. And, though she herself had designed it this way, and had remained content with it through all her months of writing, she felt perhaps a bit envious as well, and wanted to go in there now, break through their circle of exclusivity, and steal their show.

Just then, the telephone rang in the kitchen.

"I'll get it!" Ruby called, and she could hear her family calmly carrying on their conversation in the dining room, completely unfazed that she should be lurking just outside their door.

"Hi, I'm Felicity Bozeman from *Good Times Press*," said the voice at the other end of the line. It was a voice with the hip inflection and the easy, mellow, tone of a female radio announcer on a jazz/rock program. "Sorry to bother you on the weekend like this, but I just put down your book and I had to call. I read it straight through without stopping and I loved it. I'd like to publish it. And I'll tell you why: It will touch every woman's heart."

There was also the tie-in with Hollywood and Hillary Bennett, she said, and the fact that Ruby was an attractive young mother (she had enclosed a snapshot with the manuscript), a housewife, a small-town girl from way out in the middle of the Mojave Desert somewhere. "These are all major selling points."

"You really think so?"

"Absolutely," Felicity said. "And the fact that you have experience in front of audiences doesn't hurt a bit. What you're going to find, Ruby, in this field, people are not really buying what's between the covers of your book. They're buying you as a person. I mean, if you can write, that's great. And an inspirational theme is important. But frankly, you could sell them anything if you packaged it right."

So, what she wanted to do, she said, was FedEx a contract tomorrow. If Ruby signed on, she would do a preliminary run of five or six thousand copies, send her out on a publicity tour of the "self-help circuit," and see how it played. If things worked out, she would run off another ten thousand copies and send her out again, this time with some spots on local radio and TV.

"We get the word-of-mouth going," Felicity said, "we'll hit the cities, and the sky's the limit. What do you say?"

Tongue-tied for the first time in her life, Ruby could do no more than nod at the telephone receiver and whisper "Uh-huh, uh-huh, uh-huh..."

Yet, just a few moments later, she was clomping into the dining room, flinging her cane and manuscript on the table, joyously proclaiming the news at the top of her lungs: "I've just had an offer! Just had an offer!"

Halting their conversation, her family looked up at her all at once, their faces blank, mystified.

And in the instant that it took for them to register the meaning of her words, Ruby formed a candid and indelibly printed color picture of them in her mind: Seated at an oval yellow-oak table in the circular redwood paneled dining room, under an antique brass chandelier, with a panorama of desert, canyon, and mountain out the curving windows behind them, they seemed amazingly vibrant and real to her, larger than life.

Max was at the head of the table. Dominica sat across from him, handy to the kitchen. Sybil and Lonnie Jr. were together, with their backs to the sunlight, while Ned and Reno sat facing the windows. Ruby saw each of them in minute detail, more clearly than she had in ages.

Max's hair had receded in the past year and a half, and his face was heavier now, more deeply lined, masking complicated emotions.

Dominica's figure seemed fuller, more statuesque, but her beautiful, dark face remained as serene as ever.

Sybil was thinner and grayer, yet her posture and expression conveyed, as always, exceptional good health, and a formidable sense of self.

Reno had suddenly become an old man, stooped and sallow, with a quavery voice and shaking hands.

Lonnie Jr. had grown from a tot into a plump, robust boy with a mop of dirty-yellow curls, sprightly sea-green eyes, darkish skin, and a wide impish grin.

Ned, on the other hand, appeared to have atrophied at the age of twelve. Small-boned and thin, with translucent white skin, long curling lashes, and thick wavy hair that had darkened to auburn, he was almost girlishly self-conscious and beautiful. And he had developed this little tick in his left eye, like a pulling at the optical nerve. It was no more than a tremor, a ruffle on the surface. Yet, peering more deeply into his eyes (and they had grown very dark, almost gentian blue), his mother could see that it was not an optical problem at all, but a sign of some other disturbance, far below the level of consciousness. *Better not say a word about this to Max,* she thought.

When at last her family's faces lit up, and they smiled with comprehension, Ruby's own smile had already flown.

"Ned, run and get the champagne in my refrigerator," Sybil said. "This calls for a celebration!"

That night, in their cups, Ruby and Max continued the celebration in their bedroom.

"You know what, honey? And I'm not kidding," Ruby said, finishing off the last of her champagne, setting her empty glass on the dressing table. "I think that woman, Felicity, was right. I think we got us a winner here."

"Awwwwwright! Awwwwwright!" Max bellowed happily, doing a little jig on the white carpet, smearing it with his dusty boots. Then he sailed his feedstore cap across the room and belly-flopped on the bed. Ruby threw herself down beside him, and they lay together side by side for a while, laughing, bouncing up and down.

"Damn, I don't think I've been this happy since my honeymoon!" Max said. Then, taking a deep breath, as if to fortify himself against the uneasiness he felt when he got close to her nowadays, he turned and snuggled up to her ear, sniffed her hair. "The old Miramar Beach Hotel in Santa Barbara. Remember?"

"Yeah," Ruby replied, sarcastically, wondering why he had always liked the smell of her hair so much. Max himself had no identifiable smell at all. Even after he had worked all day at the garage, even if you stuck your nose in his armpit, you couldn't smell him. It was weird, it was like he wasn't all there, like he was an optical illusion or something. While Ruby felt that she had to shower once a day, twice a day during her period, or she reeked like dead meat.

"Yeah," she said again. "Our room was right under the shadow of your grandpa's mansion. You drove us up there every day to look at it. You were so proud of it. But every few moments, you imagined your aunt or uncle or one of your cousins would come out and catch you and prosecute you for trespassing."

"It wasn't half-bad though, was it? The old Miramar. With that veranda out front, remember? And the view of the islands, the moonlight on the channel. Very romantic."

"Oh, it was romantic, all right. At least we didn't have to worry about birth control. I was four months pregnant with Ned."

Max's breath had suddenly grown hotter, heavier, in her ear. He ran his hand up her cowboy shirt and started tickling her under the arm, with this very serious and intent expression on his face. And she started giggling, started wiggling about, just like when they were kids, out on the lawn in front of the Eagle Field front gate. Then his tickling got softer and softer, creeping up the side of her breast. And he started blowing in her ear and nibbling on her lobe, which he knew turned her on.

So, it was not but a minute or two before she had to ask him to draw the curtains and turn off the light.

"How come you always want it dark?" he wanted to know, but Ruby wouldn't answer.

You'll like it a lot better, she thought, *if you don't have to look at it.*

"Are you sure you know what you're doing?" she asked, when he returned to her on the bed. It had been so long since they last made love that she could barely remember what it was like. In a certain way, her writing had become a substitute, she knew, and there had been times when she barely missed it.

"No," he said.

Yet, very slowly and methodically, he pulled her boots and trousers off, slithered her panties over her hips, down her legs and off her feet. Then, while Ruby waited on the bed in an agony of anticipation, he stood up to strip himself naked, to fold and lay out his clothes on the armchair, to reach in the drawer, extract a lubricated condom, tear it open and carefully roll it over his erection. Climbing back into bed, he kissed her, hotly, wetly, for the first time in many, many moons. She opened her legs to him, and he lay between them, hard as stone. He snapped her western shirt open, and she drew him down upon her breasts. But he seemed in no hurry, and after he had kissed and nipped and sucked her there for a while, he started licking down her tummy, into her belly button, toward her pubic hair.

"No," she murmured, and stopped him with her hand, pulled his face up to hers, looking into his nearly invisible eyes. "Don't do that. I want you now."

With that, he took his own erection in his hands and cautiously guided it inside her, centimeter by centimeter, pulling back every few moments, as if to say, "Does it hurt?"

"No, no, don't stop, don't stop!" she kept crying, impatiently. And finally, she was almost screaming it, "No! No! No!"

Yet even in the midst of an exquisitely delayed orgasm, Ruby could hear a tiny, panic-stricken voice inside her, saying, "It's not like it used to be; it's not like it used to be."

Afterwards, lying quietly beside Max in front of the TV, watching the evening news, she wondered how he had been able to make love so calmly and deliberately after so many months of celibacy. And it occurred to her that of course he had not been celibate.

Ruby woke late the next morning, nursing a hangover, long after Max had left for work and Ned had gone off to YMCA day camp. Staggering to the bathroom, she popped a couple of aspirins and lay down again on her marital bed, listening to her own shallow breathing, the slow dripping of the faucet she had neglected to turn off fully.

As the medicine took effect, and the ball of nausea in her esophagus contracted, the circle of her consciousness expanded slowly outward, until she could hear Dominica's love birds cooing downstairs, and Lonnie Jr. asking questions in the kitchen.

"Why the rain fall, Mama?"

" Rain come 'cause God want it to."

"Why He want it to?"

"Doan't know. But we lucky He do. Or what we drink?"

"How the plants grow?"

"Rain."

"Why He doan't make it rain around here too much?"

"Well, you know now, Lovie, way out here in the desert, He forget 'bout it sometime, I reckon."

Ruby found the conversation comforting, and it helped to make her headache go away. Wrapping herself in a housecoat, she negotiated the stairs with only minor difficulty, and found Dominica at the breakfast counter, rolling tortillas for tonight's taco dinner, while Lonnie played beside her on the polyurethaned wooden floor, lining up little toy soldiers in squares.

"Hello, 'Uby," he chirped when she bent to kiss him.

He and his mother were both giggling, perhaps at something the boy had just said.

"You know," Dominica said, shaking her head, "this child, he a perfect caution. Sometime, I say, 'Eh, cry you little devil, cry! Why you be laughing all the time?'"

"Yeah, I know. Ned was the same way when he was little. sweet-natured. Sweeter than any girl you'd ever find."

"Run in the family, I s'pose."

"Probably so," Ruby said, pressing her sister-in-law's gray, doughy hand, acknowledging their kinship.

And then quickly, furtively, she drew closer and whispered, "Dominica, I'm worried about Ned."

"Oh," she said, smiling broadly, squeezing back, "doan't you go frettin' about that boy, now. He be alright."

"But how can you be so sure?"

"I's with him a lot more than you, lately. He just going through a stage. Like the other night he come into my room. Say he scared, want to sleep with me and Lonnie. 'Sure, why not?' I say. We not finical about that kind of thing, where I come from. But Max, he come in and raise hell with the boy. 'You too big for that. Nearly fourteen years old. Go sleep in your own room!'

Ned talk back, and Max drag him out. Boy sulk in his room for days, after that. See, this what they all go through. Happen about this age. Man-child and daddy. But they get over it. And they's plenty worse than them two, believe me."

"You know, sometimes I feel like you're years older than me, Dominica, instead of the other way around."

"Ain't a nurse for nothing, you know," she said, winking. "Now, can I get you somethin'? Cup of coffee, maybe?"

"No, dear, I'm here to help *you*."

"Help me?" Dominica laughed. "Why you doan't just lay back and take it easy for a while?"

"I don't know," Ruby said, pouring herself a cup of coffee. "I mean, you're doing such a great job around the house. How can I ever thank you? Without you, I never could've . . ."

"Now Ruby, you stop that, hear?"

"I never could've come close to finishing that book without you. Now I guess I'm just feeling kind of left out."

"You not left out, love. We just trying to leave you some space. You can come back any time. You know that. Thing is, you feelin' kind of guilty, I s'pose. But I doan't mind takin' care of folks, you see. It kind of grow on me."

Ruby thought over what Dominica had said and, after a few minutes of polite hesitation, took her at her word. She drove into Lancaster and did the grocery shopping, bought herself a *Vogue* at Walgreen's Drugstore, had her hair done, and spent the afternoon with her old friends Juanita and Sally, telling them the good news.

Returning about four, she had tea with Sybil, took a nice, long, hot bath, cast a cold eye on her wound in the mirror, was unaffected by the sight, and when Ned got home from day camp she went into his room, smiling.

He was lying on his bed, reading a book. She glanced at the title: *Of Mice and Men,* by John Steinbeck. Sitting down beside him on the bed, she patted his knee and tried to think of something to say.

"How are you, honey?"

"Not bad, Mom," he said casually, laying his book aside. But then he looked up at her and smiled, and his smile pained her, because it was like the trick in his eye. No more than a thin wavering line across his pale, delicate face, it was like a crack in a fragile jar, an involuntary display of some unknown inner flaw.

"So how was camp?" she asked, keeping her voice very calm and even, squeezing his leg hard to disguise the sudden tremor in her fingers.

"Alright."

"What'd you do today?"

"Oh, I did some drawing, some ceramics, some swimming."

"You playing any ball?"

"Naw."

"Now, don't answer this if you don't want, but how come you turned against baseball so much?"

"It's not the sport. I like the sport, Mom. It's the guys who play it I don't like."

"Why is that?"

"We don't have the same interests," he said. "I guess I'm just different from other kids my age."

"That's not necessarily a bad thing, is it?"

"Course not. I know that, Mom. But it's probably gonna take a while for Antelope Valley to find it out," he said. And he sounded so perfectly reasonable that for the moment he put her mind at rest.

That night, after she had consulted with Sybil, and her lawyer, and signed the contract with *Good Times Press*, Ruby figured it was about time she filled in Max on the details of her book

"Honey, there's something I have to tell you," she said, once they were settled in bed. "And I know it's not gonna be easy for you."

She was very careful breaking it to him, minimizing his own role, and the unsavory aspects. But halfway through, she knew she had already lost him.

"Hey, I don't care what kind of shit you got into down in Hollywood," he said, when she was done. She had never seen him angrier, yet he barely raised his voice. "But what came later is between us."

"Max, there was no other way."

"But you know, what I don't understand, how come you just didn't come right up to me in the beginning and ask me, 'Hey, what do you think about this?'"

"Okay," she said, and suddenly she knew that there was a tremendous stake in this, that she had to justify herself to him at all costs. "Okay, let's say I did that. I brought it to you, and I said, 'Max, this is gonna be the story of my life, and I'm not gonna pull any punches on myself or anyone else. What would you have said? You'd have said, 'I don't like it, Ruby. I don't want you airing our dirty laundry in public.' And I would've listened. And right now, I wouldn't have a book. I'd be the same little person I used to be. And I couldn't live with that."

"Well, that's where we're different, I guess. Because I've always been pretty happy with who I am."

"People can live with their differences, Max, they do all the time."

"Do they?" he said, and he took her face in his hands and held it very, very tight for a moment, searching her eyes. "I hope you're right."

Then he rolled over and turned off the light.

What she hadn't told him, because she knew he would be furious, was that she had chosen her maiden name, not her married name, as her pen name. Yet it seemed perfectly obvious that "Ruby Rose" had a lot more *panache* than "Mrs. Max Bauer."

Chapter Sixteen

A warm, Sunday morning in April 1976, with only a few, puffy, white clouds to mar a perfect blue sky, and Max found himself driving his sister-in-law, Dominica, down the Antelope Valley Freeway, heading southwest toward Acton, Canyon Country, and Saugus. Damn, but he did enjoy driving. Almost nothing he'd rather do. He carried this nearly perfect 1/100 topographical map around in his head; and, what he liked to do, he liked to look over the terrain, noting and naming to himself the various hills, mountains, canyons, valleys, streams, rivers, roads, and highways that he was passing by. He enjoyed it so much, in fact, that even the prospect of visiting his wayward brother-in-law in Santa Maria State Prison was not enough to kill his pleasure.

True, he thought, he had not been exactly overjoyed to learn that he had inherited this additional family obligation when Ruby went out on her second nation-wide book tour, and there were probably a hundred other things he would rather do. Yet now, sitting up in the cab of his big, old, Ford pickup, wailing along at seventy miles an hour, with Ritter Ridge, Quartz Hill, Desert View Highlands, Palmdale Airport, the Lockheed

Aerospace Plant, the California Aqueduct, and other familiar landmarks around him, he felt completely relaxed, in control, master of his fate.

If he felt like it, he thought, he could just keep going. Anywhere he liked. He had the wheels. He had the money. There was this huge state of California all around him, bigger than any nation in Europe except maybe France and Russia, and he knew it like the back of his hand. Hell, he even had a woman at his side. He could go anywhere he wanted. Never come back. If he didn't feel like it. Not that he'd ever do it. But it was a great feeling, anyway. That you could do any damn thing you pleased. It's what made him American, he thought.

Dominica was not a talkative girl, except when she got around Ruby. That's one of the things Max liked about her. They just kind of rode along together, not saying much, smiling at each other from time to time, listening to the Rock & Roll station on the radio, looking out at things, but not feeling a need to comment upon them.

Heading up through the rolling chaparral country of the San Francisquito foothills, along the flanks of snowy Strawberry Peak, over piney Soledad Pass to the flat, black, lettuce fields of the Fillmore Valley, out of the sun and into the chill coastal fog, up along the beaches and gray grassy hills of Ventura, the palmy canyons of Santa Barbara, the coves and madrone groves of Gaviota, Max was thinking all the time about how he loved this beautiful state of his. Not that he'd been to any others. Not at least since he left Paris as an infant. Yet, that was merely proof of his point.

You didn't have to go anywhere else. Most places only had one claim to fame, but Cali had it all: beaches, deserts, mountains, lakes, forests, and beautiful cities. Every climate from sub-tropical to arctic. Every terrain from tundra to rainforests, sand dunes to snowfields. Best damn state in the Union, he was thinking, as Dominica directed him to a rectangular complex of long, gray, four-story buildings surrounded by a stone wall and a high, barbed wire fence. "Santa Maria State Medium Security Facility," said a sign on the gatehouse out front.

Listing himself and Dominica as "brother-in-law and wife of inmate" on the pad presented to him by a grim, Chicano, gatehouse officer, Max drove onto the grounds, following the blacktop through a patch of thick, white, ground fog smelling of salt water and sewage, around some slick beds of water plant, past a tall ghostly stand of eucalyptus trees and a traffic circle full of dewy pink and white oleanders.

The outdoor Visitors' Center, where Dominica had her appointment with Lonnie, was situated just outside the walls of the prison, on a small grassy knoll between the Administration Building and the Correctional Officers' Club. Surrounded by a hedge of well-tended rose trees, it was divided into two unequal parts: the large Family Picnic Area—where Max could dimly perceive six or seven inmates having snacks on the lawn with their wives, parents, and children—and the smaller Conjugal Visiting Area, which consisted of five aluminum house trailers, each enclosed within a white picket fence.

In a recent letter, Lonnie had run down for Dominica the comic history of the trailers. Apparently, they'd been acquired by the State of California in a complicated deal with the State of Nevada, after the previous owner—a Winnemucca brothel-keeper—was prosecuted for non-payment of taxes. And they came equipped with French bidets, king-sized waterbeds, and elaborate medicine chests stocked with douches, prophylactics and spermatocides.

Max and Dominica got out of the car together, mounted the hill to the Family Picnic Area, and sat down across from each other at a vacant table. Still not saying much, and avoiding each other's eyes, they sat waiting uncomfortably, watching the inmates' children playing tag on the soggy grass. A tension had grown up between them since they arrived on the prison grounds, a kind of static electricity that put them both on edge.

"Nervous?" Max enquired, patting her on the arm. He patted her carefully, not too softly, not too long. Though Dominica was dressed demurely, in black sandals, a white cotton dress buttoned to the neck, and a black Panamanian shawl, an acute awareness of her extraordinary physical charms was never far from the surface of Max's consciousness ... or any other man's. The guards patrolling the grounds kept tripping over their own big feet looking at her.

"Nervous?" he asked again.

She wagged her finger at him from side to side, an oddly foreign gesture that he interpreted as "No." But then she shivered, rubbed her hands together, and smiled apologetically. "Just a little."

"Hey," he said, "the thought of Inmate Lonnie B. Rose is enough to put anyone up tight."

His intention had been to make her laugh, but she did not laugh, which was most unlike her, and they had to wait ten long minutes, in uneasy silence, before they saw her husband come striding up the hill.

In blue prison denim and a wispy blond goatee, Lonnie seemed even younger than the last time Max saw him, and he bounced along in his prison work boots like a self-conscious high school sophomore.

Watching him, Max could not help but lean across to Dominica again and whisper, out of the corner of his mouth, "The only thing I can't figure out is what you ever saw in the guy in the first place."

"Uh-huh, I just wondering about that myself," she murmured back. "But I's young then, you know, and I say to myself what they all does say."

"What's that?"

"'Well, he bad now, sho 'nough," she said, exaggerating her Jamaican accent, "but I gon' change his arse, make him a bettah mon.'"

Max laughed, bitterly, and he was still laughing when the inmate reached the table.

"Well, I'll be good goddamn, if it ain't the chief himself!" Lonnie said, after he'd squeezed into the seat beside Dominica and kissed her hello.

"So, how you keeping, Lonnie?" Max asked, and suddenly he felt his leg and arm muscles tightening up, his biceps twitching.

"Oh, I don't know," Lonnie said, sniffing, grinning crookedly, running his hand through his blond pompadour. "Same ole, same ole, I guess. Could be better. But not bad. Keeping my nose clean. Another few months and I'm up for parole. Then all I gotta do is the Fed time, ha-ha. But I hear my sis is doing pretty good."

"So damn good we hardly ever see her anymore. She's gonna be on national TV tonight. Channel 7. Ten o'clock. Try and catch it."

"I'll do that."

Lonnie had an uncustomary air of calm about him today. Prison had that effect on him, Max could see. It was a relief to him, perhaps. He no longer had to concern himself with adult cares. It was like the Air Force, where everything was provided. It was like Eagle Field, where he had been raised. It was home.

"Say, you know," Dominica said to her husband, looking through her bag. "Little Lonnie, he gimme a letter for you."

"Lonnie?"

"Yeah, your son, Lonnie Junior."

"Hey, I know who my son is."

"Well, you know, sometime I wonder."

"Now wait a second!"

"You ever send him a letter?"

"A letter? He's only . . ."

"He six years old now, Lonnie. In school in Gold Hill. He know the whole alphabet. Here, look."

Lonnie snatched the letter from her hand and sat puzzling over it—and the little cars and airplanes that his son had drawn on the side—for a long time, as if it were some lengthy official communication pertaining to his parole hearing.

Watching him, Max marveled for the hundredth time at the paradox of Lonnie's nature: slow on the uptake and dense to the point of stolidity, he was at the same time as flighty and unfeeling as a bird, insubstantial as water running through your hands.

Having perused the letter for some time, Lonnie read it out loud, slowly, carefully, enunciating every word as if it were the gospel truth: "'Dear Daddy how are you? I am fine. Miss you. Pray for you every night. Love, Lonnie Jr.'"

Finishing up, Lonnie raised his wide, lazy, remarkably innocent blue eyes from his reading and tried to compose his large, square-jawed face into what he had learned through experience was the proper response in cases of parental affection.

Watching him, watching his deep self-absorption take over and break his concentration, Max was sure that he had not thought of his little son in months.

"Oh, wow, that kid is somethin' else, ain't he?" Lonnie said, smiling so insincerely that it was almost a parody of childish deceit. "So," he went on, quickly changing the subject. "Where you stayin' now, babe?"

"Where else?"

"What? You still at Ruby and Max's place?" he asked, as if Max were not sitting right across from him.

"Where you send my letters?"

"Geez, you must be getting in their hair, by now. Why don't you go live with my dad at Eagle Field? He's sure got plenty of room."

"Your dad? We already been through that, Lonnie."

"I don't get it. Last time my dad was up here he said you and the kid was welcome any time."

"He telling you lies, Lonnie. He doan't give me the time of day, leave alone let me stay."

"Why not?"

"I tell you once, man, I tell you a hundred times. He blame me for what you do. I's the one that lead you to the life of crime."

"Well, maybe he's got something there. You know what I mean? If only you'd supported me a little more when I—"

"When what? Support you in the toilet when you shooting up? Support you when you puking whiskey? Support your mistress when you knock her up? Support the black man you knife in the back down in Panama? Support your best friend, Jim, when you rat on him?"

"Okay, okay," he said, peering furtively over each shoulder. "Calm down, babe, calm down. We only got another half hour."

"I want a divorce, Lonnie."

"A what?

"You heard me. A divorce."

"What for?" Lonnie demanded. And then, turning to Max with a cautious, feral look, winking incongruously, he added, "Say, bro, could you leave us alone for a minute?"

"No," Max said firmly, and with immense pleasure. "I'm afraid not."

"Huh?" Lonnie wondered, glancing rapidly back and forth from Max to Dominica, laughing as if it were some great joke.

"She said she wanted me to stay."

"Did you?" Lonnie demanded, twisting around to confront her, face to face. "Did you say that?"

"I . . . I need someone with me," Dominica said, drawing away from him.

"But how come, babe?" he asked, in an aggrieved tone. "How come?"

"Case you get mad."

"Mad? Mad? Why should I get mad?"

"You got rough with her before, right?" Max said, bracing himself for instant combat. "And she was afraid you might want to do it again."

"Hey, hey," Lonnie said, holding his hands up as if pleading for calm. "Let's not you and me get into it, bro. I got enough trouble on my hands."

"Fine by me," Max said, but he did not relax his guard.

"So," Lonnie said, sighing, turning to Dominica again. "What's all this shit about divorce?"

"Lonnie, I just can't go on like this no more."

"Like what?"

"The whole thing."

"You and me?"

"That only part of it," she said. "Like, I just make voting age and already my life seem half over."

"What you want to vote for? I'm a convict. Can't vote. And couldn't care less."

"You doan't understand."

"You got a boyfriend?" he asked and stopped to fix Max with the feral look again.

"Sometime, I wish."

"So, why don't you go ahead and do it?"

"Like I say, sometime, I wonder about that myself."

"Okay, I can see that," he said, suddenly modifying his tone, and reaching out to stroke her arm. Then he glanced up the hill toward the conjugal rights trailers. "So, what do you think?"

"What matter how I think?"

"Yeah," he said, and rose from his seat, pulling her up with him.

"I doan't go near that place, Lonnie," she said, shoving him away. "Less you sign the divorce papers."

"Where they at?"

"Right here in my bag."

"Lemme see."

Dominica gave him the papers; he read them over carefully, then laid them down on the picnic table in front of him. "Well, I know you been thinking about this for a long time," he said. "And you got your own life to lead, I guess."

"We still got Lonnie Junior, though. You always be his daddy; you know that."

"Sure, if that's the way you want it, babe, I'm not gonna be the one to stand in your way. But just as a matter of information," Lonnie said, holding the pen over the papers, "could you please tell me why you married me in the first place?"

Dominica thought fast.

"Well, I doan't know, Lonnie; I jus' fall for you, I s'pose," she said, with just the faintest trace of irony. "Fall like a ton o' bricks."

"Uh-huh," he scoffed. "I bet."

But her answer appeared to satisfy him in some perverse way, and he signed the document.

"Later, man," he said, winking at Max lasciviously, and led her up the hill.

Waiting for Dominica, imagining how she was fulfilling her bargain with Lonnie, Max felt neither anger, nor disgust, nor anything else he'd expected. What he felt was sexual arousal, to the point where he could barely hold his seat.

It was not the first time he had felt this way about Dominica, for she'd been a part of his fantasy life ever since she moved to the ranch. And a couple of times since Ruby went out on tour, he had felt that their long and uneasy familial relationship might suddenly take off in some exciting new direction. Once, he remembered, as they were saying goodnight outside her room, their bare skin touched inadvertently, and it was like a jolt of electricity passed through them; every hair on his arm seemed to stand on end. Another time, during a recent early hot spell, they took the boys swimming in Charlie Gonçalves' backyard swimming pool, and he rode all the way back from Lancaster with his sunburned white hand lying casually on her naked brown thigh, halfway between her dimpled knee and the line of her bathing suit. It got him so riled up that he could barely think straight when they got home, casting about wildly for some further excuse to touch her, have her touch him.

"Dominica, can you come in here a minute!" he hollered, without really planning it, just after he had stepped out of the shower. "Can you rub my shoulders and the backs of my legs with sunburn lotion?"

"Sure!" she shouted back, and came striding into the bathroom, grabbing up the lotion, squeezing it out of the tube, running her cool hands across his hot back, down his thighs, as briskly and competently as the practical nurse she was.

"Now do the front," he said, while she was still on her knees, finishing up his calves.

He had said it for a laugh, but they both grew instantly serious, mesmerized by the spectacle of his rising erection in the mirror beside them, and she quickly rose to her feet and left the room.

Then a couple of nights later, after work, he was wandering around the house in a pair of boxer shorts and heard Dominica in the bathroom, giving little Lonnie Junior a scrub. Obeying an impulse, he cracked the door and peeked in. She was bent over the tub, feet together, straight legged, naked as the day she was born. And the picture of her there—an elongated heart of shimmering brown with a tiny black question mark in the center—was almost too much for him to resist. He stood in the doorway, fixated on her, imagining himself smoothing up behind her, steely hard, springing out of his shorts and rubbing himself there, kneading her shoulder and neck muscles with his hands, while little Lonnie played with his toy sailboat, unaware. But then he backed away, slipped off down the hall, as much for his own sake as for the boy's. The one thing Ruby would never forgive, he knew, was an adventure with her sister-in-law.

Twenty minutes after Dominica went up to the conjugal meeting, she came trailing back down the hill on her own, crying into her hanky.

"What'd he do to you?" Max demanded, bolting from his seat, lunging up the hill to meet her. "What'd he do?"

"Oh, relax, man, he doan't do nothing," Dominica sniffled, as he helped her into a seat at the picnic table. "It just me. Up there in that trailer, alone with him, you know, I feel so open. Like, because of Lonnie Junior, he got some power over me. But thank Jesus, he quick with his work. He doan't like women too much, I think. No telling what he do in that joint. Anyway, he crawl off, and he standing by the door, buckling up his pants.

"'See you round, babe,' he say.

"'I give Lonnie Junior your love,' I say.

"'You do that, and I do this!' he say. Then he grab up the divorce papers from the table like he gon' rip 'em up.

"'No, no, Lonnie, please!' I holler.

"He hold the papers tight in his hands. His knuckles go red. He press harder, twist 'em up. Then he go, *"Rip!"* Pretend like he tearing 'em up.

"'You never woulda forgive me for that,' he say, and he reach for the door. 'Would you?'

"'I doan't know, Lonnie,' I say, 'I already forgive worse.'

"'I catch you with Max, or any other man, when I get out,' he say. 'I kill you both.'

"But then after he close the door, I can hear him laughing to himself outside. He whoop and holler once, then he head off down the back way. And, you know, layin' there alone, panties round my ankles, skirt yanked over my hips, I wonder why—after I get what I want from that man, and a lot cheaper than I expect—why I feelin' so low."

On the drive home, Dominica was silent, impassive, staring out the window into the fog as if she were disgusted with all men.

Watching her out of the corner of his eye, Max felt a welter of emotions, from pity to protectiveness to lust.

That night on a Denver television show, Ruby swaggered onto the set leading with her cane, wearing a cowgirl outfit and too much make-up, grinning like she had the world by the tail. She had put on weight from junk food and hotel fare and looked a bit like a red-headed Dolly Parton, or a rodeo queen limping from a bad ride. Watching her, Max sought the pretty, bouncy little aspiring actress he had fallen in love with; and her painted face, her odd costume, her crooked walk, they broke his heart.

"Ladies and gentlemen, Ms. Ruby Rose from Sand Canyon Ranch, Antelope Valley, California!" the announcer shouted, making their modest ranch sound like a Spanish Land Grant spread. And everyone at home and in the studio audience cheered.

The host and hostess—a slick little Italian-looking dude and a tall willowy blond with a nose job—rose to greet her. At first, they seemed almost frightened of her, as if they thought she might say something unspeakably vulgar. She set them at their ease almost immediately, however, by smoothly fielding their question about why she had written her book.

"As a starstruck teenager, I used to look up above my desert home and see the Tudor mansion of the silent movie queen, Hillary Bennett, standing splendidly alone and unassailable on barren Anaverde Ridge," she began, quoting without attribution from the preface of her book. "In the dog days of August one year, I borrowed my father's pickup truck and drove up the ridge and into Miss Bennett's yard."

Ruby had memorized the passage verbatim, but she rendered it in such a sincere and natural tone that even Max, who had heard parts of it read aloud at home and knew it to be composed almost entirely of bullshit, was nearly convinced.

Then they asked her about her illness. And he cringed in embarrassment to hear her describe their "last dance together at the Panama City Hilton," and their "lovemaking, perhaps for the last time," in their room at the clinic. But the audience ate it up. Even Max's own living room ate it up. Sybil and Dominica were *crying*, for Christ's sake!

Later that night when Ruby phoned, Max called her on it, and accused her of lying.

"That's not lying!" she protested. "It's fictional reality."

"What's the fucking difference?"

"Oh, I can't explain anything to you, Max," she said. "You don't understand anything."

Chapter Seventeen

Ruby woke up in a hotel room with all the lights on and could not remember where she was. She consulted her watch. 9:55. But what day it was, or whether it was a.m. or p.m., she could not say. She was lying face down on a black and gray quilted bedspread, wearing only a pair of black bikini panties. Her hair was still damp, as if from a shower. There was a cold cigarette butt between her fingers, burnt right down to the filter, and it seemed that she had to be some place soon. But she could not imagine where. Rolling over, rising from the bed, she flicked the butt in a wastebasket and went limping across the plush, pink and white, oval-shaped room to the window.

Peeking out through the heavy drapery, she could see that it was nighttime, and that she was up very high, at least forty floors, in the downtown area of a large city. But she had no idea which city, any more than she knew what hotel she was in.

Feeling faint, she staggered back across the shaggy white carpet and fell on the bed. Her heart was beating frantically, there was a loud buzzing noise in her right ear, and her head ached something fierce.

"Why do I feel this way?" she wondered out loud.

It occurred to her that perhaps she was merely tired. She could not remember how much she had slept the night before last, or even where she had slept, but she was often tired because her schedule was tight, sometimes two and three cities a day, and *Good Times Press* was always changing it to fit new demands.

Also, after all the media exposure, she sometimes found it difficult calming down at night. Her mind just kept racing, as if she were still in front of an audience. Lying in the dark sometimes, her eyes glued open, staring at the shadows on the wall, she would ask herself why she bothered. It was a harder life than she had ever imagined, and there would be months more of it when the paperback version of her book came out—including a European tour. But it was the life she had chosen, she would remind herself, the only life she had ever wanted. Besides, she was hooked now, and there was no turning back.

Pressing her thumb against the bridge of her nose, Ruby tried to think. It seemed to her that she had flown from Miami this morning, though it might have been from Charleston or Savannah.

The interior of the plane, the stewardesses who served her, she could recollect without any trouble. But the sky had been hazy, visibility limited. And when they began to circle for a landing there was little to distinguish the green and leafy city below her from any other large inland city in the southeastern United States.

An hour after her arrival, she recalled, she was in the make-up room of a downtown TV studio, preparing for her appearance on "The Inner-City Show." The assistant director, a young Black woman named Keisha, came in and escorted her out to the wings. Ruby had no idea what the set-up was, whether she was walking into a friendly or hostile environment, or who was going to interview her, except that the person's name was Dacey Woodrow. She felt the familiar adrenalin rush, the familiar jitters. It was such a wonderful sense of uncertainty, of possibility, of risk and opportunity, and she thrived on it.

"We have a special guest on our show this morning," said an avuncular male voice, slightly Black in accent and timbre, coming from just inside the curtain. "Her name is Ruby Rose, and she's written a fascinating book called DESERT LOVE."

This was apparently Ruby's cue, because off-camera Keisha was motioning her forward.

Striding out into the TV lights, swinging her cane like a weapon, Ruby found herself in a newsroom. A kindly looking old Black man was seated before her, alone in the anchor chair. He was wearing a pin-stripe suit with a vest and a gold key chain, and he was smiling at her in the sweetest and most natural way.

Yet, he seemed a bit surprised, as if he had expected someone slightly different, as if he might have assumed that Ruby Rose would be Black.

She moved toward him.

Off camera, Peggy motioned her to sit down beside him.

"Good morning, Ruby," he said, patting her on the hand, as if he had known her forever, as if indeed, red hair and freckles and all, she was as black as himself.

"Good morning, Dacey," Ruby replied in kind.

"Now, why don't you just tell us about this book you've written, honey, and about your triumph over misfortune."

Taking his cue, playing to what she had instantly perceived to be a largely Black and female viewing audience, she accentuated her struggles and pain, the troubles she had known, and her victory over adversity. And the rest of the interview was a piece of cake.

A half hour later, at another studio, she taped her usual eight-minute spot on the local *Morning Show*, to be aired tomorrow.

Her next appearance was on a radio talk show, out in some working-class suburb. Her host, whose name she had forgotten, was obscenely fat, with long, lank, black hair and a rustic, Georgia Hill Country accent. His instincts toward her were hostile—"Ladies and Gentlemen, we have a guest this morning from California, the land of the almighty shekel"—and his callers were ignorant and opinionated, but she won them all over quickly and easily with (fictionalized) talk of her late and lamented mother, Alma Stroud, "unfavored daughter of the Deep South, fugitive from a sharecropper's cabin in Beauregard Parish, Louisiana."

For an hour or so around noon, she signed books at Dalton's in the Peachtree Plaza Shopping Mall.

After lunch, she taped The *Dr. Helen Denning Show*, at another TV studio. Dr. Helen Denning was a pop psychologist, and every week her show focused on a different aspect of mental health, emphasizing self-help cures and the benefits of positive attitude. This week her theme was "Beating Cancer," and she had three other guests beside Ruby who had recovered from various forms of the disease. The show should have been a snap for Ruby because she had already done The *Dr. Joyce Brothers Show* in New York and Dr. Joyce was the queen of them all. But she'd drunk too much *Pouilly Fuisse* at lunch, her fellow guests depressed her—one had lost a leg, another her breasts—and she lost her train of thought. Fortunately, the others were even less adept, so nobody noticed.

At 4 p.m., she taped her usual five-minute spot on "The Evening News."

Afterwards, having a drink in the bar downstairs, she consulted her itinerary and discovered for the first time that she was scheduled to depart for Dallas on Delta Airlines, Flight 241 at 11 p.m., August 5, 1976, arriving at 3 a.m. on August 6, 1976.

Furious, she walked into a phone booth and called Mimi Threadgill, publicity director at *Good Times Press*, to demand an explanation.

"God, Mimi, what'd you put me on the Red-Eye for? You know I'm on The Gary Fellows Show at the crack of dawn."

"I know, I know," Mimi agonized. "And, God knows, Gary Fellows is no day at the beach. But for some reason the airlines were all booked up. This is the only flight I could get."

Ruby raised hell with her and demanded to talk to Felicity.

"Oh, I'm so sorry, Ruby, but she's in conference right now."

Ruby hung up, dialed Felicity's private number, let it ring four times, and left a message: "Phone me in ten minutes or I walk."

Ten minutes later, Felicity rang her in the booth.

"Look, relax, Ruby. I tell you what, why don't you just check into the best hotel in Atlanta for the evening and bill it to Good Times?"

"Atlanta," Ruby said. "Is that where I am today?"

"Is it Tuesday?"

"Yes."

"If it's Tuesday, then it must be Atlanta," she said, laughing at her little joke. "Now go have yourself a good soak and a nice long nap, love, and the flight will be a breeze."

She took Felicity's advice, checked into the Hyatt Regency, instructed the management to awaken her at nine thirty, threw herself on the bed and tried to sleep. But she couldn't sleep.

She kept thinking of home, of Max and Ned. Kept seeing these little, fuzzy, romanticized, blips and bursts and out-takes of their life together—Sundays at Sand Canyon Reservoir, picnics in Red Rock canyon, knapsack hikes through Devil's Postpile National Monument, vacations at Refugio Beach State Park, Christmases around the tree in the Victorian, Thanksgiving dinners at Grandma Sybil's house—choppily edited two and three second cuts running together end to end like a TV ad, with a schmaltzy musical background of electric harmonicas and weepy violins.

She turned on the light and glanced at her watch. It was 6 p.m. Eastern Standard Time. In California, it would be three in the afternoon. Her boy, Ned, a high school sophomore, would just be getting out of school. Soon he would catch the bus and head for home.

She pictured him getting off the bus alone, trudging up the driveway to the Bauer house with his books on his back, sitting down in the kitchen to his afternoon cookies and milk, and worried about him, reproached herself for neglecting him, wanted achingly to be by his side, loved him even more because he was such a bitter disappointment to his father.

Poor baby, she thought. His voice that had seemed so husky at ten was now a little boy voice. He hadn't even gotten pimples yet; his skin was still as smooth and clear as it had been at five. Little Lonnie was his only real friend. And there were big, buxom girls in his tenth-grade class who could have been his mother. He dreaded the monthly Sock Hops because they laughed at him when he asked them to dance. And since Ruby had gone out on tour, he had become almost totally reclusive, Sybil said, locking the door to his room and hiding in there for hours on end. He had even given up his music lessons, she said. Yet, when Ruby got him on the phone this morning (or was it yesterday morning?), he had acted completely normal, and laughed off any suggestion that he was feeling lonely or depressed.

"He's on good behavior with you," Max said, when—at 6 p.m. Eastern Standard Time and still unable to sleep—Ruby dialed him at the garage in Lancaster, "so you don't see his problems."

"What are his problems, Max?"

"Well," he said, "far be it from me to bother you with family matters when you're out on the road."

"Whatever it is, I gather that I'm supposed to be to blame."

"If the shoe fits, Ruby, wear it."

"You think I ought to call off the tour and come home?"

"Hey, you do what you want to do."

"And what do you care, Max? What difference would it make?"

"Who're we talking about here, Ned or us? Look, I'm just trying to tell you that he's gotten real sullen here lately, at least around the house. Sits around and mopes and won't say a word to anyone. Then I get this letter from the principal. Says in school he's just the opposite; always acting up, making noise, disturbing the class."

"Have you talked to his teacher?"

"Now when would I do that? I work till seven thirty at night."

"You ever heard of the phone?"

"Goddamnit, it's easy for you to cast stones, Ruby, because you're not the one on the spot."

"Okay, I tell you what I'll do. I'll take him with me on the coast leg of my tour. He ought to get a kick out of that. And we'll have time to talk it out."

"When does that happen?"

"In about a week and a half."

"He'll still be in school."

"So, we'll take him out a week early."

"Fine," Max said, a little too quickly, Ruby thought.

"I can tell you mean it."

"I always say what I mean."

"Not always."

"What are you talking about?"

"I love you," she said, ringing off. And then, into the dead receiver: "But I don't think you really want to see me again."

Then she had another whiskey and started feeling sorry for herself. She recalled helping Max fold his newspapers, out on the lawn in front of Eagle Field. Their rides to Antelope Valley Joint Union High School in the school bus. Their days on his motorcycle. Their nights in his pickup truck. Their secret Ruby Canyon. Their lunchtime trysts when they first got married. The birth of their son. Their trip to Panama.

She tried to imagine a future with Max. She tried to place him with herself a few months hence, after she got the TV talk show hostess spot that she was scheming for, or at a literary party in New York or Paris, at a cocktail party in her dream house in Beverly Hills with everyone in black ties and evening gowns. She saw herself beside him, wearing a black, sequined dress. She sensed how he felt, among all those elegant people, in his rented tux, his Western bulk, his plain weathered face, his barrel chest and short thick legs.

And she asked herself: Would you give up everything you want, everything you're working for, if you could get him back? And the answer, clear as the mirror before her, was difficult to support. So, she poured herself yet another whiskey, popped a couple of sleeping pills, had herself a little cry, and fell asleep on the bed with a lit cigarette in her hand.

Now, several hours later, having recalled and reassembled the missing and jumbled pieces at last, and wishing she hadn't, Ruby dragged herself off the bed, showered, made up, dressed, packed, made it down to the lobby somehow, caught a taxi for the airport, and boarded the Red-Eye for Dallas.

The plane was packed with religious fundamentalists from all over the south, heading for a convention in Fort Worth. One of the few empty seats in First Class, as it happened, was with Tom Pool, a movie actor she had met on a live panel show in Boston and then run into later at a taping session in Baltimore.

Tottering down the aisle, managing her cane and overnight bag only with some difficulty, she decided to swing in beside him.

"Mind a little company, Tom?"

"Be my guest."

"I was just wondering how I was going to get myself through the night."

"You know, that's funny. I was thinking along the same lines."

"Misery loves company, I guess."

"So, they say. Where you headed?"

"Dallas."

"What show?"

"Gary Fellows."

"Me too."

"No kidding?"

"Yeah. You know, Ruby, we oughta put our heads together on that reactionary fucker. Try to figure out how he's gonna jerk us around."

"Right on, Tom!" she said, in the voice of Dacey Woodrow. "Let's strategize, and deal with his ass."

In fact, they didn't get much strategizing done at all. But they killed some time, had a few giggles, did a lot of sipping at Ruby's bottle of Johnny Walker, got each other through a rough, bouncy take-off, and by the time they reached cruising altitude they had established a small and temporary rapport.

Tom (*né* Polatschek) was thirty-one years old and six foot, three inches, with a hatchet face, coarse, dirty-blond hair, ruddy, acne-scarred skin, and a rough, laconic speaking voice that the critics had called "compellingly working-class." A former coal miner from Port Carbon, Pennsylvania, he played street fighters, psychos, and stone killers in the movies. Though he was making the publicity rounds, touting his most recent thriller, he was furious with the studios now.

"I want leading roles," he growled, over their second Scotch. "I deserve leading roles."

"Why won't they give them to you, Tom?"

"Word's out that I'm 'hard to handle.'"

"Is it true?"

"Not with you, honey," he laughed. "With you I'm a fucking pussy cat."

The fundamentalists all went to sleep, and from then on, the flight was a breeze until, 29,000 feet above the Sabine River, the plane started to pitch and yaw, wending its way around towering banks of inky black thunderheads. Lightning lit up the sky, thunder clapped all around, charges of eerie blue electricity rippled across the wings, and everyone woke up and started to get jumpy.

At which point the bottom dropped out.

Tom, who had unstrapped himself to go to the bathroom, flailed in slow motion toward the ceiling, like a reluctant astronaut. Ruby, with a large gulp of Scotch halfway down her gullet, closed her eyes and held her breath, thinking, *Goodbye, boys; it was great while it lasted.* The flight attendant, a sweet young thing with the face of an Irish saint, went down on her knees in the aisle, clinging to the seat pedestal, and raised her eyes to heaven in agony, while Tom's drink tray spun listlessly in the air above her head, like a halo, and the fundamentalists all started screaming at the tops of their lungs for Jesus to deliver them from death. Then, having lost ten thousand feet of altitude in thirty seconds, the plane abruptly met with solid air again and everything including Tom and the tray came down with a bang. Surprisingly, only glass was broken, and a few minutes later the pilot came on the intercom to announce that he had everything under control.

"I'd like to take this opportunity to apologize for the momentary inconvenience we suffered back there, and to assure you that we'll have smooth sailing ahead, all the way into Dallas," he said, in a languorous Carolina drawl, and went on to discuss in some detail the nature and perils of "air pockets."

When he was done, passengers and cabin crew stood as one and—like skyjack victims—applauded the author of their torments with heartfelt emotion.

In Dallas, it turned out that Ruby and Tom had been booked into the same hotel, so they decided on a nightcap in Ruby's room. The nightcap turned into three or four and somewhere toward dawn there came a moment when it seemed to Ruby that they might as well just roll into bed together for the hour or two before they had to face Gary Fellows.

What's the percentage in virtue? she asked herself, as Tom thrust his tongue into her mouth and groped beneath her skirt. But at the last moment she felt the abyss open up at her feet again, just as it had the time she wore her mother's dress.

"Why not?" Tom wanted to know when she pushed him away.

"I'm a married woman," she said.

Chapter Eighteen

Max got up early, headed down to the kitchen, brewed up a pot of coffee and carried a couple of hot cups up to Dominica's room—one for himself and one for her. After he'd pushed through her door, though, he was unsure of how to proceed, so he just kind of stood there for a minute or two, looking around.

He loved Dominica's room, so different from any other in the house, so out of place amid all that Victorian clutter. He loved the straw mat floor that she had put in, the dangling vines, the rubber plants, the flowers everywhere.

With Dominica, you were never far from the rain forest, he thought, and approached her across the room, carrying the steaming coffee before him.

He sat on the bed beside her, set the coffee down on the straw mat, and leaned forward over her voluptuous hip and breast, marveling at the peacefulness of her sleep. She was such a simple organism, he thought, in comparison with himself, Ruby, and Ned. It thrilled him that she was uncomplicated, that her needs were elemental. All she asked of life was contentment. He liked that. And he liked the sweet earthy smell of her sleeping flesh, the heaviness of her eyelids, her pretty, mocha brown face smeared with lipstick and make-up, the medusa-like snarls of her thick black hair. He even loved her little son, curled up like a dark tousle-headed cupid at her breast. Yesterday, the day before yesterday, Max had crept into their room and stood silently over them, watching them sleep, and the yearning that he had felt was more than he could bear.

So, he'd hit upon this coffee scheme.

He leaned further now, nosed into her fragrant hair, kissed her ear. She smiled in her sleep. He kissed her again. He couldn't stop.

"Mmmmmmm," she said, smiling, stretching out under the sheets, and her eyes fluttered open.

"How about some coffee?" he said and reached down for the cup.

"Thank you, Max," she said, sitting up, still smiling up at him, folding the sheet around her breast. "Is my birthday, or somethin'?"

"Just a momentary inspiration," he said, handing her the cup. "But it could get to be a habit."

A couple of nights later, after the kids were in bed, they ran into each other in the upstairs hallway. "Eh, Max," she said, "friend of mine just send me a little gift from the Zone."

"What kind?"

"Want some?" she asked, and reached into a little paper bag she was carrying and pulled out a matchbox of Panama Red.

"Sure, why not?" he replied, though in fact he had never tried the stuff in his life.

They went down to the living room together, she rolled it up into a torpedo-sized joint, took a puff that nearly popped the stays on her peasant blouse, and offered it to Max. He had a toke, they passed it back and forth, and ten minutes later they were stoned out of their minds. Dominica turned the stereo up and put on Jimmy Cliff's "The Harder They Come."

"Come on," Max said. "Let's dance."

"Where you learn to reggae, man?"

"I make it up as I go along," he said, and she swayed into his arms.

Holding Dominica gave Max such a sudden rush of pleasure that his mouth fell open. It was like this *"Oooooh!"* expression that he could do nothing to prevent, and he hoped that she had not glanced in the mirror to see him. He pressed her tight, crushing her breasts up against his chest.

"Oh, the officers are trying to keep me down,"
Jimmy Cliff sang, "treating me like a clown.
Well, the harder they come, the harder they fall
one and all."

Their thighs rubbed together with every step. Her head was on his shoulder, her breath on his neck. The space between their bodies felt like it might burst into flames.

"Okay, man," she said, pushing him away. "We start that shit and they gon' be hell to pay, 'cause Ruby be my friend."

And Max instantly obeyed her, almost with relief.

It was like a teasing, childish, mildly incestuous game between them. If it ever came to fruition, they knew, all the lightness and playfulness would disappear, and the weight of adultery would descend upon their heads.

Then one evening he came in from the garage and saw her working in the kitchen. Beyond her, in the living room, he could hear the TV blaring, and assumed that Lonnie Junior was there, while Ned was probably up in his room reading. He found it exciting, somehow, that this charming vision of her was his alone. And he stopped in the doorway to watch her for a moment. She was standing at the counter, chopping vegetables into a pan of sizzling olive oil for her main course—*Liver Venetian Style*. "Chop, chop, chop," went her knife, missing her quick, sure fingers by centimeters, and the peppers and onions just flew. But her young and pretty foreign face seemed as calm and placid as that of some dark Madonna, and she even swayed slightly to the reggae music on the cassette recorder beside her on the counter.

Suddenly it seemed important to Max that he creep up behind Dominica and surprise her. Yet, as he approached her, she became aware of his step, recognized it, put down the paring knife, and turned to greet him. She was smiling as she turned, and it was such a broad, beautiful, sunlit smile, a smile of such obvious delight to see him, that he walked right up to her and took her in his arms. She offered no resistance, though they were both acutely aware of the boys nearby. He brushed her cheek and the corner of her mouth with his lips. She closed her eyes. The smile left her face. He smelled her hair, her skin; it was an aphrodisiac to him. And suddenly his tongue was in her mouth, their teeth were clicking together, and their hearts were beating like mad.

It was a kiss like no other in his life, a kiss to stir the soul and the loins, a kiss that would prevent sleep at night, a kiss that would inspire endless masturbatory fantasies, a kiss that was as good as fucking, sufficient unto itself, a kiss that would remain forever labeled in Max's imagination as "THE KISS" in capital letters. Lips, tongues, teeth pressed together, they kissed for what seemed an eternity, groping at each other instinctively, running their hands over bottoms and hips and backs and breasts, oblivious to everything, until Dominica's sauteing veggies began to smoke up the kitchen and she had to turn off the flame.

For a long time after that—long, as Max was reckoning things: two or three days—they did nothing but kiss. The kiss became their "be-all and end-all." They awaited it all day with the greatest hunger and anticipation, and when they finally managed to find a moment alone—in the service porch, the kitchen, or the hall—they were ravenous, insatiable. Sometimes their kisses went on for fifteen or twenty minutes, until their lips were bruised, their tongues ached, and they were no longer sure whose mouth was whose.

"Ruby my friend, Ruby my friend," Dominica kept protesting, and made sure they were never alone long enough for anything else to happen. Still, she could not stop the kissing any more than Max.

All his life, Max had prided himself on being a calm and deliberate person, a man of moderation. But this was not like anything he'd ever experienced before. He was as obsessed with Dominica as Ruby had been with her book. He couldn't eat, sleep, or stop thinking about her. On the job he drank too much coffee. His heart beat so fast he feared a heart attack, and he could not keep his mind on his work. He would be in the middle of overhauling a Jaguar Mark IV, with the parts spread out all around him, and he would blank out for ten minutes, imagining their last kiss, feeling her body pressed against his. He would be in the middle of an important business conversation with Charlie, and he would drift off to Dominica's bed, smelling it, feeling it.

"Max, Max, goddamnit, wake up, this is serious shit!"

He was like a teenager with a crush. His cock was always semi-hard. A couple of times a day his balls ached for her so much that he had to crawl up in the tire attic where Lonnie used to sleep and beat off into his hanky just to release the tension. He was astounded at how much sperm he was producing. There was enough to populate the world, he thought. Eventually, though, his sleeplessness wore him down. He began to feel listless and ill. He caught a cold and could barely talk. All the cliches about sexual passion, he found, were true. It sapped your energy for anything else, made you languorous, worthless for the work-a-day world. He kept thinking that once this love was consummated, then everything would be okay. But he knew he was only kidding himself.

Sometimes, riven with guilt, Max would see the whole thing as a conflict of spirit and flesh. And when he thought about Dominica, he would see her as a witch, a voodoo priestess, a devil in his flesh, and he would wish that she'd just go away. After all, he and Ruby had a life together. Maybe it wasn't the greatest life, anymore. But it was not a bad life. And it was their life. Over the years they had worked it out, and they were sometimes happy. If it ended now, it would just be such a monumental waste of time, energy, and emotion. And he had no illusions about what a divorce would do to Ned. Still, he had this terrible feeling of inevitability. It was like he and Dominica were both caught up in something they could do nothing about, something bigger than both: fate.

The next Sunday afternoon he was driving Dominica to the supermarket, and he got to talking. He did not talk about important stuff, just kind of passed the time of day. Anything to get his mind off what was on it. But it was so unlike him that Dominica had to laugh.

"Now, Max Bauer, what got into you, man?"

Thus encouraged, Max talked some more, and some more. Talked all the way into town, all the way through the supermarket and all the way back. Then, gazing out across the floor of the desert, casting about desperately for something else to say, he thought suddenly of the secret canyon. It was the one intimate family secret that Ruby had not seen fit to reveal in her book. He considered for a moment whether she had told Dominica about it, in private. She had told her many things, he knew, but he was willing to bet she had not told her about Ruby Canyon. So, he took a chance.

"Dominica, I want to tell you about something," he said, "something that's important to me. I was out hunting one morning when I was a kid. I shot a bobcat, tracked it down, and then I heard a goat bleating. I followed the sound into a hidden canyon."

He did not tell her that he had later taken Ruby there, that it had once meant everything to them. He just told her how he found the place, became captivated by it, spent much time there, and then forgot its existence for years.

"And you know, I only rediscovered it a few months ago by chance, when I was out hunting in Bitterroot Canyon," he said, while Dominica listened, as enrapt as Ruby had been when he first told the story to her. "And the funny thing is, even though the whole area is crisscrossed with RV tracks, the canyon itself is still untouched. I went inside and fell asleep on the sand, by a little spring, and dreamed of Indian girls. Some of them, I must admit, looked a little bit like you. So, I started going to the canyon more and more, just to be alone. One day I was sitting by the pool, staring at the bottom, and I saw what looked to me like gold. Right away I thought, 'Goddamn, this place was passed over by the gold rush, I bet it's another Mother Lode!' So, I took a sample down to the county assayer's office and guess what."

"I doan't know. What?"

"They said it was fool's gold."

"Well, I never hear such a story in my life!" Dominica laughed. "Never hear you talk so much neither."

"You don't like it?"

"Oh yes," she murmured. "I like it a lot."

And it was then that their bare arms touched again.

Would you like to go there now?" he asked her, breathlessly.

"I doan't think so, man."

"Why not?"

"Too much like Panama," she said, "jizzing about like that with the sand up your arse. I gon' fuck-over the best friend I ever had? It gon' be in bed."

That night, long after the TV had gone quiet, and the boys had sluffed off to bed, and the house had grown silent, Max heard Dominica close the door to her room and pad down the hallway. Instantly, his erection made a tent of the sheet.

Thrusting her head in his bedroom door, Dominica smiled, slipped in, and pushed it shut behind her. Then she loosened the tie on her robe and let it fall to her feet. For a moment she just stood there before him, tall and lithe and proud, letting him get an eyeful. Oh, but Sweet Jesus what a body that girl had! Such a tiny waist. Such round brown buttocks and breasts. Such a wondrous want of body hair. Watching her, his rod now making a Big Top of the sheet, Max could not help but reflect on how much less naked she looked than Ruby.

With her pallid, freckled skin, and her mass of red pubic hair, Ruby seemed so nude, so out of her element, so defenseless when she took off her clothes. A man might experience a greater sense of triumph in getting a woman like her naked, but he might also feel a faint, ever so faint, twinge of nastiness in doing it. Almost as if there were something slightly off-color in her soft, white vulnerability.

Ah, but Dominica! Naked, she was in her element.

"You want me now?" she whispered.

"What do you think?" he replied, and she tiptoed across the room and slipped into the bed beside him.

Her skin was dry and warm, and so smooth to the touch that when Max brushed it with his cock, he felt like it might burst a blood vessel.

"Kiss it, for God's sake, kiss it," he murmured, "before it explodes."

Rising to her knees, she took his aching penis in her hand, thrust it wetly into her mouth, and started sucking. She sucked for an eternity, it seemed, sliding it to the hilt and then gently letting go, running her fingers lightly about his scrotum and ass.

Then, without pulling out of her mouth, he scissored around, grabbed her by the hips, thrust his face in her smooth and nearly hairless cunt and stuck his tongue inside. As they "went 69," she opened her legs wider and began to undulate against his mouth. He slithered his tongue out of her vagina and lapped at her clitoris till she cried out loud. Then he came in her mouth, and she gurgled it down.

Five minutes later she got him hard again, threw a leg over him, and impaled herself on his prick with a great sigh. Rising off it, falling upon it, riding it like a pony, she went at first very slowly, then faster and faster, her large dark breasts bouncing up and down as he cupped them with his hands.

She closed her eyes in ecstasy and fell upon him, still thrusting instinctively, her long, heavy, black hair falling around his head. He ran his hands around her lunging hips and gripped her about the buttocks as hard as he could, his fingers gouging the crack of her ass. And he met her thrust for thrust. Synchronized, they accelerated like a Triumph in first gear, and he came again. She felt it spurt up inside her and shrieked with pleasure, so loud he was afraid the children would awaken. Thrusting even faster, almost frightening him with the violence of her movements, she convulsed in another orgasm.

Sated, Max was still semi-hard, and stayed inside her as he rolled her over and rested beside her. She opened her eyes. They looked at each other and smiled.

"I love you," he said. Yet, even as he said it, he knew that it was not exactly true.

What he felt was completely physical, but of such a high order that it was a quantum leap beyond anything he had known before. Her darkness was what got him, her darkness against his whiteness. He knew it was probably a racist notion, but, mounting her, he felt her ripple and swell under him like the contours of the earth. And the earth was alive, steaming, hissing, and moving under him, smelling of the primordial soup. When he kissed her mouth, he tasted eternity. When he sucked her breasts, he sucked at the fountain of life. When he lapped at her cunt, he drank of the wellspring of being. Her breath was intoxicating to him, like inhaling the scent of every tropical flower at once. When she swallowed his cock and made him come, he felt that fish eggs and pollywogs might suddenly come wriggling out of her eyes, ears, mouth, and nose.

He could never, never get enough of her.

Nor she him.

They fucked all night. They fucked till the alarm went off, till the kids were banging at the door for their breakfast. They fucked all morning, leaving Ned and Lonnie to get themselves off to school alone and run up the hill to beg breakfast from Sybil. They fucked till noon, leaving Charlie and Gil alone at the garage, fuming, phoning, screaming over the answering machine, "Where the fuck you at, Max, you sonofabitch?" They fucked all day, all the next night and the next day too. Lonnie Junior hadn't a clue what had gone wrong and cried endlessly for his mama. But Ned knew exactly what was up and he let them know it: "Come on out of there, you two, or I'm gonna tell on you!"

Meanwhile the pressure built inexorably. Chaos reigned at home, at school, at the garage. Charlie threatened a lawsuit. Juanita threatened to phone Ruby and tell her the whole story.

Sybil threatened to have them arrested for child neglect and swore she had made her last meal for the boys, washed her last pair of jeans. The truant officer of Gold Hill School District came by to ask why Ned Bauer and Lonnie Rose Jr. had been absent two days in a row with no written excuse. For a time, it seemed that the entire town of Gold Hill was outside their bedroom door, banging to be let in. But still they would not come out. For days on end they were lost, drowning in sweat and spit and sexual juices.

They were one; and they left the rest of their lives undone.

Chapter Nineteen

Ruby canceled her flight to Salt Lake City, booked a seat to Bob Hope Airport in Burbank, and all the way across the Great American Desert from Denver she was trying to figure out the best way to confront Max and Dominica with what she knew.

The most reasonable and dignified approach, she thought, was to say nothing of treachery, to assign no blame at all. She would simply ask what their intentions were. Let the chips fall where they may.

As the trip wore on, however, she felt less and less inclined toward mercy.

Then, once on home ground, she found herself strangely reluctant, almost frightened, to face the lovers at all, and thought a talk with her old man first might help put things in perspective.

So, she rented a Cadillac, drove through Palmdale, heading out toward Eagle Field, and a funny thing happened. She began to see the familiar sun-bleached landscape before her as a stranger might see it, coming from some far distant land.

Under a vast upturned bowl of blue October sky, across a dull, spilled custard of desert plain, the decrepit old air base appeared to her first as a mirage in the highway ahead, or another dry lake. Coming nearer, she caught a glimpse through the rising heat waves of concrete bunkers, overgrown runways, sand-drifted support roads, the reflecting walls of metal hangars, machine shops and Quonset huts. And the place began to take shape before her: the boarded-up administration building, the Air Force control tower with all its windows shot out, the abandoned Squadron HQ building, the PX, the BOQ, the Married Officers' Quarters, and Link Trainer buildings which after the war had become the dormitories and hospital facilities of Eagle Field State Prison and were now occupied by Reno's teeming progeny of house cats gone wild.

Turning into the pot-holed access road, she drove past the bullet-pocked "No Trespassing" sign, the derelict gatehouse, the rusted perimeter fence. Then, lost in a swirl of dust, she pulled up before the sandblasted old military barracks and corroding Quonset huts where she, Lonnie, Dee, Gil, Juanita, Sally, and Eddie Marczaly had been raised amid the demented howling of the criminally insane. And she noted, as if for the first time, that since the departure of the state not a tree or shrub or flower or blade of grass remained in the entire six hundred acre complex, except for the little patch of green around Reno's house. And it struck her that you would have to travel far and wide to discover an equally bleak or forbidding place.

"Well now, what can the matter be?" Dominica had wanted to know the day before, as soon as she got on the line, and her melodious voice was a great comfort to Ruby.

"Oh, I don't know, Dominica. The usual, I guess. Gary Fellows had me for breakfast this morning, I haven't slept a wink, I've got to catch a plane for Denver in a couple of hours, and I miss you all very much."

"We miss you too, love."

"So, where's Ned and Lonnie?"

"Oh," she said. "Oh, they with Max, I think. Over at his mama's place."

"You mean Max isn't at work?"

"Mmmmmm," Dominica said, and something in her tone sounded off. "Him and Charlie fall out again. Max say he never set foot in that garage long as he live. Say he gon' look for a mechanic job at Jimmy Fisher Ford. Be poor that way, he say, but a lot more happy."

"Oh, it'll blow over soon enough, Dominica," she said. "It always does. Give him my love when he comes in, okay? And the boys too."

But her mind was racing again.

Something did not fit.

If Max had not gone to work, what had he and Dominica done together all day while the kids were at school?

She picked up the phone again immediately after she had rung off and dialed Sybil's place.

Ned answered the phone.

"Mom? Mom? Is that you?"

At first, she was taken aback, as if she had not recognized his voice, and it took her a moment to respond.

"Oh, Ned!" she burst out. "Ned, honey, you'll never know how much I miss you!"

"I miss you too, Mom."

"How . . . how've you been?"

"Fine, fine," he said, but his voice sounded oddly lifeless.

"What is it, Honey?"

"Nothing, Mom."

"Where's your dad?"

"Dad? Uh, I dunno."

"You don't know? But Dominica said he was with you."

"Dominica says a lot of things."

"Oh, really?" she said, and decided not to pursue it. "And where's Lonnie Junior?"

"Here with me."

"Gee, I wonder where your dad could be."

"Oh, I wouldn't worry about him, Mom, if I were you."

"Why not?"

"I just wouldn't worry, that's all."

Was that sarcasm in his voice, or what? It was becoming infuriatingly difficult to pierce his defenses.

"Bye for now, honey," she said, as cheerfully as she could manage. "Can you put your grandma on for a moment?"

And then, as soon as she heard Sybil's voice, the whole elaborate defensive wall that she had constructed around herself crumbled into sand, ran through her fingers, blew away with the wind.

"Why?" she cried. "Sybil, why didn't you tell me what was going on?"

"But my dear," she replied, with genuine surprise and sympathy, "I assumed you knew."

"I never dreamed of it!"

"Surely, Ruby, you must have."

"No, not once," she said, and it occurred to her that she was lying to Sybil, lying to herself as well. Ruby could not fathom her own subconscious motivation. Self-deception, maneuvering to defeat her own best interests; these seemed utterly at odds with the image she had of herself.

"I can't tell you how sorry I am," Sybil was saying. "I've tried to talk to him. But you know how it is."

"No, I don't know. Why don't you tell me?"

"You can't change people, dear. You can't make them what they aren't."

"So, what happens to me now? What now? I mean, there's no question about who's side you will be on."

"Now stop it, Ruby. You're my daughter now, and you know it. But you've got to give this some thought. You have several choices; it seems to me."

"What would you do, Sybil? What would you do in my place?"

"I would search my heart and find out what I really want."

"You think I want this? You think l made it happen?"

"Only you know the answer to that."

"I don't know the answer to anything," Ruby said, and rang off.

How queer it is, she thought now, as she pulled up in front of her father's Quonset hut, that Daddy thrives on the solitude of Eagle Field, that he's perfectly content with just the company of his cats. Stranger yet, she reflected, is the fact that I prefer Eagle Field in its present desolation—everything smooth and white and dazzling in the sun, hurting the eyes—to either of its previous incarnations:

"Why do you like the desert?" a reporter once asked Lawrence of Arabia. "Because it's clean," he replied.

Indeed, there had been times in Ruby's past—walking with her father down the empty, silent streets, admiring the rippled white dunes that drifted to the eaves on the windward walls of the hangars, listening to the cats chasing scaley big lizards over gritty metallic walls and roofs, and the whistle of the perennial desert wind through the corrugated ribs of Quonset huts—when she had felt the thrill of a space traveler discovering the remains of an ancient civilization.

Ruby climbed out of her rented Cadillac, limped up the narrow flagstone walkway to the Quonset hut with the aid of her cane, swung open the screen door, and—experiencing a sudden and overwhelming sense of déjà vu—stepped into the air-cooled, cat-smelling living room, anxiously calling out, "Dad? Dad?"

"In here, honey!"

She found him at the kitchen table, looking ancient, shriveled, glittery-eyed, but spry as ever, sitting beside a -middle-aged woman wearing white, wedgie shoes, a soiled, flower print dress, ruby red lipstick, and a 1940s style bandana. Stubby and dark-eyed, she had the story of her life plastered across her cheerful, sagging face: GI bride, baby boom mama, divorcee, waitress, resident of trailer courts, and single occupancy hotels. She and Reno were sipping Coors from the can, and a bunch of Neapolitan cards lay spread out on the table before them in a fan shape, while tomcats and tabbies crouched all around them, on the sink and table, looking on curiously, like interested bystanders.

"Meet my friend, Madame Pauline," Reno said.

"Pleased to meet you."

"You can leave the 'Madame' out. He just calls me that to be funny."

"Met her just this morning, over at Del's Cafe. Now she's telling my fortune."

"Oh yeah? How long you gonna live, Dad?"

"He'll live to ninety-five if he lives a day," Pauline said. Her voice was even raspier than Reno's, a two-pack-a-day voice, with the remains of an Oklahoma twang.

"Mind if I pull up a chair?"

"Be my guest," said Reno.

"Now here's a fortune I'd love to tell," Pauline put in. She tried to smile at Ruby, but she was missing a few teeth, so the effort was not altogether successful.

"Hell's bells," Reno snorted, "the whole town of Gold Hill knows that already."

"Why didn't you get word to me, Dad?"

"Tried to, Ruby, right from the start. Took one look at that *chicita*, when she first came around with Lonnie, and I said, 'Bad news.' But you wouldn't listen, would you?"

"You know what the Gypsies say?" Pauline put in.

"No, what do they say?"

"Let a vixen in the door, you better hide the eggs."

"Guess I should've talked to you first."

"Oh, you're gonna do just fine, honey. Hell, you already hit the big time with that book of yours, from what I hear."

"Sure," Ruby said, "but what about when sales decline, and the talk show invitations stop coming in?"

"My advice is, let the future take care of itself."

"I'll remember that."

"I've just asked Madame Pauline to be my bride," Reno interjected. "But she won't accept me."

"Why not?"

"It's not in the cards," Pauline said, laughing.

Late that night, after drinking more beer than she should have, and putting Reno to bed, and conducting a sodden Pauline to her trailer court, Ruby finally set out for home.

She'd been disappointed to find that her father had company this afternoon; she had wanted a shoulder to cry on. But now she was glad it worked out this way. And, driving up through the Joshua tree forest, through the sleepy little one-stop sign town of Gold Hill, along the dry creek bed, the almond orchards, the steep canyon walls, watching the purple San Francisquitos, the sagey ridge of foothills, the Jules Verne turret of her tall Victorian slide by her window in brilliant moonlight, she made peace with herself at last, and with Max as well. *I never want to see this place again,* she thought.

And it came to her, from this fresh, philosophical perspective, that it was more than her struggle with illness and death, more than her book, more than Dominica, that had driven her from Max, and Max from her. It was something greater than herself, greater than Max, greater than all of them.

Ruby Rose had to be a star.

It was an illusion, of course.

And yet, and yet . . .

Leaving the Cadillac at the mailbox, she hobbled up the white dirt driveway on her cane, kicking pebbles, listening to them roll off into the underbrush, loud in the silence.

Her mind inspired by a cosmic view, her heart brimming with love and forgiveness, she had every intention of being charitable to the lovers.

She recalled something that Michael Marczaly had taught her, many years before.

"Character is fate," she whispered to herself. And a vision of her future flashed across the night sky.

She saw it clear as day.

At the divorce hearing, she would be magnanimous, refusing to blame her husband for the failure of their marriage, granting him all their community property, asking only for custody of Ned.

"I'm gonna make it big, Your Honor," she would say, much to the amusement of the court, "and I don't want him suing me for alimony. And our boy, Ned, he's not the cowboy type anyway, so he'll do far better in Hollywood than he'd ever do out here in Antelope Valley."

Yet, despite Madame Pauline's rosy prognostication, Ruby feared that she might not do any better in Hollywood this second time around than she had the first... And when her book faded from the charts, when her TV talk show viewing audience grew fickle, she knew that she would seek to prolong her moment of triumph: Write another book. Write a screenplay with herself as star. Try to sell a TV pilot. Try to start a national non-profit foundation for cancer victims with herself as president.

She would try anything and everything.

She would never, ever give up.

In later years, perhaps, after Ned had grown up and graduated from college and was working in the movies as an assistant director, she would get close again with Max and Dominica and their brood of little ones. And though they themselves would not be doing all that great—Dominica waitressing, Max, born in Paris to artsy parents, working as a garage mechanic at Jimmy Fisher Ford—Ruby would perhaps have to rely on them at times for temporary support.

"Ruby, you look younger every year!" the greying couple would ask when she breezed in on them to borrow money. "What's your secret?"

"Stay hungry," she would say, "and dye your hair."

And when Ruby died—at the age of eighty or so, only a year or two after Sybil—she would die at Sand Canyon Ranch, despite her present intentions, surrounded by Max and Dominica and Ned and Lonnie Jr. and all her great extended family.

Her spirit would rise off the body she left behind, and it would sweep like the shadow of a great Flying Wing across these airy desert places where she was born, and it would ascend to the heavens in a shower of fire. And the fire would become a star. And the star, for a moment, a mere instant in time, would shine out all over the vast Antelope Valley, flooding it with light.

CPSIA information can be obtained
at www.ICGtesting.com
Printed in the USA
LVHW040713301022
731906LV00008B/389